ADOLESCENT DIVERSITY
IN ETHNIC, ECONOMIC,
AND CULTURAL CONTEXTS

ADVANCES IN ADOLESCENT DEVELOPMENT
AN ANNUAL BOOK SERIES

Series Editors:

Gerald R. Adams, *University of Guelph, Ontario, Canada*
Raymond Montemayor, *Ohio State University*
Thomas P. Gullotta, *Child and Family Agency, Connecticut*

Advances in Adolescent Development is an annual book series designed to analyze, integrate, and critique an abundance of new research and literature in the field of adolescent development. Contributors are selected from numerous disciplines based on their creative, analytic, and influential scholarship in order to provide information pertinent to professionals as well as upper-division and graduate students. The Series Editors' goals are to evaluate the current empirical and theoretical knowledge about adolescence, and to encourage the formulation (or expansion) of new directions in research and theory development.

Volumes in This Series

ADOLESCENT DIVERSITY IN ETHNIC, ECONOMIC, AND CULTURAL CONTEXTS

Edited by

Raymond Montemayor
Gerald R. Adams
Thomas P. Gullotta

ADVANCES IN ADOLESCENT DEVELOPMENT

An Annual Book Series Volume 10

SAGE Publications
International Educational and Professional Publisher
Thousand Oaks   London   New Delhi

For information:

Sage Publications, Inc.
2455 Teller Road
Thousand Oaks, California 91320
E-mail: order@sagepub.com

Sage Publications Ltd.
6 Bonhill Street
London EC2A 4PU
United Kingdom

Sage Publications India Pvt. Ltd.
M-32 Market
Greater Kailash I
New Delhi 110 048 India

Printed in the United States of America

Library of Congress Cataloging-in-Publication Data

Main entry under title:
    Adolescent diversity in ethnic, economic, and cultural contexts /
edited by Raymond Montemayor, Gerald R. Adams, Thomas P. Gullotta.
        p.   cm.— (Advances in adolescent development ; v. 10)
    Includes bibliographical references and index.
    ISBN 0-7619-2126-5 (cloth : acid-free paper)
    ISBN 0-7619-2127-3 (pbk. : acid-free paper)
    1. Teenagers—United States—Social conditions.   2. Adolescence—
United States.   3. Minority teenagers—United States.   4. Socially
handicapped teenagers—United States.   I. Montemayor, Raymond.
    II. Adams, Gerald R., 1946-   III. Gullotta, Thomas P. IV. Series.
    HQ796 .A3342 1999
    305.235'0973—dc21   99-050651

This book is printed on acid-free paper.

00   01   02   03   04   05   06   7   6   5   4   3   2   1

Acquisition Editor:	C. Deborah Laughton
Editorial Assistant:	Eileen Carr
Production Editor:	Sanford Robinson
Editorial Assistant:	Patricia Zeman
Typesetter:	Lynn Miyata
Indexer:	Teri Greenberg

Contents

Introduction

Advances in Adolescent Development is a serial publication designed to bring together original summaries of important new developments in theory, research, and methodology on adolescents. Each chapter is written by experts who have substantially contributed to knowledge in their area or who are especially well qualified to review a topic because of their background or interests. The chapters in each volume are state-of-the-art reviews of advances in adolescent studies. Some authors also present new data from their own research. The theme of each volume is selected by the senior editor of each volume and is based on a reading of the latest published empirical work, discussions with the other editors, and ideas provided by colleagues. Chapter topics and authors are selected in a similar way.

This book is the final volume of the **Advances in Adolescent Development** series, which began in 1989 with the publication of Volume 1 on the biology of adolescent behavior and development. The 1990s have been a time of exponential growth in the field of adolescent studies. We, the editors, think that this series not only reflected that burgeoning growth but also contributed to the continuing improvement and maturity of research on adolescents. Progress in the field of adolescent research certainly will continue, but it will be left to others to decide if the field needs and can support a book series designed to summarize, integrate, and evaluate current research on a particular topic.

Many people contributed to the success of this enterprise. A book series is only as good as the chapters in it, and we think the chapters in this series have been excellent. We thank the 171 authors who wrote and revised their manuscripts more often than they might have wished. The staff at Sage Publications produced superb books and worked hard to sell them. C. Deborah Laughton at Sage has been with us from the beginning, and we are especially thankful for her support and encouragement. She was not only our editor but also a confidante, mediator, adviser, and cheerleader. Her ongoing ebullient zest for this series energized us and, for several years, convinced Sage that this was a project worth continuing. Sage Publications has been highly supportive of our little venture and has given us all the freedom and encouragement any academician could ask for or expect, given that we were spending their money. The market for a series such as this one is relatively small, however, and Sage decided that Volume 10 would be the last volume. In truth, after all these years of editing the work of others, we are also ready to pass the torch.

—RAYMOND MONTEMAYOR
Department of Psychology
Ohio State University

1. Paths to Adulthood: Adolescent Diversity in Contemporary America

Raymond Montemayor

It used to be that adolescents in the United States were a fairly homogeneous group, and they were thought of that way. When we were a less diverse nation, adolescents—as portrayed in the media or as social science research participants—were typically White, middle-class, suburban, and from a nondescript Western European background. Other kinds of adolescents lived in America, but their numbers were small, and their lives unfolded on streets rarely visited by the majority of Americans. Occasionally, stories about kids who were poor or Black appeared on the front pages to remind the majority that the United States was more than they knew, but these youth lived on the periphery of the demographic map and as dim images in the popular mind.

Neither adolescents nor Americans are as uniformly cut from the same demographic quilt anymore. Data collected by the Census Bureau document what anyone who watches TV, goes to the movies, or lives in a big city knows: The United States is becoming less White and more ethnically diverse. In 1995, the ethnic distribution of the population of Americans between the ages of 10 and 19 was 68% White, 15% Black, 13% Hispanic, 4% Asian, and 1% American Indian (U.S. Census Bureau, 1996). Projections for the future indicate a continuing decrease in the percentage of White Americans with Western European ancestry and increases in non-White groups, especially Hispanic and Asian. By the year 2050, when most of today's adolescents will be grandparents, the population of the United States is projected to be about 53% White, 25% Hispanic, 14% Black, 8% Asian, and 1% American Indian. The largest increase is expected among Hispanics, from a current population of 30 million to a projected 133 million, equivalent to the entire population of the United States in 1945.

Besides these well-known and well-publicized ethnic differences in the U.S. population, other differences exist that segment adolescents, and all of us, into different demographic niches. We are a nation of city dwellers, and we think of ourselves as such, and yet about one in four Americans lives in a town with a population of 2,500 or less (U.S. Census Bureau, 1996). Surprisingly little attention is paid to the 62 million Americans who live on farms or in rural areas unless the river rises or the crops are destroyed. Most of us know little about the daily lives of adolescents who live outside the glare of city lights or the ways in which these adolescents are similar to and different from urban youth.

The lives of adolescents are influenced not only by skin color, family origins, and community size but also, and perhaps even more deeply, by money. Family income plays a part in virtually every aspect of adolescent life, especially when adolescents are poor. Since the early 1980s, poverty rates for children under the age of 18 years have hovered around 20%. In 1994, the rate was about 21%, or about 15 million children and adolescents (U.S. Census Bureau, 1996). To put a dollar value on the meaning of poverty, for a family of three, it is defined as an annual family income of less than $11,821. Poverty is not an equal opportunity condition but is highly related to race and ethnicity. In 1994, the percentage of children 18 years of age or younger classified as poor was 16% White, 43% Black, and 41% Hispanic. Although many people think poor kids are mainly Black or Hispanic, the truth is that most are not. Of the 15 million children and adolescents classified as poor, about one half, 8 million, are White, whereas about 4 million are Black and 3 million are Hispanic.

THIS VOLUME

The purpose of this book is to bring together in a single volume recent theory and research that examine the diversity of adolescent experiences in the United States. Deciding which groups to include was a challenge. Rather than focus on a single group or present only ethnic minorities, we chose to open up the examination of diversity and go beyond traditional discussions that typically focus on the three largest ethnic minorities—African American, Mexican American, and Asian American adolescents. As important as ethnicity is, it is only one of several characteristics that not only describe subpopulation groups but also result in different demographic milieus within which adolescent lives unfold.

Our focus is on demographic diversity, defined by race, ethnicity, community size, geographic region, and wealth. These are the contexts in which adolescent growth and development, social relationships, and psychological and cognitive development unfold. This focus led to an examination of adolescents who are Native American, Mexican American, Asian American, African American, the urban poor, rural, and Appalachian. There are other interesting groups we could have examined—religious minorities, such as Mormons or the Amish, other racial and ethnic minorities, such as Eskimos or Cajuns, or the very wealthy; the list of nonmainstream groups is long. We chose groups who seemed important for our national life or who had been neglected in other reviews.

Chapter authors were selected based on their knowledge of each group. Authors are recognized experts on the group on which they write, and all have long and distinguished programs of research. Several authors have engaged in extensive clinical work with the adolescents about whom they write. Some have developed and implemented prevention and treatment programs. Authors were asked to discuss their own work in addition to reviewing current theory and research.

Authors were given wide leeway in the organization of their chapters and in what theories and research they examined. They did whatever best suited their purposes. Authors were asked to consider the important contexts of adolescent development, including community, family, peer group, and school.

Authors were asked explicitly to examine "normal" adolescent development and not to focus on problem behavior, the typical emphasis of research on minority groups. Much of the research on adolescents who are minority, poor, or rural has been based on a deficit model, in which they and their families are compared to White, middle-class, two-parent, suburban adolescents, usually to the detriment of the nonmainstream youth. More recent research, as described in the chapters in this book, has been based on an adaptation model, in which adolescent behavior is examined as a response to particular social and economic contexts.

CHAPTER SUMMARIES

The chapter by Yoshikawa and Seidman focuses on the neglected topic of competence among urban adolescents living in poverty. The first section presents a brief overview of current research on the effects of poverty on urban adolescents. The second section considers two principal reasons for the neglect of competence as a developmental outcome among urban poor adolescents: a societal and scientific focus on problem behaviors and psychopathology and the fact that competence among urban poor teenagers may not conform to the expectations of current theories of adolescent development. The authors then review relevant ethnographic and quantitative literature and consider the multiple dimensions of competence as they occur among this group; the multiple contexts within which competence develops; and the ways that current models of risk, vulnerability, and resilience may need to be revised to investigate the development of competence. Lessons are drawn from the discussion for the next generation of research and for programs and policy involving urban adolescents in poverty.

Crockett, Shanahan, and Jackson-Newsom examine rural youth. Little is known about these adolescents despite the fact that they constitute a large proportion of U.S. adolescents. The authors use four dimensions to define rural—population size and density, community ties, traditionalism, and land use—and use these dimensions to organize their chapter. One basic question about rural adolescents is "How different are they from nonrural adolescents?" Many stereotypes about rural families exist—such as that they are more traditional, authoritarian, and cohesive than urban families—but the little research that has compared urban and rural families suggests that urban and rural families are more similar than different, although some important differences have been identified. Crockett et al. examine research on psychosocial adjustment among rural youth and identity how rural adolescents are advantaged and disadvantaged relative to nonrural youth. The authors then turn to what they consider to be the central challenge facing contemporary rural youth—the need to reconcile attachment to family and place with a desire for educational and occupational mobility. Finally, they suggest conceptual and empirical guidelines for future research.

The chapter by Wilson and Peterson examines adolescents living in the Appalachian region of the United States, with special emphasis on youth from rural regions of central and southern Appalachia. According to the authors, these adolescents encounter a complex environment of social, economic, and physical conditions that differ from conditions faced by non-Appalachian youth. The chapter uses an ecological perspective to examine how these factors contribute to development of contemporary Appalachian youth. Wilson and Peterson argue that myths about the backward ways and dysfunctional social organization of Appalachian families and communities cloud understanding of the reality of the people and places in the region. The continuing marginalization of Appalachia in contemporary America is built on a long history of exploitation by outsiders. In the social sciences, this marginalization is evidenced in the underrepresentation of Appalachian youth in contemporary scholarship and research. Family reputation, name, and legacy forge strong emotional ties among extended family members. Relationship interdependence and the concept of kin are more valued than individualism. Appalachian social life and adolescent development involve the complex interplay of lingering elements of traditional folk culture and the powerful encroachment of contemporary urban influences. There appear to be three paths to adult identity in the Appalachian region: Appalachian-identified, biculturally identified, and urban-identified. Appalachian adolescents are a poorly understood but relatively large minority population in American society. The authors conclude with a plea for more systematic research on this largely invisible group of adolescents.

In the chapter on American Indian adolescents, Beauvais shows how the history of Native American peoples has led to social conditions that are inimical to healthy adolescent development. Among American Indians, socioeconomic stress has created problems in the family, educational, and community domains. Rates of social problems, which include substance abuse, school dropout rates, and violence and victimization, are elevated in many Indian communities, and psychological problems occur at higher levels than in White communities. Indian youth, however, are heirs to a rich and resilient culture that provides them with the resources to counter the many sources of disadvantage they endure. Of major importance is the support available from an extended family structure. Data describ-

6 ADOLESCENT DIVERSITY

ing other specific ingredients for healthy adolescence are rare, although many Indian youth develop in healthy ways. According to Beauvais, the sociopolitical situation is gradually improving, providing a brighter outlook for Indian youth. Tribes are regaining control over their governmental, educational, and health care delivery systems and are attempting to recover many aspects of their traditional culture. Indian youth should gain from this change and may be able to negotiate the tasks of adolescent development in a more supportive environment.

In the chapter on Mexican American adolescents, Castro, Boyer, and Balcazar answer two questions: "What constitutes normal healthy adjustment among Mexican American youth?" and "What factors promote healthy adjustment in these adolescents?" The problem of defining psychological health continues to elude social scientists, who have found it easier to identify mental illness, psychopathology, and the absence of health than the presence of competency. Mental health is especially hard to define among Mexican Americans because of the unique combination of stressors many of these youth experience and the need to reconcile English-speaking and Spanish-speaking cultures. Castro et al. do not attempt to offer a definitive statement about what it means to be a well-adjusted Mexican American adolescent, but they do indicate that such a definition must be sensitive to Mexican American culture and focus on processes, especially those that lead to personal development and interpersonal effectiveness. The fundamental challenge Mexican American youth face is learning to cope with the stressors of cultural conflict. Typical outcomes include acculturation, assimilation, or biculturalism. Another theme in this chapter is the importance of the family and the ideology of "familism" for Mexican American parents and adolescents. Several features of familism are described and contrasted with the family ideology characteristic of Anglo-American families. The authors conclude by presenting a framework to guide researchers interesting in examining the healthy development of Mexican American adolescents.

Leong, Chao, and Hardin review the literature on Asian American adolescents from the perspective that Asian Americans are a "model minority." In the introduction to a special issue of the *Journal of Social Issues* in 1973 on Asian Americans Kitano and Sue introduced the idea that Asian Americans were a model minority. According to Kitano and Sue, the majority of Americans perceive Asian Americans as a successful, nonoppressed minority. Since 1973, many scholars have shown that the model minority label is a myth that is inaccurate and misleading. The view that through academic success Asian Americans have adapted to American life successfully is an overly simple story that ignores the complexity and variety of the Asian American experience. Leong et al. provide a critical review of the research and emerging theoretical issues related to the development of Asian American adolescents. They focus on the areas of academic achievement, ethnic identity, and psychological adjustment and present a picture of Asian American adolescents that is more complex than the model minority view.

The chapter by Taylor, Jacobson, and Roberts is a review of the empirical research on African American adolescents. The authors first present a conceptual model for organizing the literature based on Urie Bronfenbrenner's ecological perspective, in which peer, school, and neighborhood contexts are viewed as having an impact on parenting practices, which, in turn, affect adolescent behavior. Based on this model, poor functioning among African American adolescents is shown to be related to having peers with negative values or attributes, attending schools in which the majority of students are poor or in which teachers have low expectations for students, and living in dangerous neighborhoods. Conversely, positive adjustment among African American adolescents is associated with affiliating with peers with positive values, attending schools with an economically diverse student body or going to schools in which teachers have high expectations for students, and living in neighborhoods with plentiful resources. Research linking social context to parenting has shown that in neighborhoods with high crime rates, parents are more likely to restrict their adolescents' behavior and are less emotionally supportive than are parents in safe neighborhoods. In general, neighborhoods with low crime rates are contexts that are associated with high parental warm and support and a stable and structured home environment, all of which are positively associated with good adolescent adjustment and school success. Taylor et al. suggest several areas where research is needed. For example, we do not know how cultural traditions influence parenting practices. Research also is needed on nonurban, middle-class African American adolescents. Finally, the authors suggest that we need to consider the ways in which adolescents help shape the contexts in which they reside.

Cunningham and Spencer take a phenomenological approach to Bronfenbrenner's ecological model and focus on adolescents' perceptions of their personal, family, and neighborhood experiences. They describe their model, the Phenomenological Variant of Ecological Systems Theory, and use it as a framework to review research done by them and others on African American adolescents. According to Cunningham and Spencer, it is essential to take into account the perceptions adolescents have of their own behavior and of their environment, especially when studying minority adolescents, because these perceptions, or meanings, are often at odds with mainstream adolescents. One methodological consequence of this discrepancy is that many questionnaires designed to measure adolescent behavior do not capture the behavior of minority adolescents accurately, because these instruments were normed on samples of White European adolescents. Cunningham and Spencer show that the perceptions African American adolescents have of their environment are a potent influence on adolescent behavior.

In the final chapter, Montemayor discusses several themes that emerged from the chapters in this volume. Of particular importance is the point made by every author that adolescents who are non-White, poor, or rural are faced with the fundamental issue of reconciling their ethnic or traditional heritage with the largely White, middle-class, urban world of modern America. How this issue is resolved and who helps the adolescents resolve it—family, peers, school, media—profoundly influence adolescent behavior.

REFERENCES

U.S. Census Bureau. (1996). *Statistical abstracts of the United States: 1996* (116th ed.). Washington, DC: Author.

2. Competence Among Urban Adolescents in Poverty: Multiple Forms, Contexts, and Developmental Processes

Hirokazu Yoshikawa
Edward Seidman

Where do American adolescents in poverty live? Census data suggest that the majority live in cities: In 1993, 77% of poor children and adolescents lived in metropolitan areas, and 45% lived in central city areas (U.S. Census Bureau, 1995). Furthermore, these data show that poverty rates of children and adolescents in 1993 were far higher in central city areas than in the nation as a whole (34% vs. 23%, respectively). When comparing near-poverty rates (i.e., less than 150% of the federal poverty threshold), which many poverty researchers consider a more accurate threshold, the comparison is just as striking (47% vs. 34%, respectively; U.S. Census Bureau, 1995).

The common image of urban poverty is that of concentrated "ghetto" or "inner-city" poverty, defined by researchers as census tracts within which more than 40% of families live in poverty. Jargowsky and Bane (1990) noted that, using this definition, the percentage of America's poor who lived in concentrated urban poverty in 1980 was 9%, much smaller than the 77% cited above. However, this 9% was made up of 21% of all African American poor persons, 16% of all Latinos, and 2% of European Americans. Census data con-

AUTHORS' NOTE: Work on this chapter was supported in part by grants from the National Institute of Mental Health (MH43084) and the Carnegie Corporation (B4850). We express appreciation to our editor, Raymond Montemayor, and two reviewers, Suniya Luthar and Andrew Fuligni, for their insightful comments on an initial draft.

firm images of inner-city poverty, in that African Americans comprised 65% of those living in concentrated poverty tracts, Latinos 22%, and all other race/ethnicity groups 13%.

The evidence is well-known: Urban poor neighborhoods, compared to urban higher-income or suburban neighborhoods, have higher crime rates; poorer-quality and more crowded housing; fewer employment opportunities; higher levels of pollution and toxins; and schools with larger classes, fewer resources, and lower levels of expenditure per pupil (Bullard & Wright, 1993; Council of the Great City Schools, 1992; McGahey, 1986; National Research Council, 1993; Parrish, Matsumoto, & Fowler, 1995; Rosenbaum, 1991; Sherman, 1994). A characteristic view of the inner-city teenager accompanies this image of urban poverty: He is violent and drug-abusing, she is pregnant or already a mother, they are African American or Latino, they have dropped out of school. Urban, low-income teenagers are indeed at high risk for delinquency, drug use, teenage pregnancy, school dropout, and HIV infection (Annie E. Casey Foundation, 1994; Jemmott & Jemmott, 1994; National Center for Education Statistics, 1993; Rotheram-Borus et al., 1992; Yoshikawa, 1994). Available data also confirm that Latino and African American adolescents are disproportionately represented among the urban poor.

These statistics present ample cause for concern and intervention. However, they mask the fact that the majority of urban poor adolescents do not become delinquent or drop out of school and that the majority of urban poor adolescent girls do not become pregnant (Seidman, 1991). Ethnographic evidence indicates that some are able to lift themselves out of poverty, despite the structural obstacles in their way (Jarrett, in press). Little is known about the processes that bring about such successful outcomes. Very few quantitative studies of normative development or competence among urban poor adolescents exist. The emphasis of quantitative developmental researchers, when studying low-income urban teenagers, has been on problem behaviors.

This chapter focuses on the neglected topic of competence among urban poor adolescents. The first section presents a brief overview of current research on the effects of poverty on urban adolescents. The second section considers two principal reasons for the neglect of competence as a developmental outcome among this group: (a) a societal and scientific focus on problem behaviors and psychopathology and (b) the fact that competence among urban poor teenagers may not conform to the expectations of mainstream theories of adolescent development. A review of relevant ethnographic and quantitative literatures then considers the multiple dimensions of competence as it occurs among this group; the multiple contexts within which competence develops; and the ways that current models of risk, vulnerability, and resilience may need to be revised to investigate the development of competence. In the final section, recommendations are made for the next generation of research, programs, and policy involving urban low-income adolescents.

POVERTY AND THE
AMERICAN ADOLESCENT

Data on poverty trends in the United States show that concern about urban poverty's effects on adolescents is well justified. Urban poor teenagers in the last decade of the 20th century confront greater income inequality and higher child poverty rates than at any time during the past 25 years (Karoly, 1993; Sherman, 1994). Factors driving these increases—the decline in real wages for less-skilled workers, restrictions on eligibility for government antipoverty programs and declines in the real value of their benefits, and increases in single-parent-headed families (Danziger & Weinberg, 1994; Wilson, 1987, 1996)—have caused the experience of adolescence among the urban poor to diverge more and more from that of higher-income teenagers. As manufacturing jobs—historically the locus of employment for adolescents and less-skilled adults—disappeared from the central city, access to the financial and social capital associated with the jobs also disappeared. The illegitimate economy became an increasingly attractive alternative to finding scarce legitimate employment. The rise in urban poverty reduced the kinds of opportunities available to develop adult "mainstream" skills such as job skills. Williams and Kornblum (1985) noted that middle-class children grow up learning how to meet and interact with strangers in unfamiliar settings all the time, experiences that make transition to the world of work relatively easy. Children from urban low-income neighborhoods have had fewer and fewer chances to be exposed to such experiences. Stigmatization and, for minority adolescents, experiences of race- and class-based discrimination may further alienate urban poor youth from participating in the central service economy, usually located in the more central, well-to-do residential or business neighborhoods of cities. Evidence suggests that these trends in urban poverty will continue, as the United States continues to shift from an industrial to an information economy.

It should be noted that differences exist in the nature of urban poverty among regions in the United States, as well as among different subgroups. A recent comparison of poverty among African Americans and Latinos in cities of the Southwest reveals several important caveats concerning assumptions about urban poverty. Cuciti and James (1990) observed that poverty among Latinos (they considered primarily Mexican Americans) in the Southwest does not always conform to current characterizations of the urban "underclass"—that is, high rates of unemployment, single-parent families, and teenage pregnancy (Wilson, 1987, 1996). The percentage of working single men, for instance (which Wilson used to calculate the Male Marriage Pool Index, measuring the availability of marriageable single men), is substantially higher for Mexican American men than for African American men in these cities. Mexican American families in poverty are also much more likely to be two-parent families. The authors also noted that deindustrialization, central to Wilson's explanation for rises in the concentration of urban poverty, did not occur in most large Southwest cities through most of the 1980s.

Poverty has been theorized to affect adolescent development not only through changes in the economy as a whole but also through the more proximal settings of neighborhood and family. Neighborood-level poverty may affect adolescent development adversely by reducing the availability of positive role models engaged in mainstream educational or occupational activities, the amount of collective supervision of children engaged in by neighborhood adults, or the availability or quality of resources and institutions necessary to facilitate the transition to adulthood. Such factors may partly explain high school dropout, teenage pregnancy, and delinquency among urban poor adolescents (Mayer & Jencks, 1989; Sampson, 1992; Tienda, 1991). Family-level poverty may affect development by reducing the attention and resources parents have available to give to their children. Reduced levels of social support of parents, increases in parent emotional distress and family conflict, reductions in availability and quality of child care, and subsequent declines in parenting quality, in this view, lead to socioemotional and academic problems in children (McLoyd, 1990). One study support for this mediational model of family-level poverty effects: Unemployment and work interruption among lower- and working-class, single African American mothers affected adolescents' depressive symptoms through mediating factors such as mothers' depressive symptoms, low levels of instrumental support, and use of punishment (McLoyd, Jayaratne, Ceballo, & Borquez, 1994). This overview suggests that the preponderance of research on urban poor adolescents considers negative outcomes. The next section considers why positive outcomes are neglected among this population.

WHY COMPETENCE AMONG URBAN POOR ADOLESCENTS IS NEGLECTED

Why is competence among the urban poor a neglected topic? Concern about the relatively high rates of problem behaviors and psychopathology in poor areas has resulted in neglect by omission of competence outcomes. In addition, there is little interest in how forms of competence in this population may differ from those expected in current theories of adolescent development. These explanations are considered in turn below.

The Pathologizing of Urban Adolescents in Poverty

Much of the current research on urban poor adolescents focuses on understanding the development of problem behaviors and psychopathology. These efforts are critical in informing policies and programs to combat the negative effects of poverty. The danger in a preponderance of this kind of research is that, by reasoning from extremes, pathologizing conclusions are drawn about this population as a whole (Seidman & Rappaport, 1986). Gans (1995) noted the historical roots of America's pathologizing of the "undeserving" poor, stretching from notions of the feeblemindedness of immigrant groups in the early 20th century to more recent labels, such as the "culture of poverty" and the "underclass." Many developmental researchers have noted that such assumptions about the poor underlie the tendency to focus on group differences in negative outcomes between poor and nonpoor children and adolescents. Emphasis on such between-group differences masks the range of individual differences among poor adolescents, particularly the range of competent outcomes that many achieve (Huston, McLoyd, & Garcia Coll, 1994; Jessor, 1993; Seidman, 1991; Slaughter-Defoe, Nakagawa, Takanishi, & Johnson, 1990). There have been few efforts to explore what leads to the statistically more numerous positive outcomes among these teenagers. Such information is potentially more important than developmental risk research in informing prevention- and competence-promotion programs (Seidman, 1991).

Traditional Theories of Adolescent Development and the Experience of Poor Urban Adolescents

There is also little interest in the particular forms competence may take among urban poor teenagers. Indicators of successful development may diverge substantially from those expected in much of the literature on adolescence. Current developmental theories stress both universal and culture-specific aspects of adolescence. Biological changes of puberty are indeed universal and consistent, whereas changes in adolescent thinking, though most likely universal, differ in content according to the situation and among cultures (Brooks-Gunn & Reiter, 1990; Cole, 1992; Linn, 1983). Other developmental tasks considered central in theories of adolescence include achieving greater autonomy from parents, engaging in dating behaviors, and acquiring skills required in adulthood (Elliott & Feldman, 1990; Erikson, 1968). Researchers have noted that these theories are often based on observations and research conducted with primarily European American, middle-class adolescents (Burton, Allison, & Obeidallah, 1995; Seidman, 1991). Some aspects of the theories are vulnerable to overgeneralization when considering culturally or economically diverse teenagers, particularly emphases on individuation from parents and assumptions about the nature of dating behaviors and adult skills.

For several reasons, the experience of urban poor adolescents may differ from expectations about adolescent development. First, ethnographic researchers have noted the early assumption of adult roles among African American and Latino children in urban poor families (Burton et al., 1995; Jarrett, in press; Tyler, Tyler, Tommasello, & Zhang, 1992). Due to the lack of resources available for child care and other family functions, older children often help with sibling caregiving and other household tasks. Adolescence, defined as an intermediate stage between childhood and adulthood, may not apply to urban poor teenagers who have been performing adult roles for years. This form of competence often goes unnoticed, not only by researchers but also by people in urban adolescents' lives. Burton et al. (1995) quoted a 15-year-old's view of his schoolteacher: "I take care of my mother and have raised my sisters. Then I come here and this know-nothing teacher treat me like I'm some dumb kid with no responsibilities. . . . Don't they understand I'm a man and I been a man longer than they been a woman" (p. 129).

There is another reason why traditional theories of adolescence may need to be revised when considering urban poor adolescents: The face of urban youth in the United States is changing. The majority of the estimated 8 million children of the post-1965 wave of immigration to the United States live in the nation's urban centers and have transformed them. Unlike previous waves of immigration, comprised primarily of Europeans, post-1965 immigrants are over-whelmingly non-European (77%; Portes & Zhou, 1993). This trend contributes substantially to recent increases in the proportion of the U.S. population who are of ethnic-minority or immigrant status. The Census Bureau projects that the increases will continue: The percentage of adolescents (14 to 17 years old) who are of Hispanic origin is expected to increase from 12% of all U.S. adolescents in 1990 to 23% in 2020, with an even greater proportional jump for Asian and Pacific Islander adolescents (4% to 10%, respectively) and a somewhat smaller one for Black adolescents (15% to 21%; U.S. Census Bureau, 1993a).

Although rates of poverty vary greatly among and within immigrant groups (see Rumbaut, 1997), children and adolescents from immigrant families are twice as likely to live in poverty as are all U.S. children and adolescents (U.S. Census Bureau, 1993b). Traditional notions of adolescent development may not capture the experience of the minority or immigrant adolescents who do live in poverty. For example, a value central to some Latino cultures—familism—places needs of the family before needs of individuals. This emphasis may conflict with values of autonomy and individualism central to some theorists' view of adolescence (Cuciti & James, 1990; Erikson, 1968).

It is clear that urban poor adolescents are a diverse group who may diverge in their normative development, not only from expected norms but also from each other. It is vital, therefore, in an investigation of competence among this population, to consider multiple dimensions as well as how those dimensions differ among the variety of physical and cultural settings that they inhabit.

COMPETENCE:
MULTIPLE DIMENSIONS

What is competence, and what forms does it take? The early literature on competence among children and adolescents in poverty still shapes current research in its emphasis on cognitive competence, as measured by IQ and school achievement. This relatively narrow focus emerged from concerns in the 1960s that poor children were falling far behind their more well-to-do peers on these two outcomes. The combination of developmental theories suggesting the primary importance of early experience for future development and the policy context of the War on Poverty produced a national program—Head Start—whose initial evaluations were cognitive in focus (despite the broader goals set forth by the committee that developed Head Start; Zigler & Muenchow, 1992). Although the purpose of Head Start was to encourage competence, the program often was labeled "compensatory" education, making up for the deficit assumed to be inherent in the "culture of poverty."

Due to the overemphasis on cognitive outcomes, researchers called for a broadening of goals of programs for children in poverty (Zigler & Trickett, 1978). As a result, social competence has in the past decade become an additional form of competence studied by child and adolescent researchers. In many cases, however, social competence is defined globally, with little effort to separate out types of social competence, such as peer-based competence; romantic competence; HIV risk reduction behaviors; social skills; or involvement in peer, school, neighborhood, and other activities.

Recent quantitative work on multiple dimensions of competence begins to address the issue of multiple forms of competence among urban poor teenagers and how such forms may relate to one another. Luthar (1995, 1997) investigated forms of school-based competence among inner-city, largely African American and Latino adolescents. Four dimensions of competence (teacher-rated assertiveness, peer-rated leadership and sociability, and academic grade point average) and four measures of psychological symptoms (anxiety, depression, and internalizing and externalizing symptoms) were measured at the beginning of the school year as predictors of the four forms of competence measured 6 months later. Although most measures of competence revealed substantial stability across the 6-month interval, exploration of cross-domain associations revealed that peer-rated sociability early in the year was associated with lower levels of peer-rated leadership late in the year, as well as with lower academic achievement.

Multidimensional measurement of competence among urban poor adolescents may reveal unexpected associations across domains. Other cross-sectional work by Luthar, using a demographically similar sample, revealed interactive effects among different forms of competence. Under high levels of stress, cognitive competence predicted low levels of social competence and lower academic achievement. Cognitive competence predicted higher school grades only when students reported low levels of stress or internal locus of control, and such competence predicted higher teacher-rated assertiveness and responsibility only when students reported low levels of stress or high levels of ego development (moral development, impulse control, and interpersonal relationships; Luthar, 1991; Luthar & Zigler, 1992). Luthar and Zigler (1992) concluded that the more intelligent children in her sample may be more susceptible to the levels of stress in their environments and may be less tempted to turn away from academic pursuits if they have internal locus of control or impulse control. Mehan, Hubbard, and Villanueva (1994) found another instance of unexpected associations among dimensions of competence in their study of Latino and African American students in an "untracking" program in inner-city San Diego high schools. Students who had been through this program, which targeted students of high academic potential whose performance was suffering, showed both increases in belief in schooling and continued awareness of racism and discrimination. Prior research had found that attachment to school and awareness of discrimination were negatively related to each other among African American (Fordham & Ogbu, 1986) and Mexican American students (Alva, 1991).

Recent ethnographic work points to forms of competence specific to certain groups of urban poor adolescents. For example, early caretaking skills are associated with the extended kin networks of African American families (Allison & Takei, 1993; Burton et al., 1995) and also with adolescent children of immigrant parents helping their parents to negotiate the difficulties of a foreign culture (Tyler et al., 1992). Urban poor teenagers are also often called on to work to help supplement family income. Much of this work may involve informal employment or jobs off the books, especially in neighborhoods in which traditional employment is scarce (Williams & Kornblum, 1985).

Relations among domains of competence may also be specific to ethnocultural subgroups within the larger group of urban poor teenagers. Recent research on the new second-generation (i.e., children of the post-1965 wave of immigration) indicates that historical links between assimilation and academic and occupational success may be reversed among this group. Among children of immigrants from Latin America and the Caribbean, *bilingualism,* defined as retention of the parental language coupled with fluency in English, predicted higher school achievement and educational and job aspirations (Portes & Schauffler, 1994). Waters (1994) similarly found, in a sample of West Indian and Haitian American second-generation immigrant adolescents, that social mobility in the inner city was associated with retention of immigrant identity and distancing from Black Americans. Among a sample of Indochinese refugee children and their families, parents who indicated that retention of the past was important had children with higher grade point averages than did those who did not (Caplan, Choy, & Whitmore, 1992). Finally, in an ethnographic study of children of immigrants from Haiti, Vietnam, Cuba, Nicaragua, and Mexico, Fernandez-Kelly and Schauffler (1994) found some evidence that having an immigrant identity can protect adolescents from negative stereotypes and pressures from popular peer groups not to conform to adult mainstream goals.

Some forms of competence among poor urban adolescents represent their own responses to their often marginalized status in American society. Personal responses to marginalization may include such aspects of identity as positive feelings about one's ethnic identity or coming out as a lesbian, gay, or bisexual adolescent, both of which have been associated with more global self-esteem (Bat-Chava, Allen, Seidman, Aber, & Ventura, 1996; Savin-Williams, 1995). Ethnographic researchers have described urban teenagers' development of critical consciousness, the ability to observe their social world critically to overcome the pressures of marginalization based on class, race, gender, or sexuality (Ward, 1996). Ward described how parents of African American urban girls in poverty foster the development of such awareness through a variety of techniques, such as teaching their daughters about detecting racial stereotypes in the media and elsewhere. However, Pastor, McCormick, and Fine (1996), in a study of Latina and Afro-Caribbean female adolescents in New York, found that critical consciousness, without the perception of opportunities to overcome oppression, may be associated with lower aspirations, self-esteem, and academic achievement. This finding also was noted in a study of a multi-ethnic urban high school by Fine (1991).

Multiple dimensions of competence may have different relations with problem outcomes, ranging from psychological or academic difficulties to conduct problems. For example, preliminary analyses from the Adolescent Pathways Project, a large-scale investigation of ethnically diverse adolescents in three cities, show that involvement/ participation in neighborhood action activities are associated with high levels of self-efficacy but also with high levels of antisocial behavior. The association of academic competence with low peer popularity is a well-known phenomenon in some poor urban high schools, particularly among African American students (Fordham & Ogbu, 1986; Luthar, 1995; Steinberg, Darling, Fletcher, Brown, & Dornbusch, 1995). Luthar (1995) found that high levels of anxiety among inner-city adolescent girls early in the school year were associated with improvements in their grades over the year.

These studies, although few in number, demonstrate the rich multidimensionality of competence among urban adolescents in poverty. Considering competence as a single global construct, or even as two broadband dimensions (academic and social), does not do justice to the complexity of these adolescents' lives. Future research should expand our notions of competence to encompass the full range of possible forms it can take.

COMPETENCE:
MULTIPLE CONTEXTS

How do multiple dimensions of competence and their sources differ across multiple contexts? Adolescents are involved in a greater variety of settings—including family, peer, school, neighborhood, and institutional contexts—than are younger children. Attention not only to multiple competence dimensions but also to the variety of contexts within which they occur is vital to ecologically sensitive accounts of urban poor teenagers' lives, as well as to ecologically sensitive programs and policies to improve them. The following section reviews findings on how dimensions and sources of competence appear and may influence one another in different contexts. Unfortunately, few of the studies investigate multiple dimensions, and fewer consider even part of the full matrix of dimensions across settings—the ones that do are highlighted.

Family Contexts

Not surprisingly, much of the research on the family contexts of competence has focused on academic achievement. The areas of parenting and parent involvement in school have received the most attention. In the best of this research, family sources of competence are considered with attention not only to the larger context of poverty but also to that of culture. For example, Caplan et al. (1992) found that cultural norms emphasizing family involvement in children's schooling were associated with higher academic achievement among refugee families from Laos and Vietnam. Data from this sample show a reversal of the usual association of greater family size with lower academic achievement. School achievement of children in larger families was higher than that of children in smaller families (up to a point; children in families with six or more siblings showed lower grade point averages). The authors found an explanation for this unexpected association in their data: Older siblings were highly involved in teaching younger ones at home. This involvement is consonant with Asian cultures' emphases on harmony and support within the family.

Other studies have found that forms of parenting leading to academic competence among low-income teenagers may differ from those among their higher-income counterparts. Alfred and Clara Baldwin and their colleagues, for example, found that parental restrictiveness, emphasis on self-control, and lack of justification of parent policies was positively correlated with adolescents' academic achievement among their high-risk families and negatively correlated among the low-risk ones. This finding held whether *high-risk* was defined as a composite of family-level minority status, father absence, and family educational and occupational status, or as neighborhood-level crime rate (Baldwin, Baldwin, & Cole, 1990). A later study by the same authors duplicated this finding, but in relation to mental health and psychological well-being (Baldwin et al., 1993).

Research on family sources of competence has begun to expand beyond academic achievement to consider other forms of competence. Authoritative parenting, found to predict academic achievement among adolescents in mixed-income communities (Steinberg et al., 1995), predicted self-reliance in a study of urban low-income African American adolescents (Taylor, Casten, & Flickinger, 1993). Taylor et al. (1993) found, in addition, that the positive relation of kinship support to self-reliance was mediated by the positive effects of authoritative parenting. Similarly, emotional support from parents has been found in middle-class samples to predict adolescent well-being; a recent study found that such support from fathers was associated with higher life satisfaction and global self-esteem among African American male teenagers in inner-city neighborhoods (Zimmerman, Salem, & Maton, 1995).

Some family studies have considered competence outcomes particularly salient in the lives of adolescents in poverty. Stack and Burton (1993) note that, among African American adolescents, early caretaking activities take place in a family network in which the conscription of kin for collective family tasks is not only normative but itself a measure of family-level competence. This hypothesis is supported by data showing that African American adolescent mothers who experience greater support from their families (their mothers, in particular) are more likely to finish school (Colletta & Lee, 1983). In addition, a recent study of African American families living in an urban low-income neighborhood found that adult kinship support of the mother was associated with self-reliance among their adolescent children (Taylor & Roberts, 1995). However, other data caution against simple generalizations of the effect of extended family networks on African American adolescents. For example, Chase-Lansdale, Brooks-Gunn, and Zamsky (1994) found that grandmother coresidence with young African American mothers was associated with less optimal parenting practices among both the mothers and grandmothers. However, among the youngest (adolescent) mothers, coresiding grandmothers showed higher quality parenting than did non-coresiding grandmothers.

Peer Contexts

Much attention has been paid to the negative impact of peer popularity and social support on academic competence among urban low-income adolescents (Fordham & Ogbu, 1986; Luthar, 1995). For example, a study of poor African American and Latino adolescents in New Haven found that social support from peers was associated with lower school grades (Cauce, Felner & Primavera, 1982). It has been hypothesized that minority teenagers in cities, and particularly African American teenagers, face a trade-off in school between perceived allegiance to same-ethnicity peers (and, by extension, their own ethnic identity) and allegiance to school achievement. More recent research by Cauce, Mason, Gonzales, Hiraga, and Liu (1994) expanded the study of peer support to encompass not only multiple dimensions of competence but also peer values. In this study of African American urban adolescents (of whom half were living in poverty), peer support was related positively to all four forms of competence: global self-worth and social, school, and romantic competence. An interaction was found, such that the positive relation between peer support and school competence only held when peers were perceived to support academic goals (Cauce et al., 1994). Thus, the assumption that peer support in urban low-income neighborhoods lowers school competence may not always hold true. Luthar and McMahon (1996) found similar evidence that among a group of largely African American and Latino inner-city adolescents, a subgroup exists who maintain high levels of acceptance by their peers as well as high academic achievement and responsible behavior.

Peer influence may be an important factor in the development of other competence outcomes, as well. Walter et al. (1992) investigated the role of peer influence in HIV risk reduction behaviors among a sample of primarily African American and Latino poor adolescents in New York City. They found a positive relation between reports of consistent condom use and sexual abstinence among peers and the adolescents' own engagement in these behaviors. Evidence from an intervention for homeless urban adolescents supports this link. An intensive 20-session program providing mainly peer-based support for HIV risk reduction led to increases in runaways' reports of consistent condom use, with a dose-response effect for number of sessions (Rotheram-Borus, Koopman, Haignere, & Davies, 1991).

School Contexts

Research on the influence of the school setting on urban poor adolescents has focused, not surprisingly, on academic achievement. Research on the ecology of school, however, has yet to catch up with public concern over the quality of schools in low-income neighborhoods (Kozol, 1991). Concern over the negative effects of school transitions on adolescents is especially warranted among the urban poor, who often make transitions to schools that are not only huge but also resource-poor. Seidman, Allen, Aber, Mitchell, and Feinman (1994) conducted a study as part of the Adolescent Pathways Project on the influence of normative school transitions on a large sample of African American, European American, and Latino urban poor adolescents. They found that the transition to junior high school was associated with drops in self-esteem, class preparation, and grade point average. Changes in perception of the school and peer contexts accompanied these effects: rises in school-specific hassles; declines in school social support, extracurricular involvement, and peer-specific hassles; and perceptions of peers' values as more antisocial. Additional analyses of a further wave of data suggest that these effects were specific to the transition year and not developmental trends (Seidman, Clements, Aber, & Allen, 1996). The authors concluded that the findings support the hypothesis (Eccles & Midgley, 1989) that the junior high school transition—with its move to an unfamiliar peer context, brief contacts with numerous teachers rather than extended contact with one, and a much larger school environment—is developmentally inappropriate for early adolescents. Moreover, such transitions may be particularly problematic in the context of resource-poor urban schools.

Results of urban school reform programs support and extend these basic research findings, although rigorous evaluations have been few. The creation of smaller, more intimate schools within existing huge school buildings is one strategy that has begun to be evaluated (Oxley, in press). In an informal evaluation of one of the first smaller-school efforts, a sample of early adolescent students graduating from Deborah Meier's Central Park East public elementary schools in Harlem went on to achieve a 90% high school graduation rate, substantially higher than the rate in the district as a whole (Meier, 1993). James Comer's well-known intervention, involving the creation of schoolwide planning teams to improve relations

among staff and between staff and parents, succeeded in transforming the culture of two low-performing elementary schools in New
Haven, Connecticut. Over a period of years, the two schools moved
from the bottom of the list of New Haven schools in reading and
math achievement to the top (Comer, 1980). The Comer model has
been replicated in several sites across the country and is being evaluated in Maryland by Amy Anson, Thomas Cook, and colleagues
(Anson et al., 1991; Carnegie Council on Adolescent Development,
1989).

Neighborhood Contexts

   Conventional wisdom would suggest that neighborhood poverty
has a large effect on multiple competence outcomes among adolescents. The existing research is almost entirely limited to neighborhood income effects on education and employment. This literature
shows that when family-level poverty is controlled, most neighborhood income effects are quite modest (Jencks & Mayer, 1990).
Jencks and Mayer noted that very little data exist on such important questions as what difference a move from a low-income
neighborhood to a higher-income neighborhood makes in the lives
of children. However, data from a study of a housing voucher program in Chicago show quite a large effect on children of moving
from inner-city poverty neighborhoods to suburban neighborhoods.
Rosenbaum (1991) was able to compare African American families
that had moved to the suburbs to those that had moved within urban
areas to better neighborhoods (the housing voucher program set up
what was, in essence, a quasi-experiment; initial analyses revealed
that the two groups showed only one minor preprogram difference
across a range of 11 demographic variables). Children of suburb
movers, compared to children of city movers 9 years after their
moves, showed lower levels of high school dropout (5% vs. 20%,
respectively), higher levels of college attendance (54% vs. 21%) and
employment (75% vs. 41%), and higher levels of employment benefits when they were employed (55% vs. 23%). "Although preliminary concerns about discrimination and initial disadvantage were
legitimate, . . . most low-income families were able to overcome difficulties and benefit from the new opportunities" (Rosenbaum, 1991,
p. 1204). Competence may be linked to length of stay in low-income
neighborhoods—one ethnographic study found that African Ameri-

can adolescents more recently arrived in a housing project had higher aspirations for occupational success than did European American adolescents who had lived in the project for a longer period of time (McLeod, 1995).

Very little research has taken a look at other characteristics of neighborhoods besides poverty level. Urban low-income neighborhoods vary in access to material and institutional resources and in indicators of social capital, such as coherence of networks and degree of collective monitoring of children (Coleman, 1988; Jarrett, in press). Differences among family networks in degree of dispersal across neighborhoods and consequent access to varying levels of resources can directly affect the competence of adolescents. Although much of the ethnographic data suggest that families face enormous challenges in coping with the high level of stressors in urban poor neighborhoods, some ethnographic evidence counters prevailing views of urban low-income neighborhoods having only negative effects on adolescent development. Fernandez-Kelly and Schauffler (1994), for example, documented the relative social mobility that characterizes Cuban immigrant youth in Miami's Little Havana. They attributed this mobility to the economic diversity of the original waves of immigrants from Cuba in the 1960s and their reconstitution in Miami of some of the social and economic institutions to which they had been accustomed (Cubans also benefited from government programs such as the Cuban Loan Program; Portes & Zhou, 1993). In contrast, Nicaraguan immigrant youth in Miami lack access to such institutions and, in fact, report that Cubans discriminate against them. Data from a study of Vietnamese youth in the New Orleans neighborhood of Versailles suggest that the availability to youth of Vietnamese community organizations (such as civic associations and the Vietnamese Catholic Church) may contribute to the continued strong ethnic identity and academic success of a substantial proportion of them (Zhou & Bankston, 1994).

Other Contexts Specific to Urban
Low-Income Neighborhoods

Microsystems relevant to urban poor adolescents include some relevant to all adolescents, such as the school, family, peer, and neighborhood contexts, but also some specific to urban poor neighborhoods, such as the housing project community, the urban church, mosque, temple, and other religious institutions, and the vast array of community-based youth organizations. Relatively little research has been carried out on the effects of these settings on urban poor adolescents' competence, with the exception of church involvement, which has been linked to academic achievement among African American (Spencer & Dornbusch, 1990) and Vietnamese immigrant (Zhou & Bankston, 1994) adolescents.

As the above review shows, very little research has investigated how forms and sources of competence may differ across settings. Research on family settings has begun to consider multiple dimensions of competence. In contrast, studies of school influences have been limited to academic competence, and those of neighborhood influences have been limited to academic and employment competence. Almost no quantitative data exist on such important questions as whether school or neighborhood characteristics affect dimensions of competence other than education or employment. One study from the Adolescent Pathways Project presented measure development and validation data concerning involvement/participation of poor urban youth in multiple settings—peer, family, school, neighborhood action, neighborhood social, and athletic activities. Factor analysis revealed that the items of the scale did, indeed, fall into setting-based factors (Seidman et al., 1995). Findings concerning the correlates, sources, and consequences of such setting-based forms of competence would expand greatly our understanding of urban teenagers in poverty.

DEVELOPMENTAL AND CONCEPTUAL MODELS APPROPRIATE TO THE STUDY OF COMPETENCE

Our review has focused on different kinds of competence among urban poor adolescents and how they may differ across multiple contexts. Little attention has been paid thus far to the nature of developmental processes leading to competence. The following section considers the applicability and limitations of current conceptual models of resilience to the study of competence and suggestions for other developmental models that remain to be investigated.

The societal and scientific focus on negative outcomes among urban poor adolescents—low school achievement, delinquency, mental health problems, and teenage pregnancy—has led to the development of models that explain what leads to negative outcomes in adolescence (vulnerability), or what protects against them (resilience) (Garmezy, 1974; Rutter, 1979; Werner & Smith, 1992). *Vulnerability* has been defined as trait-like qualities that can leave one vulnerable to risk effects on negative outcomes. These qualities often have been posited as having sources early in development and often include factors such as temperament or genetic vulnerabilities. They are theorized to increase the chances that proximal or later risks, such as harsh parenting or a poor school environment, will impair development.

Resilience has been defined as overcoming the odds of risk effects, the employment of successful coping in the face of stress, or recovery from past trauma (Masten, Best, & Garmezy, 1990). In all three approaches, resilience counters the probability of a negative outcome. Although this framework has been important and useful in disentangling the influence of multiple factors in the development of negative outcomes and providing implications for preventive interventions (Coie et al., 1993; Yoshikawa, 1994), it may need to be expanded to consider a greater variety of developmental processes leading to positive outcomes. In particular, resilience is often associated with protection against the effects of risk on negative outcomes, an interactive model of resilience that neglects the possibility of direct, cumulative, mediated, or indirect chain effects on positive outcomes. These processes are discussed in turn.

Direct effects are simple bivariate associations that, although not very informative concerning developmental processes, are vital in developing initial theories of what may lead to competence. The study of cumulative effects (Rutter, 1990) answers the question of how multiple direct effects may act together to increase the probability of youth developing competence outcomes. Such effects may be (a) additive, in which the effect of multiple factors represents a simple summing of the separate effects; (b) multiplicative, in which the effect of the factors together leads to a much greater probability of competent outcomes than the sum of the separate effects; or (c) neither, in which there is no summing up of effects. Such effects often are hypothesized to accumulate across time, although much of the research in this area measures multiple predictors at a single point in development, neglecting the importance of timing of exposure to particular factors (e.g., Newcomb & Felix-Ortiz, 1992; Seifer,

Sameroff, Baldwin, & Baldwin, 1992). Most of this research has examined cumulative effects on negative outcomes, whether in the risk or protective direction; none has looked at how predictors may accumulate across time to facilitate the development of competence among urban poor adolescents.

Interactions, in which the effect of a predictor on competence is weakened or strengthened in the presence of another factor, may involve not just protection (the weakening of a risk or vulnerability effect) but also the "piling up" of the positive effects of two factors (a "synergistic" interaction; Rutter, 1990). The prior process most often is associated with resilience and has been investigated quite extensively, though again in predicting lack of negative outcomes rather than the presence of competent outcomes (e.g., research investigating the well-known social support buffering hypothesis). The latter mechanism, which is similar to the cumulative process in its finding of the "piling up" of single direct effects on competence, has been studied rarely (for an exception, see the previous discussion of Luthar's studies of school-based competence, locus of control, and ego development).

Evidence of *statistical mediation* can hint at how direct effects on competence may occur by suggesting that the effect of a given predictor on a competence dimension can be explained by its effect on a mediating factor (Baron & Kenny, 1986). A few studies have begun to look at the possibility of such effects; for example, Taylor et al. (1993) found that authoritative parenting mediates the relation of kinship social support to self-reliance among their sample of African American urban teenagers. Fewer studies, however, have investigated possible mediated effects across time. If a mediating factor is measured chronologically between a predictor and an outcome, one can begin to posit a developmental process (e.g., that authoritative parenting in early adolescence mediates the effects of late childhood peer popularity on the likelihood of high school graduation).

Finally, there may exist *indirect* or *chain effects* of competence dimensions across time—for example, sociability in early childhood leading to leadership qualities in late childhood and involvement in community activities in adolescence. Such indirect effects may or may not reveal instances of statistical mediation.

In addition to the investigation of this variety of mechanisms involved in the development of competence, the impact of normative or non-normative life events and transitions on forms of competence needs to be studied. Such research could consider a wide range of events, such as divorce, school transitions, puberty, exposure to family or community violence, and immigration. The question of developmental specificity of such events can be investigated (e.g., are there points in development when divorce is least likely to affect the development of competence?).

Relatively little research has investigated this range of possible types of effects on competence. Even less has examined these kinds of processes across time. Although much valuable information regarding these effects can be gleaned from cross-sectional observation of naturally occurring developmental phenomena (Rutter, 1994), prospective longitudinal data would greatly enrich our knowledge of how competence develops across time.

Longitudinal data are essential in investigating questions of continuity and discontinuity in dimensions of competence, questions that also remain largely unexplored. Masten et al. (1995) undertook a study that begins to fill this gap in our knowledge. Their data, from a sample of children from mixed-income neighborhoods in the Twin Cities of Minnesota, enabled them to consider the stability of social conduct (the absence of conduct problems), and academic competence from late childhood to late adolescence. Using latent variable modeling, they did, in fact, find stability in all three kinds of competence, with continuity strongest for conduct and somewhat weaker for social and academic areas.

Although the research of Masten et al. (1995) presented evidence supporting homotypic continuity (i.e., continuity in roughly the same behavior across time), there may be other instances in which heterotypic continuity in competence dimensions occurs (i.e., a strong association between two behaviors across time that are different in form but that reflect the same developmental process). Rutter (1989) proposed that heterotypic continuity requires demonstration of the two behaviors sharing common predictors, consequences, or both. With reference to competence, an instance of heterotypic continuity might consist of peer social skills in middle childhood predicting romantic competence in adolescence, with the two constructs showing similar relations to other factors, such as popularity or self-esteem. Attention to heterotypic continuity in competence dimensions may broaden the range of possible competence-enhancing programs and policies for adolescents: By considering the possibility of continuity across seemingly different domains, programs could expand their focus beyond simply enhancing one type of competence at one point in the hope that the same type will be affected later.

Finally, it should be noted that most quantitative research on competence among the urban poor, like most quantitative developmental work in general, uses nomothetic approaches to data, such as regression and analysis of variance models. It has been noted that nomothetic approaches, which focus on variables that represent groups of people, tend toward uniformity of explanation of phenomena (Rapkin & Luke, 1993). Although nomothetic approaches can consider multiple dimensions of competence, in using summary variables as the unit of analysis, they mask how individuals differ from each other on the dimensions. In contrast, idiographic approaches, such as cluster analysis, use the individual as the unit of analysis and can ascertain profiles of competence dimensions. Idiographic approaches therefore may be particularly suited to examining diversity among urban poor adolescents in their forms of competence.

Recent analyses on Adolescent Pathways Project data use just such an approach (cluster analysis) to categorize individuals on six dimensions of competence, broadly defined: academic competence, social skills, self-perceived social competence, self-esteem, positive feelings about one's ethnic identity, and employment (Yoshikawa, Seidman, Aber, Allen, & Friedman, 1998). This methodology enables the investigation of how urban poor teenagers differ from each other on the dimensions of competence rather than simply the investigation of how the dimensions interrelate in the sample as a whole (as correlations or regressions would reveal). Preliminary results show the existence of six profiles: a bravado group, characterized by relatively low levels of social skills and academic competence but high levels of self-perceived social competence; an ethnically disidentified group, characterized by extremely low levels of positive feelings about their ethnic identity; an unhappy underemployed group, characterized by low levels of self-esteem and employment; two competent groups, with generally high levels of competence across the dimensions, distinguished by high and low levels of employment; and an intrapsychically vulnerable group, characterized by low levels of self-perceived social competence and self-esteem.

Future phases of analysis will investigate some of the developmental models described here to answer the following questions: Do competence profiles demonstrate continuity or discontinuity across early to late adolescence? If they demonstrate continuity, is the continuity homotypic or heterotypic (i.e., do associations between profiles of competence across time reflect similar or different relations to predictors and/or consequences)? Do profiles of competence differ when investigated within race-ethnicity (separately for African Americans, European Americans, and Latinos)? How do profiles of competence relate to other developmental outcomes, such as psychological symptoms or antisocial behavior? Do risk or protective bases in earlier development—depth of family or neighborhood poverty, family structure, stressful life events—relate to later competence profiles in direct, cumulative, indirect, or mediated ways? Do indirect or mediated effects of these factors on competence occur differentially through the adolescents' experience of hassles, support, or involvement across different proximal settings, such as family, peer, school, neighborhood, or church? How are profiles of competence dimensions affected by normative or non-normative events, such as transitions to junior high school and high school, divorce, exposure to community violence, and recency of immigration? Finally, what are the implications of these data for enhancement of competence among urban poor adolescents as a whole and among different ethnocultural subgroups?

RECOMMENDATIONS FOR RESEARCH, PROGRAMS, AND POLICIES ADDRESSING COMPETENCE AMONG URBAN POOR ADOLESCENTS

This review was organized not only to present state-of-the-art research on competence among urban poor adolescents but also to indicate, through its subtopics, promising areas for future research. In this respect, this conclusion in part recapitulates the topics covered previously. However, throughout this final section, research recommendations with implications for the promotion of competence through programs and policy are emphasized. Recommendations are made in the following four areas: measurement of competence, sources and mechanisms of competence development, the relation of competence to other outcomes, and the effects of poverty and antipoverty policies on competence.

Measure the Multiple Forms and
Contexts of Competence

The literature reviewed considered multiple forms of competence
and multiple contexts within which they unfold. Many gaps remain
within the topics discussed. As a first step, studies of urban poor
adolescents should include, whenever possible, measures of multiple forms of competence in the relevant contexts within which they
appear. The positive outcomes considered in this chapter reflect
numerous possible areas to investigate, ranging from traditional
forms of academic competence to HIV risk reduction behaviors,
employment, involvement with the extended family, and positive
feelings about ethnic identity. Many of the abilities discussed in
the ethnographic literature, in particular, have not been explored
in the much smaller quantitative literature on competence among
the urban poor. Ethnographic studies also have forged ahead of
quantitative studies in their appreciation of the diversity of competence across cultural groups. Attention to how competence differs across subgroups is necessary in evolving culturally appropriate competence-promotion efforts.

Explore Sources and Processes of Competence
Development to Inform Promotion Efforts

Experimental and observational data can inform each other in the
development of preventive interventions (Price, 1987). The same is
true for the development of health- or competence-promoting interventions, which have been relatively neglected for the same reasons
that study of competence itself has been neglected. Prevention researchers have acknowledged the importance of longitudinal risk
and resilience research for developing theory to guide preventive
interventions (Institute of Medicine, 1994; National Institute of
Mental Health, 1993). Longitudinal research on competence is
equally critical in developing programs and policies to promote
competence among urban poor adolescents.

Information on sources of competence is particularly important
in guiding competence promotion. The following questions remain
largely unanswered: What resources within the child or across
settings (family, peer, neighborhood, etc.) are important in the de-

velopment and continuity of profiles of competence dimensions? How do changes in the availability of such resources relate to changes in competence profiles? Are developmental pathways to those forms of competence common or unique across subgroups? Are there dimensions of competence unique to different developmental periods? Such knowledge could inform decisions concerning the content, timing, and targeting of competence-promotion efforts.

In addition to information on sources of competence, data on processes in its development can have important implications for competence promotion. As mentioned previously, conceptual models of competence development may differ from prevailing models of resilience and may involve direct, cumulative, interactive, indirect, or mediated relations among predictors, between predictors and competence outcomes, and/or among competence outcomes. These different kinds of relations illuminate different processes in the development of competence and may have different implications for intervention (Yoshikawa, 1995). Evidence of the cumulative effect of multiple competence-promoting factors may indicate the promise of combining components of a program targeted to each factor, as long as the effect of each factor is independent. For example, if separate programs have been developed to enhance the quality of parental and school involvement in adolescents' lives, and if these two factors have been shown to have cumulative effects on one or more dimensions of competence, the programs could be combined to have a greater effect than either alone. Evidence of mediation, on the other hand, may imply that attention to the predictor's effects on competence without attention to the mediator's effects may hinder the effectiveness of an intervention aimed at increasing the effect of the predictor. For example, consider hypothetical findings that the effects of retention of the parent language on school-based competence among immigrant adolescents are mediated by identification with immigrant identity. Programs that encourage bilingualism among this population may benefit from tracking their effect on immigrant identity or including components that acknowledge or even maintain it.

Several problematic issues arise when using developmental research on competence to inform programs and policies. First, given the diversity of the urban poor and the variety in dimensions of competence, the degree of targeting and specifying of outcomes becomes an extremely important aspect of program and policy design. Interaction effects, in which developmental processes leading to competence dimensions differ across subgroups or dimensions, may suggest that interventions designed to promote one form of competence in one group are inappropriate for other groups or for other forms (Seidman, 1994). On the other hand, certain forms of competence may be common to multiple groups (e.g., school achievement); broadly targeted interventions may then be appropriate (i.e., school restructuring programs). Second, care must be taken to consider the question of who is defining competence. Adolescents, members of their families, members of their communities, and researchers may have very different ideas concerning what forms of competence are important, what should be done to enhance them, and, indeed, whether they need to be encouraged at all. Community-based competence-promotion programs may benefit from models such as those evaluated by Hawkins, Catalano, and Associates (1992), in which community members come together to choose which risk factors for drug abuse to address in their prevention efforts.

Explore How Competence Relates to Other Outcomes
to Guide Prevention and Promotion

Through much of this chapter, research on competence has been highlighted as a contrast to the prevailing emphasis on problematic outcomes among urban poor teenagers. It is important, however, to place competence in the context of such outcomes, to guide the twin goals of prevention and competence promotion. As Luthar's research showed, for some urban poor adolescents, competence dimensions may coexist with other outcomes, such as anxiety. In addition, indicators of difficulty may share certain predictors with indicators of competence.

Research on how problematic and successful outcomes do or do not share common developmental pathways will serve to answer the question of when problem prevention overlaps with competence promotion and when it does not. For example, findings of associations between HIV risk reduction behaviors and low levels of anxiety, depression, and substance use have implications for intervention (Rotheram-Borus, Rosario, Reid, & Koopman, 1995): The authors suggest that future HIV risk reduction programs for adolescents should focus not just on the target behaviors but on mental health needs, as well. Another example: Evaluators may shortchange a particular program's effects if they consider only reductions in negative outcomes, such as delinquency, and ignore other, possibly complementary, positive outcomes, such as employment (Yoshikawa, 1995).

Explore the Effects of Poverty and Antipoverty Policies on Competence Outcomes

Although the literature on poverty and school achievement is quite large, very little data exist on the relation of poverty to other forms of competence. Many questions remain to be explored concerning the effects of poverty on adolescent competence, such as: What are the effects of depth of poverty (near-poverty to extreme poverty) on forms of competence? How do neighborhood-level poverty and family-level poverty affect competence profiles? Are effects of poverty on competence dimensions mediated by effects on other aspects of adolescents' lives? Do changes in poverty, income, or employment status of parents or adolescents lead to changes in the adolescents' profiles of competence?

Competence-promoting efforts for this population also should be considered in the context of antipoverty policies and programs. Many questions arise concerning the relation between competence-promotion and antipoverty initiatives. Do the two goals complement each other or work at cross-purposes? For example, do different types of welfare reform efforts (ranging from time limits and sanctions to job training and "make work pay" efforts) help or hinder the development of competence among adolescents? Do economic empowerment initiatives, taking place at the level of the neighborhood, have effects on competence dimensions? Do policy changes, such as those in Medicaid coverage or immigration policy, affect competence dimensions? Do these effects occur directly or are they mediated through effects on neighborhood or family factors? Competence promotion among urban low-income adolescents, like competence itself, needs to be placed in the context of changes in urban poverty in America.

CONCLUSION

This chapter has considered the range of what we now know about the competence of urban adolescents in poverty. Much progress has been made in the last decade in delineating more clearly than before how teenagers facing the challenges of poverty develop a wide range of skills and abilities. Our findings suggest, however, that an expansion of the field of study to encompass new forms and contexts of adolescent competence, as well as the variety of developmental processes through which they develop, would enrich our vision of this population. Such knowledge, in turn, can serve to inform new policies and programs based on models of strength rather than deficit and help counter prevailing negative images of urban adolescents in poverty.

REFERENCES

Allison, K., & Takei, Y. (1993). Diversity: The cultural contexts of adolescents and their families. In R. M. Lerner (Ed.), *Early adolescence: Perspectives on research, policy, and intervention* (pp. 51-69). Hillsdale, NJ: Lawrence Erlbaum.

Alva, S. A. (1991). Academic invulnerability among Mexican-American students: The importance of protective resources and appraisals. *Hispanic Journal of Behavioral Sciences, 13,* 18-34.

Annie E. Casey Foundation. (1994). *Kids Count data book: 1993.* Baltimore: Author.

Anson, A. R., Cook, T. D., Habib, F., Grady, M. K., Haynes, N., & Comer, J. P. (1991). The Comer school development program: A theoretical analysis. *Urban Education, 26,* 56-82.

Baldwin, A. L., Baldwin, C., & Cole, R. E. (1990). Stress-resistant families and stress-resistant children. In J. Rolf, A. S. Masten, D. Cicchetti, K. H. Nuechterlein, & S. Weintraub (Eds.), *Risk and protective factors in the development of psychopathology* (pp. 257-280). New York: Cambridge University Press.

Baldwin, A. L., Baldwin, C. P., Kasser, T., Zax, M., Sameroff, A., & Seifer, R. (1993). Contextual risk and resiliency during late adolescence. *Development and Psychopathology, 5,* 741-762.

Baron, R. M., & Kenny, D. A. (1986). The moderator-mediator variable distinction in social psychological research: Conceptual, strategic, and statistical considerations. *Journal of Personality and Social Psychology, 51,* 1173-1182.

Bat-Chava, Y., Allen, L., Seidman, E., Aber, J. L., & Ventura, A. M. (1996). *Ethnic identity among African-American, Latino, and White urban adolescents: Nomothetic and idiographic approaches.* Unpublished manuscript, New York University.

Brooks-Gunn, J., & Reiter, E. O. (1990). The role of pubertal processes. In S. S. Feldman & G. R. Elliott (Eds.), *At the threshold: The developing adolescent* (pp. 16-53). Cambridge, MA: Harvard University Press.

Bullard, R. D., & Wright, B. H. (1993). Environmental justice for all: Community perspectives on health and research needs. *Toxicology and Industrial Health, 9,* 821-841.

Burton, L. M., Allison, K. W., & Obeidallah, D. (1995). Social context and adolescence: Perspectives on development among inner-city African-American teens. In L. J. Crockett & A. C. Crouter (Eds.), *Pathways through adolescence* (pp. 119-138). Hillsdale, NJ: Lawrence Erlbaum.

Caplan, N., Choy, M. H., & Whitmore, J. K. (1992, February). Indochinese refugee families and academic achievement. *Scientific American, 266*(2), 36-42.

Carnegie Council on Adolescent Development. (1989). *Turning points: Preparing American youth for the 21st century.* Washington, DC: Author.

Cauce, A. M., Felner, R. D., & Primavera, J. (1982). Social support in high-risk adolescents: Structural components and adaptive impact. *American Journal of Community Psychology, 10,* 417-428.

Cauce, A. M., Mason, C., Gonzales, N., Hiraga, Y., & Liu, G. (1994). Social support during adolescence: Methodological and theoretical considerations. In F. Nestmann & K. Hurrelmann (Eds.), *Social networks and social support in childhood and adolescence* (pp. 89-108). Berlin, Germany: de Gruyter.

Chase-Lansdale, P. L., Brooks-Gunn, J., & Zamsky, E. S. (1994). Young African-American multigenerational families in poverty: Quality of mothering and grandmothering. *Child Development, 65,* 373-393.

Coie, J. D., Watt, N. F., West, S. G., Hawkins, J. D., Asarnow, J. R., Markman, H. J., Ramey, S. L., Shure, M. B., & Long, B. (1993). The science of prevention: A conceptual framework and some directions for a national research program. *American Psychologist, 48,* 1013-1022.

Cole, M. (1992). Culture in development. In M. H. Bornstein & M. E. Lamb (Eds.), *Developmental psychology: An advanced textbook* (pp. 731-789). Hillsdale, NJ: Lawrence Erlbaum.

Coleman, J. S. (1988). Social capital in the creation of human capital. *American Journal of Sociology, 94*(Suppl. 1), S95-S120.

Colletta, N. D., & Lee, D. (1983). The impact of support for Black adolescent mothers. *Journal of Family Issues, 4,* 127-143.

Comer, J. P. (1980). *School power.* New York: Free Press.

Council of the Great City Schools. (1992). *National urban education goals: Baseline indicators, 1990-91.* Washington, DC: Author.

Cuciti, P., & James, F. (1990). A comparison of Black and Hispanic poverty in large cities of the Southwest. *Hispanic Journal of Behavioral Sciences, 12,* 50-75.

Danziger, S. H., & Weinberg, D. H. (1994). The historical record: Trends in family income, inequality, and poverty. In S. H. Danziger, G. D. Sandefur, & D. H. Weinberg (Eds.), *Confronting poverty: Prescriptions for change* (pp. 18-50). Cambridge, MA: Harvard University Press.

Eccles, J. S., & Midgley, C. (1989). Stage/environment fit: Developmentally appropriate classrooms for young adolescents. In R. E. Ames & C. Ames (Eds.), *Research on motivation in education* (Vol. 3, pp. 139-186). New York: Academic Press.

Elliott, G. R. & Feldman, S.S. (1990). Capturing the adolescent experience. In S. S. Feldman & G. R. Elliott (Eds.), *At the threshold: The developing adolescent* (pp. 1-13). Cambridge, MA: Harvard University Press.

Erikson, E. H. (1968). *Identity: Youth in crisis.* New York: Norton.

Fernandez-Kelly, M. P., & Schauffler, R. (1994). Divided fates: Immigrant children in
    a restructured U.S. economy. *International Migration Review, 28,* 662-689.
Fine, M. (1991). *Framing dropouts: Notes on the politics of an urban high school.* Albany:
    State University of New York Press.
Fordham, S., & Ogbu, J. U. (1986). Black students' school success: Coping with the
    burden of "acting White." *Urban Review, 18,* 176-206.
Gans, H. J. (1995). *The war against the poor: The underclass and antipoverty policy.*
    New York: Basic Books.
Garmezy, N. (1974). The study of competence in children at risk for severe
    psychopathology. In E. J. Anthony & C. Koupernik (Eds.), *Children at psychiatric
    risk* (pp. 77-97). New York: John Wiley.
Hawkins, J. D., Catalano, R. F., & Associates (1992). *Communities that care: Action for
    drug abuse prevention.* San Francisco: Jossey-Bass.
Huston, A. C., McLoyd, V. C., & Garcia Coll, C. (1994). Children and poverty:
    Issues in contemporary research. *Child Development, 65,* 275-282.
Institute of Medicine. (1994). *Reducing risks for mental disorders: Frontiers for preven-
    tive intervention research.* Washington, DC: National Academy Press.
Jargowsky, P. A., & Bane, M. J. (1990). Ghetto poverty: Basic questions. In L. E. Lynn
    & M. G. H. McGeary (Eds.), *Inner-city poverty in the United States* (pp. 16-67).
    Washington, DC: National Academy Press.
Jarrett, R. L. (in press). Community context, intrafamilial processes and social mo-
    bility outcomes: Ethnographic contributions to the study of African-American
    families. In M. B. Spencer & G. K. Brookins (Eds.), *Ethnicity and diversity.*
    Hillsdale, NJ: Lawrence Erlbaum.
Jemmott, J. B., & Jemmott, L. S. (1994). Interventions for adolescents in community
    settings. In R. J. DiClemente & J. L. Peterson (Eds.), *Preventing AIDS: Theories and
    methods of behavioral interventions* (pp. 141-174). New York: Plenum.
Jencks, C., & Mayer, S. E. (1990). The social consequences of growing up in a poor
    neighborhood. In L. E. Lynn & M. G. H. McGeary (Eds.), *Inner-city poverty in the
    United States* (pp. 111-186). Washington, DC: National Academy Press.
Jessor, R. (1993). Successful adolescent development among youth in high-risk set-
    tings. *American Psychologist, 48,* 117-126.
Karoly, L. A. (1993). The trend in inequality among families, individuals, and
    workers in the United States: A twenty-five year perspective. In S. Danziger &
    P. Gottschalk (Eds.), *Uneven tides: Rising inequality in America* (pp. 19-97). New
    York: Russell Sage Foundation.
Kozol, J. (1991). *Savage inequalities: Children in America's schools.* New York: Crown.
Linn, M. C. (1983). Content, context and process in reasoning. *Journal of Early Adoles-
    cence, 3,* 63-82.
Luthar, S. S. (1991). Vulnerability and resilience: A study of high-risk adolescents.
    Child Development, 62, 600-616.
Luthar, S. S. (1995). Social competence in the school setting: Prospective cross-
    domain associations among inner-city teens. *Child Development, 66,* 416-429.
Luthar, S. S. (1997). Sociodemographic disadvantage and psychosocial adjustment:
    Perspectives from developmental psychopathology. In S. S. Luthar, J. Burack,
    D. Cicchetti, & J. Weisz (Eds.), *Developmental psychopathology: Perspectives on
    adjustment, risk, and disorder.* New York: Cambridge University Press.

Luthar, S. S., & McMahon, T. J. (1996). Peer reputation among inner-city adolescents: Structure and correlates. *Journal of Research on Adolescence, 6,* 581-603.

Luthar, S. S., & Zigler, E. (1992). Intelligence and social competence among high-risk adolescents. *Development and Psychopathology, 4,* 287-300.

Masten, A. S., Best, K. M., & Garmezy, N. (1990). Resilience and development: Contributions from the study of children who overcome adversity. *Development and Psychopathology, 2,* 425-444.

Masten, A. S., Coatsworth, J. D., Neemann, J., Gest, S. D., Tellegen, A., & Garmezy, N. (1995). The structure and coherence of competence from childhood through adolescence. *Child Development, 66,* 1635-1659.

Mayer, S. E., & Jencks, C. (1989). Growing up in poor neighborhoods: How much does it matter? *Science, 243,* 1441-1445.

McGahey, R. M. (1986). Economic conditions, neighborhood organization, and urban crime. In A. J. Reiss & M. Tonry (Eds.), *Crime and justice: A review of research: Vol. 8. Communities and crime* (pp. 231-270). Chicago: University of Chicago Press.

McLeod, J. (1995). *Ain't no making it: Aspirations and attainment in a low-income community.* Boulder, CO: Westview.

McLoyd, V. C. (1990). The impact of economic hardship on Black families and children: Psychological distress, parenting, and socioemotional development. *Child Development, 61,* 311-346.

McLoyd, V. C., Jayaratne, T. E., Ceballo, R., & Borquez, J. (1994). Unemployment and work interruption among African American single mothers: Effects on parenting and adolescent socioemotional functioning. *Child Development, 65,* 562-589.

Mehan, H., Hubbard, L., & Villanueva, I. (1994). Forming academic identities: Accommodation without assimilation among involuntary minorities. *Anthropology and Education Quarterly, 25,* 91-117.

Meier, D. (1993). Transforming schools into powerful communities. *Teachers College Record, 94,* 454-458.

National Center for Education Statistics. (1993). *Dropout rates in the United States: 1992.* Washington, DC: U.S. Department of Education.

National Institute of Mental Health. (1993). *The prevention of mental disorders: A national research agenda.* Washington, DC: Government Printing Office.

National Research Council, Commission on Behavioral and Social Sciences and Education, Panel on High-Risk Youth. (1993). *Losing generations: Adolescents in high-risk settings.* Washington, DC: National Academy Press.

Newcomb, M. D., & Felix-Ortiz, M. (1992). Multiple protective and risk factors for drug use and abuse: Cross-sectional and prospective findings. *Journal of Personality and Social Psychology, 63,* 280-296.

Oxley, D. (in press). The school reform movement: Opportunities for community psychology. In J. Rappaport & E. Seidman (Eds.), *Handbook of community psychology.* New York: Plenum.

Parrish, T. B., Matsumoto, C. S., & Fowler, W. J. (1995). *Disparities in public school district spending: 1989-1990* (U.S. Department of Education, National Center for Education Statistics). Washington, DC: Government Printing Office.

Pastor, J., McCormick, J., & Fine, M. (1996). Makin' homes: An urban girl thing. In B. J. R. Leadbeater & N. Way (Eds.), *Urban girls: Resisting stereotypes, creating identities* (pp. 15-34). New York: New York University Press.

Portes, A., & Schauffler, R. (1994). Language and the second generation: Bilingualism yesterday and today. *International Migration Review, 28,* 640-661.

Portes, A., & Zhou, M. (1993). The new second generation: Segmented assimilation. *Annals of the American Academy of Political and Social Sciences, 530,* 74-97.

Price, R. H. (1987). Linking intervention research and risk factor research. In J. A. Steinberg & M. M. Silverman (Eds.), *Preventing mental disorders: A research perspective* (DHHS Publication No. ADM 87-1492, pp. 48-56). Washington, DC: Government Printing Office.

Rapkin, B. D., & Luke, D. A. (1993). Cluster analysis in community research: Epistemology and practice. *American Journal of Community Psychology, 21,* 247-277.

Rosenbaum, J. E. (1991). Black pioneers—Do their moves to the suburbs increase economic opportunity for mothers and children? *Housing Policy Debate, 2,* 1179-1213.

Rotheram-Borus, M. J., Koopman, C., Haignere, C., & Davies, M. (1991). Reducing HIV sexual risk behaviors among runaway adolescents. *Journal of the American Medical Association, 266,* 1237-1241.

Rotheram-Borus, M. J., Meyer-Bahlburg, H. F. L., Koopman, C., Rosario, M., Exner, T. M., Henderson, R., Matthieu, M., & Gruen, R. S. (1992). Lifetime sexual behaviors among runaway males and females. *Journal of Sex Research, 29,* 15-29.

Rotheram-Borus, M. J., Rosario, M., Reid, H., & Koopman, C. (1995). Predicting patterns of sexual acts among homosexual and bisexual youths. *American Journal of Psychiatry, 152,* 588-595.

Rumbaut, R. G. (1997). Ties that bind: Immigration and immigrant families in the United States. In A. Booth, A. C. Crouter, & N. S. Landale (Eds.), *Immigration and the family: Research and policy on U.S. immigrants* (pp. 3-46). Mahwah, NJ: Lawrence Erlbaum.

Rutter, M. (1979). Protective factors in children's responses to stress and disadvantage. In M. W. Kent & J. E. Rolf (Eds.), *Primary prevention of psychopathology: Vol. 3. Social competence in children* (pp. 49-74). Hanover, NH: University Press of New England.

Rutter, M. (1989). Pathways from childhood to adult life. *Journal of Child Psychology and Psychiatry and Allied Disciplines, 30,* 23-51.

Rutter, M. (1990). Psychosocial resilience and protective mechanisms. In J. Rolf, A. S. Masten, D. Cicchetti, K. H. Nuechterlein, & S. Weintraub (Eds.), *Risk and protective factors in the development of psychopathology* (pp. 181-214). New York: Cambridge University Press.

Rutter, M. (1994). Beyond longitudinal data: Causes, consequences, changes, and continuity. *Journal of Consulting and Clinical Psychology, 62,* 928-940.

Sampson, R. J. (1992). Family management and child development: Insights from social disorganization theory. In J. McCord (Ed.), *Facts, frameworks and forecasts: Advances in criminological theory* (Vol. 3, pp. 63-93). New Brunswick, NJ: Transaction Publishing.

Savin-Williams, R. C. (1995). Lesbian, gay male, and bisexual adolescents. In A. R. D'Augelli & C. J. Patterson (Eds.), *Lesbian, gay, and bisexual identities over the lifespan* (pp. 165-189). New York: Oxford University Press.

Seidman, E. (1991). Growing up the hard way: Pathways of urban adolescents. *American Journal of Community Psychology, 19,* 173-205.

Seidman, E. (1994, Winter). Ecological theory and research: Dilemmas for action scientists. *Community Psychologist, 21*(4), 6-8.

Seidman, E., Allen, L., Aber, J. L., Mitchell, C., & Feinman, J. (1994). The impact of school transitions in early adolescence on the self-system and perceived social context of poor urban youth. *Child Development, 65,* 507-522.

Seidman, E., Allen, L., Aber, J. L., Mitchell, C., Feinman, J., Yoshikawa, H., Comtois, K. A., Golz, J., Miller, R. L., Ortiz-Torres, B., & Roper, G. C. (1995). Development and validation of adolescent-perceived microsystem scales: Social support, daily hassles, and involvement. *American Journal of Community Psychology, 23,* 355-388.

Seidman, E., Clements, M., Aber, J. L., & Allen, L. (1996). *One year later: Longitudinal effects on poor urban youth of the transition to junior high school.* Unpublished manuscript, New York University.

Seidman, E., & Rappaport, J. (1986). Introduction. In E. Seidman & J. Rappaport (Eds.), *Redefining social problems* (pp. 1-9). New York: Plenum.

Seifer, R., Sameroff, A. J., Baldwin, C. P., & Baldwin, A. (1992). Child and family factors that ameliorate risk between 4 and 13 years of age. *Journal of the American Academy of Child and Adolescent Psychiatry, 31,* 893-903.

Sherman, A. (1994). *Wasting America's future: The Children's Defense Fund report on the costs of child poverty.* Boston: Beacon.

Slaughter-Defoe, D. T., Nakagawa, K., Takanishi, R., & Johnson, D. J. (1990). Toward cultural/ecological perspectives on schooling and achievement in African- and Asian-American children. *Child Development, 61,* 363-383.

Spencer, M. B., & Dornbusch, S. M. (1990). Challenges in studying minority youth. In S. S. Feldman & G. R. Elliott (Eds.), *At the threshold: The developing adolescent* (pp. 123-146). Cambridge, MA: Harvard University Press.

Stack, C. B., & Burton, L. M. (1993). Kinscripts. *Journal of Comparative Family Studies, 24,* 157-170.

Steinberg, L., Darling, N. E., Fletcher, A. C., Brown, B. B., & Dornbusch, S. M. (1995). Authoritative parenting and adolescent adjustment: An ecological journey. In P. Moen, G. H. Elder, & K. Luscher (Eds.), *Examining lives in context: Perspectives on the ecology of human development* (pp. 423-466). Washington, DC: American Psychological Association.

Taylor, R. D., Casten, R., & Flickinger, S. M. (1993). Influence of kinship social support on the parenting experiences and psychosocial adjustment of African-American adolescents. *Developmental Psychology, 29,* 382-388.

Taylor, R. D., & Roberts, D. (1995). Kinship support and material and adolescent well-being in economically disadvantaged African-American families. *Child Development, 66,* 1585-1597.

Tienda, M. (1991). Poor people and poor places: Deciphering neighborhood effects on poverty outcomes. In J. Huber (Ed.), *Macro-micro linkages in sociology* (pp. 244-262). Newbury Park, CA: Sage.

Tyler, F. B., Tyler, S. L., Tommasello, A., & Zhang, Y. (1992). Psychosocial characteristics of marginal immigrant Latino youth. *Youth and Society, 24,* 92-115.

U.S. Census Bureau. (1993a). *Population projections of the United States, by age, sex, race, and Hispanic origin: 1993 to 2050.* Washington, DC: Government Printing Office.

U.S. Census Bureau. (1993b). *We the American foreign born.* Washington, DC: Government Printing Office.

U.S. Census Bureau. (1995). *Income, poverty, and valuation of noncash benefits: 1993* (Current Population Reports Series P60-188). Washington, DC: Government Printing Office.

Walter, H. J., Vaughan, R. D., Gladis, M. M., Ragin, D. F., Kasen, S., & Cohall, A. T. (1992). Factors associated with AIDS risk behaviors among high school students in an AIDS epicenter. *American Journal of Public Health, 82,* 528-532.

Ward, J. V. (1996). Raising resisters: The role of truth telling in the psychological development of African American girls. In B. J. R. Leadbeater & N. Way (Eds.), *Urban girls: Resisting stereotypes, creating identities* (pp. 85-99). New York: New York University Press.

Waters, M. C. (1994). Ethnic and racial identities of second-generation Black immigrants in New York City. *International Migration Review, 28,* 795-820.

Werner, E. E., & Smith, R. S. (1992). *Overcoming the odds: High risk children from birth to adulthood.* Ithaca, NY: Cornell University Press.

Williams, T. M., & Kornblum, W. (1985). *Growing up poor.* Lexington, MA: Lexington Books.

Wilson, W. J. (1987). *The truly disadvantaged: The inner city, the underclass, and public policy.* Chicago: University of Chicago Press.

Wilson, W. J. (1996). *When work disappears: The world of the new urban poor.* New York: Knopf.

Yoshikawa, H. (1994). Prevention as cumulative protection: Effects of early family support and education on chronic delinquency and its risks. *Psychological Bulletin, 105,* 28-54.

Yoshikawa, H. (1995, Winter). Long-term effects of early childhood programs on social outcomes and delinquency. *The Future of Children, 5*(3), 51-75.

Yoshikawa, H., Seidman, E., Aber, J. L., Allen, L., & Friedman, J. (1998). *Multidimensional profiles of competence among urban adolescents in poverty.* Manuscript submitted for publication.

Zhou, M., & Bankston, C. L. (1994). Social capital and the adaptation of the second generation: The case of Vietnamese youth in New Orleans. *International Migration Review, 28,* 821-845.

Zigler, E., & Muenchow, S. (1992). *Head Start: The inside story of America's most successful educational experiment.* New York: Basic Books.

Zigler, E., & Trickett, P. K. (1978). IQ, social competence, and evaluation of early childhood intervention programs. *American Psychologist, 33,* 789-98.

Zimmerman, M. A., Salem, D. A., & Maton, K. I. (1995). Family structure and psychosocial correlates among urban African-American adolescent males. *Child Development, 66,* 1598-1613.

3. Rural Youth: Ecological and Life Course Perspectives

Lisa J. Crockett
Michael J. Shanahan
Julia Jackson-Newsom

Until recently, rural youth were largely neglected within the socio-logical and psychological literature. Within sociology, there is a long and distinguished tradition of research on rural-urban differences (Adair-Toteff, 1995; Nelson, 1952), but typically these studies have focused on adults or on the rural population as a whole, with little attention to adolescents as an important subgroup. Conversely, within psychology, adolescents are recognized as a distinct develop-mental subgroup, but there has been little attempt to determine how and to what extent rural youth differ from their urban and suburban counterparts. From an ecological perspective (Bronfenbrenner, 1979; Ianni, 1989), differences would be expected, because rural settings differ from metropolitan settings in important ways, creating dis-tinct contexts for development. Yet, few studies have focused on the distinctive features of the rural ecology and their implications for adolescent development.

In part, this neglect may reflect the perception that rural adoles-cents are few in number. However, a substantial percentage of U.S. adolescents are growing up in rural America. Data from the 1990 census indicate that rural youth (i.e., those who live in towns of fewer than 2,500 or unincorporated areas that are not near metropol-itan areas) account for 15.5% of U.S. adolescents between the ages of 10 and 19; rural metropolitan youth (who live in small towns or out-side incorporated areas but adjacent to a fairly large city) account for another 11.5% (U.S. Census Bureau, 1992). Thus, more than one in four adolescents in the United States (almost 9.5 million youth) live in rural settings.

Inattention to rural youth also may reflect the perception that their problems are less pressing than those of inner-city and minority adolescents and that rural adolescents are insulated from the problems of contemporary urban America by virtue of their geographic isolation and strong ties to family and community. Indeed, traditional rural communities would appear to be high in *social capital* (see Coleman, 1988), defined as "social relationships that serve as resources for individuals to draw upon in implementing their goals" (Furstenberg, 1994, p. 5). Specifically, social capital depends on dense ties among family, kin, schools, religious institutions, and local community organizations. Such ties provide a framework of shared norms, mutual obligations, and access to information that supplements an individual's personal resources. Furthermore, communities rich in social capital are high in both investments in youth and in informal social control (Coleman, 1988), making them supportive environments for development. From this perspective, rural communities should promote adaptive functioning among adolescents. Yet, the sweeping social, economic, and demographic changes that have engulfed rural America define a context of risk for children and adolescents. During this century, technological advances, global competition, and spreading urbanization have transformed rural settings and ways of life radically. The number of jobs in farming and extractive industries has declined steadily since the early 1900s, eroding the traditional economic bases of rural communities (Freudenburg, 1992; Hobbs, 1994). More recently, the farm crisis of the early 1980s led to the loss of large numbers of family farms in the Midwest (Conger & Elder, 1994).

These changes have brought increased disadvantage to rural areas. Currently, poverty rates are higher in nonmetropolitan areas than in metropolitan areas (Jensen & McLaughlin, 1995), especially among children (Hobbs, 1994), and unemployment is more common and more prolonged (Swaim, 1995). Moreover, rural-urban migration patterns have favored metropolitan areas strongly: Rural areas have witnessed large losses of the young, educated, and skilled (Lichter, McLaughlin, & Cornwell, 1995), raising the specter of increasing concentrations of poverty in some rural areas (Fitchen, 1995; Lichter, 1993). In small towns of fewer than 2,500 inhabitants, rapid depopulation and the growing concentration of elderly have been accompanied by precipitous declines in the availability of retail and professional services (Johansen, 1993). Models of social change suggest that such economic and demographic shifts disrupt traditional patterns of social organization, producing strain in the family and community (Conger & Elder, 1994). In addition, economic decline and the outmigration of talented young adults conspire to reduce resources for schools and youth services (Hobbs, 1994). Thus, the social changes transforming rural America create challenges for successful adolescent development. In recognition of these and other problems, several reports published in the past few decades have identified rural children and youth as being "disadvantaged" or "at-risk" (e.g., Edington, 1970; Ehly & Retish, 1990; Helge, 1990; William T. Grant Foundation, 1988).

A third reason for the lack of attention to rural adolescents may relate to the difficulties inherent in studying such a diverse group of youth. Although rural communities may share important characteristics that distinguish them from metropolitan communities, they also differ from each other along such potentially important dimensions as geographic region, ethnic composition, occupational structure, and access to major cities. Thus, life for adolescents in rural Mississippi is different from life for rural youth in the small mining towns of Pennsylvania or the farming communities of rural Iowa. Because of this diversity of settings, many of which have not yet been studied adequately, generalizations about rural youth at this point are difficult.

Despite the scientific challenges, the study of rural adolescents has much to contribute to the field of adolescence and to social policy. From a policy perspective, a focus on rural youth can identify areas of risk or disadvantage that call for intervention; it also can provide insight into the sources of resilience among rural youth that may apply in other settings as well. From a theoretical perspective, the study of rural adolescents can enhance our understanding of basic developmental and ecological processes. In particular, the confluence of social change and social capital in rural communities offers a unique opportunity to study both the challenges to healthy development created by social change and the dynamic processes of family and community adaptation.

Drawing on the themes of social change, ecological risk, and their implications for the life course, this chapter is intended as a point of departure for future research on rural adolescents. We begin by con-

sidering the basic but difficult issue of defining the ecology of rural
youth, noting possible sources of risk and resilience. We then examine research on psychosocial adjustment among rural youth, identifying how they are advantaged and disadvantaged relative to other
youth. Third, we turn to a central challenge facing contemporary
rural youth: the need to reconcile attachments to family and place
with a desire for educational and occupational mobility. Finally, we
suggest conceptual and empirical guidelines for future research.

DEFINING THE ECOLOGY
OF "RURAL" YOUTH

Rural typically has been defined comparatively, relative to the
qualities of urban life. Within this comparative framework, some
researchers have relied on a rural-urban dichotomy. The census criteria are illustrative of this approach: Since at least 1874, the census
has defined rural residents as anyone living in or near towns of some
specified size (e.g., fewer than 2,500 residents). The limitation of this
approach is readily apparent: Even if the complexities of rural communities can be distilled into measurable dimensions, cutoff levels
for dichotomous classifications are imprecise and inherently arbitrary. One example of this problem involves densely populated
areas outside cities and towns. Under earlier census definitions,
these unincorporated areas would be considered "rural"; yet, based
on population density, these areas should be counted as "urban." In
recognition of this problem, the census definition of "town" and
"city" has been modified repeatedly to accommodate increasing
population density within unincorporated areas (Truesdell, 1949).

A second comparative strategy assumes that, rather than representing an absolute dichotomy, rural and urban communities fall
along a continuum defined by multiple dimensions, such as population heterogeneity, size and density, and the predominance of agriculture (e.g., Sorokin & Zimmerman, 1929; Wirth, 1938). Thus, the
"purely rural" community is sparsely populated, lacking in diversity, and based on farming as a way of life and livelihood.

Problems also have arisen with this approach. First, rural-urban
typologies reflect so many criteria that the validity of the distinction
is questionable (Dewey, 1960). Second, empirical investigations
have found that variables thought to underlie the rural-urban con-

tinuum are not always closely interrelated. For example, Willits and Bealer (1967) examined correlations among three dimensions of rurality: ecological (e.g., population density), occupational (e.g., proportion of farmers in the area), and sociocultural (prevalence of traditionalism in the area) and found that these relations were uniformly low. Such results are contrary to the notion of an underlying continuum. Indeed, Beers (1957) suggested that the rural-urban distinction, although initially valid, has become less meaningful during the 20th century as interstate highways and mass communication have strengthened the connection between rural and urban areas and as the predominance of agriculture has waned in rural areas. Similarly, Hobbs (1994) noted, "Cities have deconcentrated into the countryside, and rural and urban lifestyles have converged under the effects of a mass society with its mass media and mass consumption" (p. 149).

Nonetheless, people readily make use of the rural-urban distinction to characterize places and persons (Jacob & Luloff, 1995). Thus, a third measurement strategy relies on an individual's perception of place. For example, based on interviews with a small group of Californians, Hummon (1986) reported that self-identified small-town residents defined themselves as coming from a place of more intimate bonds, domesticity, and tradition than city dwellers; they also rejected "spurious" urban values (e.g., materialism, conformity). "Country people," a popular self-designation of rural town residents, viewed themselves and their community as being independent, practical, plain, broadly skilled, and close to nature because of outdoor activities (see also Bell, 1992). This research suggests that, although the rural-urban distinction cannot be quantified easily, it remains an important social category and a basis for self-definition and community identity. As such, it may have important implications for the socialization of young people.

The preceding discussion alerts us to the challenges of defining "rural" and to the caveats one must keep in mind when interpreting empirical findings. Clearly, there is no consensus about how "rurality" should be defined and measured. Still, it can be argued that four dimensions—population size and density, community ties, traditionalism, and land use—have figured prominently in discussions of rural life and serve as a possible basis for defining rural settings. Importantly, these ecological dimensions also appear to have important implications for adolescent development. We turn next to a discussion of these four dimensions and their possible influences on rural youth.

Population Size and Density

Rural areas generally have been characterized by low population density and small community size. These demographic criteria may be important for adolescent adjustment because of their effects on social participation and psychological well-being. Barker has argued that "undermanned" settings, in which relatively few people are available to fill a large number of roles, require greater levels of participation by individuals in the system. In such settings, individuals are actively recruited to fill important roles. For example, Barker and Gump (1964) found that students from small schools participate in twice as many extracurricular activities as do those in large schools; they are also more likely to report feeling needed, responsible, and confident. Similarly, small communities may constitute undermanned settings in which adolescent participation is actively solicited. Rural adolescents may be highly involved in their schools and communities, with resulting psychological benefits.

Retrospective accounts of former graduates of small rural high schools in Iowa confirm some of the advantages of these educational settings (Schonert-Reichl, Elliott, & Bills, 1995). Many graduates commented on the benefits of being involved in multiple extracurricular activities, including opportunities to assume leadership roles and to develop self-confidence. Many also emphasized the personal attention they received from teachers.

Undermanned settings also may affect adolescent peer networks. Because of their greater levels of participation, rural adolescents may have a larger pool of familiar age-mates to draw on in forming smaller, intimate groups; they also may possess enhanced "people skills." In fact, several studies indicate that a larger percentage of rural adolescents are designated "popular" when compared with their urban counterparts, whereas fewer are rejected or neglected (Darling, Munsch, & Foster-Clark, 1991). This finding supports the notion that rural youth are more likely to be known and liked by their peers.

On the other hand, because of the extensive connections found in rural peer networks, those rural adolescents who are rejected or neglected tend to be evaluated in these terms by a larger percentage of their associates, as was found by Darling et al. (1991):

> Continuing contact between children in multiple settings will allow even children with low social impact to find a niche within the peer group. . . . Unfortunately, these same structural characteristics also increase the likelihood that individuals with strong negative characteristics will carry their reputation with them. (p. 6)

In line with this conclusion, a retrospective study of graduates of small rural high schools indicated that the choice of peer groups in high school was limited and that adolescents who were not mainstream were marginalized (Schonert-Reichl et al., 1995). Thus, population size and density may be important correlates of psychosocial adjustment because of their impact on peer networks.

A related consideration concerns the homogeneity of rural communities and rural schools. Recent studies indicate that urban settings are more culturally diverse, more tolerant of differences, and less conventional than rural settings (Fischer, 1995). Thus, rural settings may seem more constraining to adolescents who do not fit the conventional mold. In line with this notion, some graduates of small rural schools expressed dissatisfaction with the lack of diversity in their communities and with attitudes that they described as narrow-minded (Schonert-Reichl et al., 1995). Other graduates noted that there was insufficient emphasis in their schools on higher education and a limited awareness of career options; women, in particular, reported that schools did little to expand their knowledge of non-traditional jobs. Thus, the homogeneity of rural communities may limit adolescents' perceptions of educational and occupational opportunities and constrain the range of acceptable identities.

Finally, population size may be related to the levels of psychological distress felt by rural adolescents in times of social change. Hoyt, O'Donnell, and Mack (1995) argued that economic hardship has been particularly damaging to small rural communities (i.e., villages with fewer than 2,500 inhabitants) in terms of both regional structure and culture. Small communities lost much of their commercial base during the farm crisis of the 1980s, and this loss promoted out-migration of the young and educated. In turn, social services—hospitals, government offices, and schools—were consolidated, with the result that residents who remained had less immediate access to important resources. Consolidation and the resulting loss of local services contributed to feelings of isolation, dissatisfaction, and lower cohesion among the residents of small rural communities, although such distress was less evident in larger rural towns and among farmers. Hoyt et al.'s analysis of psychological distress by place size revealed that, after controlling for individual hardship and social and personal resources, persons living in smaller communities had significantly greater depressive symptoms. Thus, in the context of recent economic downturns, small population size may be associated with increased psychological risk among rural adolescents.

Community Ties

    Rural communities also have been characterized as places of dense social networks and strong community ties. Residents of smaller, rural places express both greater satisfaction with their communities than do residents of more densely populated areas (Hummon, 1992) and more regret at the prospect of leaving (Kasarda & Janowitz, 1974). Smaller community size is also associated with greater life satisfaction among rural Appalachian young adults, as is proximity to one's childhood home (Wilson & Peterson, 1988). Among adolescents, attachment to community may be fostered by strong intergenerational networks (Schneider & Borman, 1993); this can be seen in the reflections of one young adult:

> My dream is to someday come back to the rural area and find a good steady job and raise my children. I miss the friendly people, being able to help one another out and knowing that if you need a helping hand there's someone there. In the small town I felt safe and loved, needed. I want my kids to grow up in a rural area like I did so they can go to the smaller school where the teachers are able to spend time with each individual. I want my kids to be part of a community that cares about each other and not just about themselves. (Schonert-Reichl & Elliott, 1994, p. 8)

    From a social capital perspective, the strong social networks of rural communities constitute a potential resource. The dense social networks, homogeneity, and smaller populations of rural communities may increase the integration of adolescents into the community and also the consistency of socialization pressures, contributing to a sense of social responsibility and security. On the other hand, as noted previously, the resulting pressure toward conformity may be experienced by some adolescents as restrictive and narrow-minded.

Traditionalism

Rural traditionalism is thought to encompass lower materialism, greater cooperation, more conservative attitudes, and more traditional gender roles. Yet, the empirical support for this assumption is weak, in part because rural-urban comparisons are rare, and in part because the comparisons that do exist are inconsistent (Provorse, 1996). For example, several studies have demonstrated that the attitudes, beliefs, and values of rural residents are generally traditional and conservative (Fischer, 1975; Nelsen & Yokley, 1970; Schnaiberg, 1970), but the accuracy of this conclusion has been questioned (e.g., Melton, 1983). Similarly, the assumption that rural residents are more religious than urban residents and hold more conservative religious beliefs has received some empirical support (e.g., McCartin & Freehill, 1986; Meystedt, 1984), but the findings are inconsistent (Melton, 1983).

Rural-urban comparisons using adolescent samples are virtually nonexistent. Instead, a few researchers have compared farm residents with rural town dwellers. For example, drawing on a sample of rural Pennsylvania high school sophomores in 1959-1960, Willits and Bealer (1963) found a pattern of less conservatism among rural town youth as compared to farm youth or youth residing in open nonfarm country. Although this could be taken as evidence of greater traditionalism in less urban areas, the amount of variance accounted for by place of residence was quite small, indicating that, although statistically significant, such differences are substantively unimportant.

Research on gender roles has produced similarly equivocal results. Demographic studies show that rural women marry earlier than do women from metropolitan areas (e.g., McLaughlin, Lichter, & Johnston, 1993), a pattern that could indicate greater endorsement of traditional gender roles among rural women but that also may reflect limited occupational opportunities for women. Furthermore,

there is some evidence that rural women are less likely to work outside the home than are urban women (Schnore, 1966) and that rural
women who do work outside the home spend more time on house-
work than their urban counterparts (Lawrence, Draughn, Tasker, &
Wozniak, 1987).

Relatedly, research on children's household chores points to possible rural-urban differences in gender role socialization. White and
Brinkerhoff (1981) examined the gender-typing of children's chores
in a representative sample of families from Nebraska. A comparison
of children and adolescents in farm, rural nonfarm, and urban families revealed that although rural nonfarm families were most likely
to assign chores differentially based on gender, farm families were
the least likely to do so; urban families fell in between. The authors
speculate that when labor demands are high, the gender stereo-
typing of work becomes dysfunctional. Thus, the hypothesis of
greater traditionalism in rural areas was supported for nonfarm
families but not for farm families. To date, the premise of greater
traditionalism in rural areas has not been well tested, and the results that are available provide only mixed support.

Land Use and the Predominance of Agriculture

Although agriculture was traditionally the dominant occupation
in rural America, the number of jobs in agriculture has been declining consistently for more than a century, and other industries have
come to predominate in many rural counties. Extractive industries,
such as mining and logging, along with railroad employment, also
are considered traditionally rural industries (Freudenberg, 1992).
In recent decades, there has been increased diversification of rural
land use as a function of declines in agricultural employment, the
deconcentration of urban areas, and regional changes in economic
opportunities (Hobbs, 1994). A recent classification system of nonmetropolitan counties includes seven designations: agricultural-
dependent, manufacturing-dependent, mining-dependent, and
government-dependent counties, along with federal lands, retirement destinations, and persistent poverty areas (Bender et al., 1985).
The proportion of rural residents living in these various types of
counties attests to the changing occupational profile of rural
America: In 1990, 39% of the nonmetropolitan population lived in
manufacturing-dependent counties and 24% lived in retirement

counties; only 14% lived in agricultural counties (U.S. Department of Agriculture, 1993).

Both occupational structure and demographic trends differ across these different types of counties. For example, during the 1980s, retirement counties increased in population largely as a result of in-migration of older adults, whereas farming-dependent counties had an overall loss of 10%, due to out-migration of young adults and lower rates of births relative to deaths (Johnson, 1993). Even though both types of counties experienced an increase in the proportion of older people, the underlying process is different (influx of retirees from metropolitan areas vs. out-migration of young adults) and may have different implications for adolescent development (Hobbs, 1994).

Yet another dimension of ecological variation in rural counties concerns the proximity to a metropolitan area. Closeness to metropolitan areas expands the range of employment opportunities available to rural residents, making them less likely to relocate; it also increases the probability that metropolitan residents will move into the county. In turn, these trends influence population size and growth in the county (Johnson, 1993). Such regional and county differences underscore the importance of land use in shaping the local economy and ecology; they further attest to the diversity of rural settings with respect to population size, employment opportunities, poverty, and ethnic composition. As noted previously, such differences influence the community setting, creating diverse ecologies for adolescent development.

The picture that emerges from this discussion of rural settings is one of both developmental supports and constraints. The extensive ties within the peer group and throughout the rural community should provide ample social support and access to social capital for adolescents who can take advantage of them. On the other hand, youth who are unconventional or who have nontraditional aspirations may feel constrained by the pressure toward conformity arising from dense social networks; worse yet, they may feel excluded and marginalized. Thus, the effects of a rural upbringing may be different for youth with distinct individual characteristics: Conventionally oriented youth with good social skills may benefit considerably, as may adolescents who need a high degree of consistency and structure. Youth who do not fit the patterns endorsed by the local community, however, may fare more poorly. In addition, regional and county-level differences in economic and demographic profiles and in patterns of social change suggest that rural communities comprise a multiplicity of ecological niches, each presenting distinct opportunities and challenges for developing youth.

PATTERNS OF
PSYCHOSOCIAL ADJUSTMENT

To the extent that rural settings provide a context for development that is distinct from urban settings, rural-nonrural differences in adolescent psychological, social, and behavioral patterns would be expected. Comparisons of rural and nonrural adolescents to date have pointed to several differences that have implications for the development of rural youth. Some of these represent a rural advantage (e.g., in terms of social capital), whereas others suggest that rural youth are at risk.

Family and Kin Relationships

Many hypotheses about the rural family and kin system have been advanced. For example, rural families are thought to be more traditional, more authoritarian, and more cohesive than urban families. Yet, very little empirical research has examined the distinctiveness of rural family life. Indeed, a large body of research suggests that family processes in rural settings are quite similar to those found in other ecologies. For example, Conger, Patterson, and Ge's (1995) study of families in central Iowa and urban Oregon demonstrated that the processes linking stressful life events to marital relations and parenting were similar in both samples.

However, research by Elder and his colleagues (e.g., Elder & Conger, 1999) has identified several distinctive features of Iowa farm families that distinguish them from other rural families and, potentially, from families in metropolitan settings. Of course, these distinctive features may not be typical of all rural farm families; yet, to the extent that the Iowa sample is demographically similar to many rural areas and insofar as farm families in other settings are also subject to economic fluctuations, these findings offer a reasonable basis for future study.

First, family relationships on the farm were found to be highly interdependent, because they were focused on the maintenance of the farm as a business and way of life (Elder & Conger, 1999). For example, compared to nonfarm children, farm children spent considerably more time with their fathers, working and participating in community activities. Low-achieving adolescents from farm backgrounds (who are more likely to remain in the community and continue with farming) expressed greater levels of warmth toward their fathers and were more often sought out by their parents for advice. Thus, it appears that farm adolescents who plan to remain on the farm are more highly integrated in the family business and enjoy better relationships with parents.

Second, grandparents in farm families, especially paternal grandparents, were more involved in their adolescent grandchildren's lives than was true in nonfarm families (King & Elder, 1995). Grandparents in farm families were more likely to participate in activities with their adolescent grandchildren and to serve as a companion, in large part because they lived closer to them. Whether these relationships promoted healthy development is difficult to determine, however, because most adolescents who had close and nurturant relationships with their grandparents also enjoyed better relationships with their parents. However, qualitative data indicated that grandparents act in a wide range of roles in farm families and were frequently evaluated in very positive terms (Elder & Conger, 1999). This was especially true among the small groups of adolescents who had relatively poor relationships with their parents but lived close to a grandparent. Thus, there is evidence that grandparents may play a more important role in the lives of adolescents growing up on farms, with possible psychological benefits for adolescents, particularly those without close relationships with parents.

Third, families who lived on a farm or who had a farm background were more likely to have strong community ties (i.e., both parents had an established history of involvement in a diverse range of community organizations such as the PTA, church, and civic organizations) when compared with nonfarm families. Mekos and Elder (1996) argued that such ties facilitate development by bringing adolescents into a wider network of supportive adults and by promoting participation in youth activities that are valuable socialization experiences. In other words, extensive ties to the community should increase an adolescent's access to social capital. Mekos and

Elder reported that adolescents growing up in families with strong community ties have better grades and are rated as more socially competent by teachers than are adolescents with weak ties, even when parents' education is statistically controlled. Thus, some evidence suggests that adolescents growing up in rural families with extensive community ties are more likely to succeed at the central tasks of adolescence.

Findings to date suggest that many of the presumed strengths of rural families, such as connections to extended family and involvement in a supportive community network, may be more characteristic of farm families. If so, adolescents in farm families may show greater resilience than nonfarm youth in times of social change.

Productive Roles

Although there is considerable interest in contemporary adolescent productive roles (Greenberger & Steinberg, 1986; Mortimer, Finch, Ryu, Shanahan, & Call, 1996; Steinberg & Dornbusch, 1991), very little attention has been devoted to rural-nonrural differences in work experiences. Yet, historically, productive activities of the young represented an important path to adulthood (Modell, 1989), especially in rural settings (Zelizer, 1985). Recent research suggests that adolescent work contributes little to the economic well-being of contemporary urban families (Greenberger & Steinberg, 1986; Mortimer et al., 1996), but both historical and contemporary records indicate the potentially substantial role of adolescents in the rural household economy (Bartlett, 1993; Friedmann, 1978).

Some adolescent rural work is thought unique for its involvement of extended kin and close family associates, its delegation of serious responsibilities, and its important consequences for the family. Drawing on his analysis of Depression-era cohorts, Elder (1974) reported that when adolescent work constitutes a genuine contribution to the family's well-being, personal maturity, self-conceptions, and relationships with parents are enhanced. Thus, rural work experience may offer greater psychological and interpersonal rewards than do other forms of adolescent work.

Indeed, studies that have compared urban with rural samples suggest large ecological differences in the meaning of work, often favoring the social development of rural youth. For example, in a series of studies, Shanahan, Elder, Burchinal, and Conger (1995,

1996a, 1996b) have shown that rural youth are more likely to work in response to family need. Although both urban and rural adolescents reported being employed for reasons of immediate gratification, more than half of all rural teenagers in the Iowa sample reported assuming additional chores and paid labor in response to family need. Also, rural adolescents were more likely to spend earnings in ways not immediately connected to their enjoyment. Among those reporting wages, roughly one third of rural 9th and 10th graders spent money on the family, compared to about 10% of youth in the urban sample.

Importantly, both earnings and nonleisure spending appeared to improve relationships with parents in the rural sample (Shanahan et al., 1996a, 1996b). Earnings and nonleisure spending were related to less parental monitoring, more sharing of advice within the family, and the affective quality of the relationship. Although nonleisure spending also improved parent-child relationships in the urban sample, there was some indication that too much nonleisure spending led to a deterioration of these relationships. Finally, rural, but not urban, earnings enhanced adolescents' self-efficacy (Shanahan et al., 1995).

Not all the rural-urban differences connoted advantages for rural youth, however. Some evidence suggests that involvement in chores leads to a decline in efficacy among farm boys, especially by mid-adolescence (Shanahan et al., 1995). This may reflect difficulties that adolescent farm boys who do not plan to become farmers have in disengaging from the family farm. Also, some rural work (especially chores) may involve an element of coercion and thus foster feelings of resentment and hostility between the generations. Thus, the evidence suggests that some but not all aspects of rural work are beneficial to adolescent social development; in particular, chores may entail some costs, especially for older farm boys.

Achievement and Aspirations

Educational attainment. National studies demonstrate a clear difference in educational attainment between rural and nonrural residents. In 1988, the average educational level of nonmetropolitan workers aged 18 to 64 was 12.7 years, as compared to a national average of 13.2 years (McGranahan & Ghelfi, 1991). Relatedly, the high school drop-out rate is higher in rural areas than in metropolitan areas; for example, in 1985, the nonmetropolitan drop-out rate was 15.2%, as compared to 13.9% in metropolitan areas (Swaim & Teixera, 1991). In 1990, the drop-out rate among youth aged 16 to 24 was 13.6% in rural areas, 10.7% in suburban areas, and 17% in central cities (Lichter, Cornwell, & Eggebeen, 1993). Thus, aggregate rural drop-out rates fell between suburban and central city rates.

Using 1990 census data, Lichter et al. (1993) examined family background variables that could help explain the rural-suburban difference in high school drop-out rates. For unmarried youth aged 16 to 18 living with parents, family structure variables, such as living with only one parent, being a parent oneself, and residing in a large household, all increased the likelihood of dropping out; however, these variables failed to account for the rural-suburban difference. In contrast, controlling family poverty status reduced the rural-suburban difference to nonsignificance, indicating that differential family poverty accounts for the differences in high school drop-out rates.

Although Lichter et al. (1993) could not address the mechanisms through which poverty affects the educational attainment of rural youth, other research has provided insight into these processes. In a small-scale study of 90 rural African American preadolescents aged 9 to 12, Brody, Stoneman, and Flor (1995) found that family financial resources were associated with more harmonious family interactions, which, in turn, were associated with better academic competence. In addition, financial resources were associated with self-regulation, which, in turn, predicted academic competence. Apart from its impact on family functioning, rural poverty may affect educational attainment by influencing educational aspirations or by undermining school quality.

Despite the legitimate concern over rural-urban differences in educational attainment, not all rural adolescents are at educational risk. For example, Schonert-Reichl et al. (1995) found that approximately 80% of their rural Iowa sample received some form of post-secondary education. Such findings highlight the diversity of rural youth and the need to consider the nature of the specific rural context when examining issues of developmental risk.

Educational and occupational aspirations. Studies have indicated consistently that the educational expectations of rural youth fall below those of nonrural adolescents (e.g., Cobb, McIntire, & Pratt, 1989; Hansen & McIntire, 1989; Sarigiani, Wilson, Petersen, & Vicary, 1990), although the size of these differences may be small (Haller & Virkler, 1993). Because educational aspirations influence educational attainment and, hence, social mobility, the lower aspirations of rural youth may represent a disadvantage meriting intervention (e.g., Breen, 1989; Cobb et al., 1989; Preble, Phillips, & McGinley, 1989).

In part, the rural-nonrural discrepancy in educational aspirations reflects differences in family socioeconomic status (SES). The SES of rural families is, on average, somewhat lower than that of nonrural families (e.g., Swanson & Butler, 1988), although, in part, this is due to the low occupational prestige scores associated with farming. Family SES, in turn, is positively associated with children's educational aspirations. In one study, about one third of the rural-nonrural difference in educational aspirations was explained by differences in family SES (Haller & Virkler, 1993).

A second explanation for the rural-nonrural difference focuses on the occupational structure within rural areas. According to this perspective, rural economies are less diversified than urban ones and offer a restricted range of occupational opportunities (Reid, 1989). In particular, rural industries, which tend to involve agriculture or the extraction of raw materials (e.g., mining, forestry), primarily provide manual and service jobs. To the extent that adolescents' vocational aspirations are shaped by the jobs they see in their communities (Ianni, 1989), we would expect rural adolescents to aspire more to manual and service occupations than would be true of suburban and urban youth, who receive greater exposure to managerial and technical occupations (Haller & Virkler, 1993). Furthermore, because traditional rural jobs require relatively little education, educational aspirations should be lower for rural youth than for nonrural adolescents.

In support of this structural explanation, several studies have shown that somewhat fewer rural than nonrural youth expect to hold professional and technical jobs (e.g., Cobb et al., 1989; Haller & Virkler, 1993). In addition, slightly more rural than nonrural students expect to have a lower-level white-collar job or a blue-collar job at age 30 (Haller & Virkler, 1993). Moreover, when both family SES and occupational aspirations are controlled, the initial difference in educational aspirations diminishes considerably (Haller &

Virkler, 1993). Research on rural Appalachian high school students also supports the notion that limited economic opportunities are associated with lower educational ambitions (Schwarzweller, 1973).

At the same time, the rural-nonrural difference in educational aspirations is not exceedingly large. Drawing on the 1980 High School and Beyond data set, Haller and Virkler (1993) found an effect size for nonrural residence of only .23, amounting to one half point on a 9-point scale. Furthermore, the aspirations of rural youth are not uniformly low. In a national sample, 51% of rural seniors, as compared to 60% of nonrural youth, expected to attend at least some college (Haller & Virkler, 1993). Studies of more circumscribed samples also have found that more than half of rural adolescents expect to go to college (e.g., Hektner, 1995). Regarding occupational aspirations, Haller and Virkler reported that 50% of rural youth (vs. 59% of nonrural youth) anticipated holding professional and technical jobs, whereas 34% of rural youth (vs. 29% of nonrural youth) expected to hold blue-collar or white-collar jobs at age 30. These findings indicate that the aspirations of rural youth are not highly constrained, although they are somewhat lower than those of nonrural adolescents.

Research suggests that more recent cohorts of rural youth perceive a wider array of occupational options. A comparison of two ninth grade cohorts from the same high school in 1967 and 1979 indicated that the younger cohort was aware of many more occupations and viewed more of them as possible for themselves (Sundberg, Tyler, & Poole, 1984). In the absence of a nonrural comparison group, it is impossible to determine whether this difference reflected an increasing awareness of vocations among rural youth relative to nonrural youth (i.e., a catch-up effect) or a general cohort-related increase. It seems plausible, however, that the spread of urbanization and mass communication, as well as local concerns about the more limited aspirations of rural youth, would lead to an increment in occupational awareness among rural adolescents.

Health and Well-Being

Psychological well-being. Rural-nonrural comparisons of specific psychological dimensions yield somewhat equivocal findings. Several studies have examined differences in self-image, producing mixed results. Trowbridge, Trowbridge, and Trowbridge (1972) reported that rural children in the third through eighth grades had higher self-image than did nonrural children. Prendergrast, Zdep, and Sepulveda (1974), however, found no differences in self-image between rural and nonrural girls aged 9 through 17. More recent studies found that rural adolescents have lower self-image than do their nonrural counterparts (Petersen, Offer, & Kaplan, 1979; Sarigiani et al., 1990).

There is also some suggestion that rural adolescents have more psychological symptoms than do nonrural youth. Both Petersen et al. (1979) and Sarigiani et al. (1990) found that rural youth score lower on emotional tone, a measure assessing positive psychological functioning and an absence of depression and anxiety. Similarly, Helge (1990) reported higher rates of depression for rural secondary school students than for their urban and suburban counterparts. As with metropolitan adolescents, depression in rural adolescents is related to family financial stress (Clark-Lempers, Lempers, & Netusil, 1990; Simons, Whitbeck, & Wu, 1994). Given that poverty rates are higher in rural areas than in nonrural areas, depression may be of particular concern for rural adolescents.

Drug and alcohol use. Though once thought to be a problem primarily in urban areas, recent data reveal that alcohol and drug use among adolescents is now a cause for concern in rural areas, as well. According to the 1993 data from the Monitoring the Future Study (Johnston, O'Malley, & Bachman, 1994), only small differences in alcohol and drug use now exist between adolescents in metropolitan and nonmetropolitan areas. Although more rapid increases in the use of drugs and alcohol in metropolitan areas during the late 1970s produced higher rates of use in urban areas, recent declines in metropolitan drug use have reduced these differences significantly.

Rates of alcohol use are similar for nonmetropolitan and metropolitan youth. Among 12th graders, the 30-day prevalence of alcohol use in 1993 was 51.9% in nonmetropolitan areas, as compared to 52.3% in large metropolitan areas and 49.8% in other metropolitan areas (Johnston et al., 1994). A similar pattern is found for lifetime prevalence, with 12th graders from nonmetropolitan areas reporting rates of alcohol use nearly identical to those in metropolitan areas (86.8%, 88.0%, and 86.7%, for rural, large metropolitan, and other metropolitan areas, respectively). However, youth in nonmetropolitan areas report slightly higher rates of binge drinking than do those in metropolitan areas (32.0%, as compared to 29.9% and 26.4% for large and other metropolitan areas, respectively).

In contrast, marijuana use is somewhat lower among rural adolescents as compared to metropolitan adolescents. In 1993, the 30-day prevalence of marijuana use for 12th graders was 13.8% for nonmetropolitan areas, 15.3% for other metropolitan areas, and 18.0% for large metropolitan areas (Johnston et al., 1994). The lifetime prevalence of use showed similar patterns: 32.7% for nonmetropolitan areas, 36.3% for other metropolitan areas, and 36.5% for large metropolitan areas. Use of other illicit drugs is low and similar for nonmetropolitan and metropolitan youth.

Another area of concern, particularly for rural youth, is tobacco use. Nonmetropolitan and metropolitan youth are equally likely to use cigarettes (30.3%, 29.8%, and 29.5%, for nonmetropolitan, other metropolitan, and large metropolitan areas, respectively; Johnston et al., 1994). However, rural youth are much more likely to use smokeless tobacco than youth from metropolitan areas (15.0%, as compared to 9.9% and 7.1% for other and large metropolitan areas, respectively).

The correlates of drug use are similar for rural and nonrural adolescents. In a review of the literature on rural adolescent alcohol and drug use, Donnermeyer (1992) found that risk factors for rural adolescent drug and alcohol use are similar to those identified for nonrural and nationally representative samples (e.g., age, gender, ethnicity, academic performance, attachment to school, religion, quality of relationship with parents, parental monitoring, and peer use). Although it is clear that adolescent substance use is a problem in both rural and nonrural areas, there are issues related to this trend that are unique to rural youth. Leukefeld, Clayton, and Myers (1992) suggested that problems with transportation, availability of services, and rural-urban differences in help-seeking behavior may have implications for the treatment of alcohol and drug use for rural adolescents. For example, many rural communities do not have primary prevention programs due to a lack of financial resources and personnel, problems that have been exacerbated by the ongoing demographic changes in rural areas. Thus, rural youth may have less access to preventive services than do nonrural youth. In addition, research on mental health service utilization suggests that rural residents are less likely to seek help than are residents of nonrural areas, controlling for levels of psychiatric disturbance (Kelleher, Taylor, & Rickert, 1992). Possible explanations for this difference include cultural norms favoring self-reliance; concerns about confidentiality in close-knit communities; and distrust of physicians and social service agencies, who may be viewed as "outsiders" (Bushy, 1994; Kelleher et al., 1992). Similar considerations may keep rural adolescents from seeking treatment for drug-related problems.

TURNING POINTS IN THE RURAL LIFE COURSE

Adolescence is the period when young people make decisions that will shape their adult life course. Many of these decisions revolve around educational and occupational goals, two key areas of planning for adolescents in modern societies (Nurmi, 1991). Others involve expectations concerning future family goals. What distinguishes rural youth is the need to consider where these goals can best be realized: in the community of origin or elsewhere. The limited occupational structure of rural communities and the ongoing economic decline in many rural areas have increased the salience of this issue.

Transition to Adulthood

One important question concerns the timing and nature of the transition to adulthood. Because of lower family SES and lower educational aspirations, rural youth may anticipate an accelerated transition into adult roles compared to metropolitan youth. Preliminary examination of this issue has supported this proposition. Bingham, Crockett, Stemmler, and Petersen (1994) compared a sample of rural youth with a sample of suburban youth in terms of their anticipated ages at reaching several young adult milestones: finishing their education, entering the workforce, marrying, and becoming a parent. In each case, the rural sample anticipated a significantly earlier transition to adult status. In part, the difference was a function of differences in family SES; however, controlling parents' educational attainment did not fully account for the difference. Additional analyses of the same rural sample indicated that the anticipated timing of adult role transitions was related to school performance and adolescent educational aspirations for both genders but also to family structure and traditional gender role attitudes for boys and to parental educational attainment, family relationships, and problem behavior for girls (Crockett & Bingham, 1996). Whether these variables also can explain the rural-suburban differences in the expected timing of role transitions has yet to be determined.

Residential Plans

As noted previously, many rural young adults leave their home communities to seek educational and employment opportunities. During the 1980s, nonmetropolitan areas experienced a net loss of approximately 1.5 million young people (Hobbs, 1994; see also Fugitt, Brown, & Beale, 1989). Even during the 1970s, when migration into rural areas temporarily increased, talented rural youth continued to show high rates of out-migration (Rudkin, Elder, & Conger, 1994). Studies of migrants from rural areas suggest that migration is often advantageous. Although the success of out-migrants may be due in part to selection factors (migrants tend to be better educated and more highly skilled), recent research suggests that rural out-migration confers benefits even for the poor and disadvantaged. Wenk and Hardesty (1993) found that poor rural men who migrated found work more quickly than did those who stayed in their rural communities, and poor rural women who migrated were less likely to remain in poverty. Thus, migration is not only a rational strategy for many rural youth but one that has important implications for the subsequent life course. Residential decisions are thus of critical importance for rural youth.

Yet, such decisions may be difficult, because realizing educational and vocational goals often means leaving one's family and home community; in this respect, the desire for social mobility is in conflict with attachments to family and place. Staying or leaving also may represent a choice between a traditional lifestyle and a more "modern" one. Donaldson (1986) casts the decision to stay or leave as involving a tension between the "native culture" and becoming part of the American mainstream (p. 121).

Several studies provide evidence of this residential dilemma among rural youth. Drawing on interviews with youth residing in a village in Maine in the mid-1970s, Donaldson (1986) reported that remaining in the village was important to all of them and that "for most, a central theme was the attempt to reconcile attachments to community and past with a desire—or economic need—to be a part of the modern American mainstream" (p. 122). In a retrospective study of former high school students from small rural schools in Iowa, Schonert-Reichl and Elliott (1994) also found evidence of a residential conflict among their participants: Many young adults expressed the desire to return to a rural way of life but felt that their economic futures were tied to metropolitan areas. Finally, a study of ninth graders from rural Iowa revealed that one third of the sample reported both a desire to live near their parents and intentions to live elsewhere after completing their schooling— clearly conflicting goals (Elder, King, & Conger, 1996).

In the only comparative study of this residential dilemma, Hektner (1995) compared adolescents from rural, urban, and suburban sites in Illinois. Rural youth were more likely to experience conflict, defined as a dual desire to live close to parents and relatives and to "get away from this area of the country," than were urban or suburban adolescents, but the difference was significant only for male youth and only among 10th graders (not among 8th or 12th graders). At 10th grade, more than half the rural adolescents held conflicting desires, as compared to just less than 40% of nonrural youth. Thus, the conflict was more prevalent among rural youth, but it was also experienced by adolescents from other settings.

Several researchers have suggested that the conflict between residential preferences and occupational aspirations may be stressful for rural youth (Sarigiani et al., 1990; Schonert-Reichl & Elliott, 1994). Research on this issue is sparse, however, and provides mixed support for this notion. Hektner (1995) finds that rural students and those with conflicting residential desires are significantly more likely to report feelings of anger and emptiness. Similarly, Elder et al. (1996) report that Iowa students who have conflicting goals (i.e., a desire to remain close to family but an intent to settle elsewhere) express marginally higher depression and unhappiness than do students who plan to stay in their home communities. However, their depression is not significantly higher than that of unconflicted students who plan to relocate; in fact, only the two unconflicted groups differ significantly. Thus, in the Iowa sample, the intention to leave per se, rather than conflict between community-family attachments and the desire to relocate, is associated with greater psychological vulnerability.

Whether or not the dilemma jeopardizes psychological well-being, the tension between community attachment and occupational goals appears to affect the choices of rural youth. Some youth may reduce their educational and occupational aspirations, bringing them into line with realistic employment prospects within their home community. For those who do leave the community, there is some evidence that appreciation of the rural community influences later residential choices. Schonert-Reichl and Elliott (1996) found that many of their young adult participants effected a compromise between the competing pulls of career and rural living by residing in rural communities and commuting considerable distances to their jobs in metropolitan areas. This allowed them to have the best of both worlds: to pursue their chosen careers and still live and raise their children in a more rural setting. These findings support the presence of the tension described by Donaldson (1986) and Hektner (1995) and also indicate that an appreciation of rural living (if not attachment to a particular rural community) affects the residential decisions of some youth with rural backgrounds.

FUTURE DIRECTIONS IN THE
STUDY OF RURAL YOUTH

The preceding discussion raises several issues that need to be addressed in future research with rural youth. One key issue is the diversity among rural communities. Although generalizations about rural youth may have been possible when rural America was largely agrarian, they are far less valid today, given the diversification of land use in rural areas and accompanying differences in economic and demographic trends. Regional differences, which in part reflect variation in ethnic and racial composition, also may contribute to ecological diversity in rural settings, as do differences in poverty levels and proximity to metropolitan areas. In light of community differences, research on carefully defined local samples is needed, along with research on nationally representative samples that examines regional and county-level differences (MacBrayne, 1987).

In addition, there are important within-community differences that have implications for adolescent development. A clear example is the farm-nonfarm distinction. Elder and his colleagues identified differences between farm families and nonfarm families in adolescents' relationships to fathers and grandparents, in work patterns, and in community involvement. Taken together, these findings underscore the uniqueness of farm families as contexts for adolescent development. More broadly, distinct family ecologies set the stage for distinct life course trajectories. Such family differences, as well as individual characteristics, need to be taken into account in future research. In accordance with an ecological perspective (Bronfenbrenner, 1979), rural youth must be viewed through a more differentiated lens that is sensitive to regional, county, community, and family-level differences and their potential influences on development. General patterns may emerge after systematic study but cannot be presumed a priori.

Second, any distinctive features of rural life need to be documented carefully, through rural-nonrural comparisons. Currently, there is surprisingly little research supporting some of our most basic assumptions about rural life: those related to family life, community cohesion, and traditionalism. Given the argument that rural-urban differences have dwindled under the effects of mass society (Hobbs, 1994), it is critical to document the size and consistency of remaining rural-nonrural differences. Moreover, given that rural-urban differences may partly reflect differences in ethnic composition and SES, such confounding factors must be taken into account.

Third, notions of risk, resilience, and social capital also should be applied in a more refined way. Rather than arguing that rural adolescents in the aggregate are disadvantaged or advantaged relative to nonrural youth, more careful attention should be paid to the sources of risk in particular rural populations and to the types of protective strategies that could be applied to foster positive outcomes. Clearly, some rural youth are at risk: those living in poverty, those with abusive parents, those exposed to marital conflict, and possibly those who deviate from community norms. Similarly, mitigating factors such as close family relationships and community support are not evenly distributed across rural America. For instance, the presumed benefits of rural families and rural communities may be concentrated in certain kinds of families (e.g., farm families) or in certain kinds of communities. Determining which rural youth are at risk and which youth have access to important family and community resources (e.g., social support, social capital) would be a logical first step in developing a more differentiated perspective on rural risk and resilience. Risk usually is assessed in terms of individual and family characteristics but could be assessed at the community level, in terms of the amount and severity of dislocation brought about by social change. Similarly, the operation of social capital in rural communities has only begun to be explored and remains a rich area for future research.

CONCLUSIONS

Long-term trends of social change involving economic reorganization and migration continue to characterize rural life. In this context, there is an urgent need for the study of rural youth as they negotiate pathways into adulthood. At the same time, rural America often is viewed as a place rich in capital, including a heightened sense of individualism and self-reliance but also a sense of commitment to community and public life (Dalecki & Coughenour, 1992).

This interplay of social change and social capital serves as a useful frame for analysis and may contribute to a more basic understanding of youth, ecological context, and the life course. What are the sources of vulnerability and risk found in rural settings? What are the distinct processes that detract from adolescent psychosocial adjustment, as reflected in the emergence of competence, health and well-being, and the transition into adult roles? It may be that young people figure more prominently in rural places by way of their extensive involvements in school, extracurricular activities, and unique work roles. In turn, they may be more highly integrated into adult social networks and engaged in activities that involve less role segmentation. However, there is very little research on ecological differences in the availability of social capital.

As our chapter suggests, there is considerable diversity in rural areas. Much of this diversity is related to varied patterns of land use. In turn, economic diversity in rural areas has coincided with new and often complicated patterns of work in the rural household: Mothers and fathers engage in combinations involving farming, light manufacturing, and gray-collar work; rural residents commute to white-collar jobs in metropolitan areas. The complexities of the contemporary rural landscape and the ongoing economic and demographic changes in rural areas raise the challenges inherent in studying changing persons in changing contexts. Yet, the rewards of this endeavor are likely to be rich, contributing to our understanding of the diversity of youth in time and place.

REFERENCES

Adair-Toteff, C. (1995). Ferdinand Tönnies: Utopian visionary. *Sociological Theory,* 13, 58-65.

Barker, R. G., & Gump, P. V. (1964). *Big school-small school, high school size and student behavior.* Stanford, CA: Stanford University Press.

Bartlett, P. F. (1993). *American dreams, rural realities: Farm families in crisis.* Chapel Hill, NC: University of North Carolina Press.

Beers, H. W. (1957). The rural community. In *Review of sociology: Analysis of a decade* (pp. 186-220). New York: John Wiley.

Bell, M. M. (1992). The fruit of the difference: The rural-urban continuum as a system of identity. *Rural Sociology, 57*(1), 65-82.

Bender, L. D., Green, B. I., Hady, T. F., Kuehn, J. A., Nelson, M. K., Perkinson, I. B., & Ross, P. J. (1985). *The diverse social and economic structure of non-metropolitan America.* (Rural Development Research Rep. No. 49). Washington, DC: U.S. Department of Agriculture, Economic Research Service.

Bingham, C. R., Crockett, L. J., Stemmler, M., & Petersen, A. C. (1994). *Community differences in adolescents' expectations about the transition to adulthood.* Unpublished manuscript.

Breen, D. T. (1989). Enhancing student aspirations: A goal for comprehensive developmental guidance programs. *Research in Rural Education, 6,* 35-38.

Brody, G. H., Stoneman, Z., & Flor, D. (1995). Linking family processes and academic competence among rural African American youths. *Journal of Marriage and the Family, 57,* 567-579.

Bronfenbrenner, U. (1979). *The ecology of human development: Experiments by nature and design.* Cambridge, MA: Harvard University Press.

Bushy, A. (1994). Implementing primary prevention programs for adolescents in rural environments. *Journal of Primary Prevention, 14,* 209-229.

Clark-Lempers, D. S., Lempers, J. D., & Netusil, A. J. (1990). Family financial stress, parental support, and young adolescents' academic achievement and depressive symptoms. *Journal of Early Adolescence, 10*(1), 21-36.

Cobb, R. A., McIntire, W. G., & Pratt, P. A. (1989). Vocational and educational aspirations of high school students: A problem for rural America. *Journal of Research on Rural Education, 6*(2), 11-16.

Coleman, J. S. (1988). Social capital in the creation of human capital. *American Journal of Sociology, 94,* 95-120.

Conger, R. D., & Elder, G. H. (1994). *Families in troubled times: Adapting to change in rural America.* Hawthorne, NY: Aldine de Gruyter.

Conger, R. D., Patterson G., & Ge, X. (1995). It takes two to replicate: A mediational model for the impact of parents' stress on adolescent adjustment. *Child Development, 66,* 80-97.

Crockett, L. J., & Bingham, C. R. (1996, March). *Anticipating adulthood: The impact of family ecology and adolescent behavior on the expected timing of adult role transitions.* Paper presented at the biennial meeting of the Society for Research on Adolescence, Boston.

Dalecki, M. G, & Coughenour, C. M. (1992). Agrarianism in American society. *Rural Sociology, 57,* 48-64.

Darling, N., Munsch, J., & Foster-Clark, F. S. (1991). *Functional characteristics of the social networks of more and less competent early adolescents.* Paper presented at the Hartman Conference on Children and Their Families, New London, CT.

Dewey, R. (1960). The rural-urban continuum: Real but relatively unimportant. *American Journal of Sociology, 66,* 60-66.

Donaldson, G. A. (1986). Do you need to leave home to grow up? The rural adolescents' dilemma. *Research on Rural Education, 3*(3), 121-125.

Donnermeyer, J. F. (1992). The use of alcohol, marijuana, and hard drugs by rural adolescents: A review of recent research. *Drugs and Society, 7*(1-2), 31-75.

Edington, E. E. (1970). Disadvantaged rural youth. *Review of Educational Research, 40,* 69-85.

Ehly, S. & Retish, P. (1990). *Children at risk: A review of the literature.* Des Moines: FINE Foundation. University of Iowa.

Elder, G. H., Jr. (1974). *Children of the Great Depression: Social change and life experience.* Chicago: University of Chicago Press.

Elder, G. H., & Conger, R. D., in collaboration with Russell, S. T., Shanahan, M. J., Mekos, D., King, V., & Matthews, L. S. (1996). *New worlds, new lives: Rural generations at century's end.* Chicago: Univ. of Chicago Press.

Elder, G. H., King, V., & Conger, R. D. (1996). Attachment to place and migration prospects: A developmental perspective. *Journal of Research on Adolescence 6,* 397-423.

Fischer, C. S. (1975). The effect of urban life on traditional values. *Social Forces, 53,* 420-432.

Fischer, C. S. (1995). The subcultural theory of urbanism: A twentieth-year assessment. *American Journal of Sociology, 101,* 543-577.

Fitchen, J. M. (1995). Spatial redistribution of poverty through migration of poor people to depressed rural communities. *Rural Sociology, 60,* 181-201.

Freudenburg, W. R. (1992). Addictive economies: Extractive industries and vulnerable localities in a changing world economy. *Rural Sociology, 57,* 305-332.

Friedmann, H. (1978). World market, state, and family farm: Social bases of household production in an era of wage labor. *Comparative Studies in Society and History, 20,* 545-586.

Fugitt, G. V., Brown, D. L., & Beale, C. L. (1989). *Rural and small town America.* New York: Russell Sage Foundation.

Furstenberg, F. F. (1994, November). *The influence of neighborhoods on children's development. A theoretical perspective and research agenda.* Paper presented at the Indicators of Children's Well-Being conference, Bethesda, MD.

Greenberger, E., & Steinberg, L. D. (1986). *When teenagers work: The psychological and social costs of adolescent employment.* New York: Basic Books.

Haller, E. J., & Virkler, S. J. (1993). Another look at rural-nonrural differences in students' educational aspirations. *Journal of Research in Rural Education, 9*(3), 170-178.

Hansen, T. D., & McIntire, W. G. (1989). Family structure variables as predictors of educational and vocational aspirations of high school seniors. *Research in Rural Education, 6,* 39-50.

Hektner, J. M. (1995). When moving up implies moving out: Rural adolescent conflict in the transition to adulthood. *Journal of Research in Rural Education, 11*(1), 3-14.

Helge, D. (1990). *A national study regarding at-risk students.* National Rural Development Institute, Woodring College of Education, Western Washington University, Bellingham, WA.

Hobbs, D. (1994). Demographic trends in nonmetropolitan America. *Journal of Research in Rural Education, 10*(3), 149-160.

Hoyt, D. R., O'Donnell, D., & Mack, K. Y. (1995). Psychological distress and size of place: The epidemiology of rural economic stress. *Rural Sociology, 60,* 707-720.

Hummon, D. M. (1986). City mouse, country mouse: The persistence of community identity. *Qualitative Sociology, 9,* 3-25.

Hummon, D. M. (1992). Community attachment: Local sentiment and sense of place. In I. Altman & S. M. Low (Eds.), *Place attachment* (pp. 253-278). New York: Plenum.

Ianni, F. A. (1989). *The search for structure: A report on American youth today.* New York: Free Press.

Jacob, S., & Luloff, A. E. (1995). Exploring the meaning of rural through cognitive maps. *Rural Sociology, 60,* 260-273.

Jensen, L., & McLaughlin, D. K. (1995). Human capital and nonmetropolitan poverty. In L. J. Beaulieu & D. Mulkey (Eds.), *Investing in people: The human capital needs of rural America* (pp. 111-138). Boulder, CO: Westview.

Johansen, H. E. (1993). The small town in urbanized society. In D. L. Brown, D. Field, & J. J. Zuiches (Eds.), *The demography of rural life* (pp. 58-82). University Park, PA: Northeast Regional Center for Rural Development.

Johnson, K. M. (1993). Demographic change in nonmetropolitan America, 1980-1990. *Rural Sociology, 58*(3), 347-365.

Johnston, L. D., O'Malley, P. M., & Bachman, J. G. (1994). *Drug use among American high school students: National trends through 1993.* Rockville, MD: National Institute of Drug Abuse.

Kasarda, J. D., & Janowitz, M. (1974). Community attachment in mass society. *American Sociological Review, 39,* 328-339.

Kelleher, K. J., Taylor, J. L., & Rickert, V. I. (1992). Mental health services for rural children and adolescents. *Clinical Psychology Review, 12,* 841-852.

King, V., & Elder, G. H., Jr. (1995). American children view their grandparents: Linked lives across three rural generations. *Rural Sociology, 57,* 165-178.

Lawrence, F. C., Draughn, P. S., Tasker, G. E., & Wozniak, P. H. (1987). Sex differences in household labor time: A comparison of rural and urban couples. *Sex Roles, 17,* 489-502.

Leukefeld, C. G., Clayton, R. B., & Myers, J. A. (1992). Rural drug and alcohol treatment. *Drugs and Society, 7*(1-2), 95-116.

Lichter, D. T. (1993). Migration, population redistribution, and the new spatial inequality. In D. L. Brown, D. Field, & J. J. Zuiches (Eds.), *The demography of rural life* (pp. 19-46). University Park, PA: Northeast Regional Center for Rural Development.

Lichter, D. T., Cornwell, G. T., & Eggebeen, D. J. (1993). Harvesting human capital: Family structure and education among rural youth. *Rural Sociology, 58*(1), 53-75.

Lichter, D. T., McLaughlin, D. K., & Cornwell, G. T. (1995). Migration and the loss of human resources in rural areas. In L. J. Beaulieu & D. Mulkey (Eds.), *Investing in people: The human capital needs of rural America* (pp. 235-256). Boulder, CO: Westview.

MacBrayne, P. (1987). Educational and occupational aspirations of rural youth: A review of the literature. *Research on Rural Education, 4*, 135-141.

McCartin, R., & Freehill, M. (1986). Values of early adolescents compared by type of school. *Journal of Early Adolescence, 6*, 369-380.

McGranahan, D. A., & Ghelfi, L. M. (1991). The education crisis and rural stagnation in the 1980s. In *Education and rural economic development: Strategies for the 1990s* (Economic Research Service, Staff Report No. AGES 9153, pp. 40-92). Washington, DC: U.S. Department of Agriculture, Agriculture and Rural Economy Division.

McLaughlin, D. K., Lichter, D. T., & Johnston, G. M. (1993). Some women marry young: Transitions to first marriage in metropolitan and nonmetropolitan areas. *Journal of Marriage and the Family, 55*, 827-838.

Mekos, D., & Elder, G. H. (1996, March). *Community ties and the development of competence in rural youth.* Paper presented at the biennial meeting of the Society for Research in Adolescence, Boston.

Melton, G. B. (1983). Ruralness as a psychological construct. In A. W. Childs & G. B. Melton (Eds.), *Rural psychology* (pp. 1-13). New York: Plenum.

Meystedt, D. M. (1984). Religion and the rural population: Implications for social work. *Social Casework, 65*, 219-226.

Modell, J. (1989). *Into one's own: From youth to adulthood in the United States 1920-1975.* Berkeley: University of California Press.

Mortimer, J. T., Finch, M. D., Ryu, S., Shanahan, M. J., & Call, K. T. (1996). Work experiences, mental health, and behavioral adjustment: New evidence from a prospective study. *Child Development, 67*, 1243-1261.

Nelsen, H. M., & Yokley, R. T. (1970). Civil rights attitudes of rural and urban Presbyterians. *Rural Sociology, 35*, 161-174.

Nelson, L. (1952). *Rural sociology.* New York: American Books.

Nurmi, J. E. (1991). How do adolescents see their future? A review of the development of future orientation and planning. *Developmental Review, 11*, 1-59.

Petersen, A. C., Offer, D., & Kaplan, E. (1979). The self-image of rural adolescent girls. In M. Sugar (Ed.), *Female adolescent development* (pp.141-155). New York: Brunner/Mazel.

Preble, B., Phillips, P., & McGinley, H. (1989). Maine's aspirations movement: Reaching out to youth. *Research in Rural Education, 6*, 35-38.

Prendergrast, P., Zdep, S. M., & Sepulveda, P. (1974). Self-image among a national probability sample of girls. *Child Study Journal, 4*, 103-114.

Provorse, D. (1996). *The search for the rural mindset: An empirical comparison of alternative definitions of reality.* Unpublished doctoral dissertation, University of Nebraska-Lincoln, Lincoln, Nebraska.

Reid, J. N. (1989). The rural economy and rural youth: Challenges for the future. *Journal of Research in Rural Education, 6*(2), 17-23.

Rudkin, L., Elder, G. H., & Conger, R. (1994). Influences on the migration intentions of rural adolescents. *Sociological Studies of Children, 6,* 87-106.

Sarigiani, P. A., Wilson, J. L., Petersen, A. C., & Vicary, J. R. (1990). Self-image and educational plans of adolescents from two contrasting communities. *Journal of Early Adolescence, 10,* 37-55.

Schnaiberg, A. (1970). Rural-urban residence and modernism. *Demography, 7,* 71-85.

Schneider, B. & Borman, K. (1993, April). *Thinking about the future: Adolescents in a small town.* Paper presented at the annual meeting of the American Educational Research Association, Atlanta, GA.

Schnore, L. (1966). The rural-urban variable: An urbanite's perspective. *Rural Sociology, 31,* 131-143.

Schonert-Reichl, K. A., & Elliott, J. P. (1994, February). *Rural pathways: Stability and change during the transition to young adulthood.* Paper presented at the meeting of the Society for Research on Adolescence, San Diego, CA.

Schonert-Reichl, K. A., & Elliott, J. P. (1996, March). *"There's no place like home:" A longitudinal investigation of rural adolescents' efforts to recreate their rural communities during adulthood.* Paper presented at the biennial meeting of the Society for Research in Adolescence, Boston.

Schonert-Reichl, K. A., Elliott, J. P., & Bills, D. B. (1995, April). *"I feel that a rural education is a wonderful thing": Rural school students' narratives of their rural school education ten years after high school graduation.* Paper presented at the annual meeting of the American Educational Research Association, New Orleans, LA.

Schwarzweller, H. K. (1973). Regional variations in the educational plans of rural youth: Norway, Germany and the United States. *Rural Sociology, 38*(2), 139-158.

Shanahan, M. J., Elder, G. H., Jr., Burchinal, M., & Conger, R. D. (1995, April). *Ecological patterns in adolescent productive activities: Predictors of involvement and consequences for self-identity.* Paper presented at the biennial meetings of the Society for Research in Child Development, Indianapolis, IN.

Shanahan, M. J., Elder, G. H., Jr., Burchinal, M., & Conger, R. D. (1996a). Adolescent earnings and relationships with parents: The work-family nexus in urban and rural ecologies. In J. T. Mortimer & M. D. Finch (Eds.), *Adolescents, work, and family: An intergenerational, developmental analysis* (pp. 97-128). Newbury Park, CA: Sage.

Shanahan, M. J., Elder, G. H., Jr., Burchinal, M., & Conger, R. D. (1996b). Adolescent paid labor and relationships with parents: Early work-family linkages. *Child Development, 67,* 2183-2200.

Simons, R. L, Whitbeck, L. B., & Wu, C. (1994). Resilient and vulnerable adolescents. In R. D. Conger & G. H. Elder (Eds.), *Families in troubled times* (pp. 223-234). Hawthorne, NY: Aldine de Gruyter.

Sorokin, P., & Zimmerman, C. C. (1929). *Principles of rural-urban sociology.* New York: Henry Holt.

Steinberg, L. D., & Dornbusch. S. M. (1991). Negative correlates of part-time employment during adolescence: Replication and elaboration. *Developmental Psychology, 27,* 304-313.

Sundberg, N. D., Tyler, L. E., & Poole, M. E. (1984). Decade differences in rural adolescents' views of life possibilities. *Journal of Youth and Adolescence, 13,* 45-56.

Swaim, P. (1995). Adapting to economic change: The case of displaced workers. In
    L. J. Beaulieu & D. Mulkey (Eds.), *Investing in people: The human capital needs of
    rural America* (pp. 213-234). Boulder, CO: Westview.
Swaim, P., & Teixera, R. A. (1991). Education and training policy: Skill upgrading
    options for the rural workforce. In *Education and rural economic development: Strat-
    egies for the 1990s* (Economic Research Service, Staff Report No. AGES 9153,
    pp. 122-162). Washington, DC: U.S. Department of Agriculture, Agriculture and
    Rural Economy Division.
Swanson, L. L., & Butler, M. A. (1988). Human resource base of rural economies. In
    D. L. Brown, J. N. Reid, H. Bluestone, D. A. McGranahan, & S. M. Mazie (Eds.),
    Rural economic development in the 1980s: Prospects for the future (RDRR-69, pp. 159-
    179). Washington, DC: U.S. Department of Agriculture, Economic Research
    Service.
Trowbridge, N., Trowbridge, L., & Trowbridge, L. (1972). Self-concept and socio-
    economic status. *Child Study Journal, 2*, 123-142.
Truesdell, L. E. (1949). The development of the urban-rural classification in the
    United States: 1874 to 1949. *Current Populations Reports, Population Characteristics,
    P-23*, 1-16.
U.S. Census Bureau. (1992). *1990 census of population: General population characteristics.*
    Washington, DC: Government Printing Office.
U.S. Department of Agriculture. (1993). *Rural conditions and trends, 4*(3). Washington,
    DC: Economic Research Service, U.S. Department of Agriculture.
Wenk, D., & Hardesty, C. (1993). The effects of rural-to-urban migration on the pov-
    erty status of youth in the 1980s. *Rural Sociology, 58*(1), 76-92.
White, L. K., Brinkerhoff, D. B. (1981). The sexual division of labor: Evidence from
    childhood. *Social Forces, 60*(1), 170-181.
William T. Grant Foundation Commission on Work, Family, and Citizenship. (1988).
    The forgotten half: Pathways to success for America's youth and young families.
    Washington, DC: Author.
Willits, F. K., & Bealer, R. C. (1963). The utility of residence for differentiating social
    conservation in rural youth. *Rural Sociology, 28*(1), 70-80.
Willits, F. K., & Bealer, R. C. (1967). An evaluation of a composite definition of
    "rurality." *Rural Sociology, 32*, 163-177.
Wilson, S. M., & Peterson, G. W. (1988). Life satisfaction among young adults from
    rural families. *Family Relations, 37*, 84-91.
Wirth, L. (1938). Urbanism as a way of life. *American Journal of Sociology, 44*, 18.
Zelizer, V. A. R. (1985). *Pricing the priceless child: The changing social value of children.*
    New York: Basic Books.

4. Growing Up in Appalachia: Ecological Influences on Adolescent Development

Stephan M. Wilson
Gary W. Peterson

Adolescents from rural Appalachia have their origins in a very complex social, economic, and physical environment characterized by much diversity and many contradictions. The experience of growing up in this region cannot be understood effectively, therefore, unless we come to grasp the ecological circumstances within which these adolescents develop. Historic, geographic, social, and economic forces in Appalachia have forged many commonalities between the youth of this region and those of the larger American society. Seemingly in contrast, however, these same forces may have fostered a somewhat distinctive sociocultural context that, in turn, may have led to developmental consequences that differ to some extent from the larger society. Given these contradictory but coexisting trends as a backdrop, the purpose of this chapter is to describe the major themes and contemporary issues that define the experience of adolescence in Appalachia, with special emphasis devoted to those youth from rural portions of the central and southern areas of this region. This task involves descriptions of regional demographics, historic social developments, the central role of family life, socialization patterns, and examinations of several psychological outcomes that are characteristic of adolescents from the region.

For a variety of reasons, therefore, the objectives of this chapter are not easy tasks to accomplish. In the first place, any understanding of what is unique about "youthful development in Appalachia" must be examined in terms of the region's complicated but distinctive ecological context (real or legendary, historic and current) that

75

has provided the circumstances in which the adolescent years are experienced. Consequently, an ecological perspective is used in this chapter to examine a complicated array of historic, geographic, social, and economic circumstances that have shaped and are continuing to influence in more limited ways the current development of Appalachian youth (Bronfenbrenner, 1979; Lerner, 1991, 1995).

Moreover, despite considerable 20th century intervention by the federal government, the quality of empirically based social science research on Appalachian adolescents can only be described as seriously deficient. The primary result of this circumstance is that we are forced to examine and synthesize the experience of Appalachian adolescents from the perspective of scholarship that is more speculative than is desirable and than is most research-based social science. Much of what is known about Appalachian adolescents must be acquired from studies on considerably broader themes, such as the social ecology, rural community life, family relationships, and economic circumstances of this region. Therefore, a realistic starting point is to recognize that Appalachian adolescents are a woefully underresearched and poorly understood minority population in American society.

BACKGROUND

The larger region of Appalachia is comprised of 406 counties, including parts of 12 states and all of West Virginia. The region runs along the Appalachian mountains and foothills, from upstate New York to northern Mississippi. Adolescents of the central and southern highlands, the focus of this chapter, reside in the mountainous rural areas of West Virginia, Kentucky, Virginia, North Carolina, and Tennessee. Especially for this portion of the region, some scholars have argued that elements of a distinctive Appalachian culture may have taken root—a source of social influence that may continue today in somewhat attenuated forms (Tribe, 1995).

The geographic context of youth from central and southern Appalachia was elevated politically into the national consciousness in 1965 when the federal government created the Appalachian Regional Commission (ARC) to deal with a number of pressing problems, such as poverty, high levels of illiteracy, and health problems, as well as deficiencies in the transportation, communications, and human services infrastructure. The central and southern portions of Appalachia, in particular, are mostly rural areas with low population density, except for Standard Metropolitan Areas such as Pittsburgh, Pennsylvania, in northern Appalachia (Obermiller & Maloney, 1994) and Charleston, West Virginia, Pikeville, Kentucky, and Knoxville, Tennessee, in central and southern Appalachia. Although the enormous out-migration of earlier decades (1940-1970) has slowed for most of the states in the region, this trend has continued for some Appalachian states during the 1980s and 1990s (e.g., population losses from 1980 to 1990: West Virginia −10.7%; Virginia −8%; Kentucky −7.9%). The resulting transition to northern mill towns and cities has complicated choices for older adolescents as more Appalachians today have come to live, for example, in the Miami Valley of Ohio than in the whole of Appalachian Kentucky. An important migration index is that there are more than 100,000 Appalachians who are living in each of the nearby cities of Cincinnati and Columbus, Ohio (Maloney, 1995).

The more than 21 million residents of Appalachia (i.e., not counting Appalachians who reside outside the region) live in 6 million families (i.e., approximately 3 or 4 persons per household). There are 1.63 million children under 6 years old, 3.44 million preadolescents, early adolescents, and middle adolescents (i.e., 6- to 17-year-olds), and another 2.2 million older adolescents (i.e., 18- to 24-year-olds) who live in the region (ARC, 1994). Despite Appalachian stereotypes of large families bursting with multitudes of youngsters, there is a lower percentage of children and young adults who reside in Appalachia than in each of the comparable age categories for the nation's population as a whole. Moreover, the more than 5.6 million preadolescents, adolescents, and youth (i.e., older adolescents) represent more than 8% of the same age categories for the United States as a whole—a population about whom our current empirical knowledge remains profoundly deficient.

A CONTEXTUAL PERSPECTIVE
FOR APPALACHIAN ADOLESCENCE

Adolescents from rural areas of central and southern Appalachia are best understood in terms of their larger historic, economic, and social heritage. The broader ecological context experienced by

Appalachian youth involves the interplay between rapidly growing influences from urban America and lingering elements of a rural folk culture. These complicated circumstances require that Appalachian adolescents and their families cope with developmental expectations that originate somewhere on a continuum between two worlds (Peters, Wilson, & Peterson, 1986), that is, Appalachian youth face traditional expectations for family loyalty, connectedness to nuclear families, and obligations to extended kin, combined with more urban-contemporary demands for greater individuality, personal achievement, and geographic mobility. As a result, youth from the mountains of Appalachia seem to share circumstances with several minority populations that, during the process of socialization (or acculturation), must accommodate to social expectations and practices that originate in more than one American subculture (Padilla, 1980; Szapocznik & Kurtines, 1980).

Recent ecological or systemic models of human and adolescent development are useful mechanisms to understand how individuals adapt to such complex social environments with diverse expectations (Bronfenbrenner, 1986; Ford & Lerner, 1992). Specifically, much of the current scholarship on adolescent development rejects exclusive reliance on "individual models" in favor of more realistic perspectives that view each person as engaged in inseparable relationships with his or her surrounding social environment (Belsky, 1981, 1984; Broderick, 1993; Bronfenbrenner, 1979, 1986; Elder, 1991; Lerner, 1991, 1995; Peterson & Hahn, 1999). According to this viewpoint, development involves relationships with both near and more distant environments, such as the physical context, immediate social contexts (e.g., the family), economic circumstances (e.g., in the workplace), communities, educational institutions, socioeconomic circumstances, and elements of the cultural context (e.g., aesthetic, religious).

These components of the adolescent's environment are organized into multiple levels that (a) are interconnected, (b) vary in terms of proximity to the developing adolescent, and (c) function to directly or indirectly shape the lives of youth. Added to this systems model are such complexities as the elements of time and history, with the result being that adolescent development and their environments are subject to forces that are unique to a given time period and products of what transpired in previous eras. As such, the purpose of this chapter is to examine the nature of adolescent development within the larger ecological context of rural Appalachia, both in terms of its present forms and unique historical experience.

ECOLOGICAL EFFECTS OF
APPALACHIAN HISTORY

Despite being treated as a geographic entity, the region is not homogeneous with respect to economic development or virtually any other socioeconomic or demographic characteristic. More specifically, central and southern Appalachia is a portion of modern America characterized by great contrasts—extreme poverty amidst great riches, glaring inequalities in the midst of wealth, love and reverence for nature despite environmental abuses (e.g., strip mining and clear cutting), and low levels of literacy in an area where some of the greatest 20th-century American poets, essayists, and novelists have been creative (e.g., James Still, Jesse Stuart, and Harriet Arnow).

Very limited amounts of research exist that specifically address the traditional topics of adolescent scholarship in an empirically sound manner with samples specifically identified as youth from rural Appalachian areas (for notable exceptions, see Dail, 1994; Kenkel, 1986a, 1986b; Peterson & Stivers, 1986a, 1986b; Peterson, Stivers, & Peters, 1986; Wilson, Peterson, & Wilson, 1993). This article attempts to synthesize what is known about youth from Appalachia from a very narrow and often unsystematically acquired knowledge base. Much of our existing conceptions of adolescents from these contexts must be gleaned from impressionistic writings on Appalachia, qualitative descriptions of Appalachian culture in mountain communities, as well as research that addresses adolescent development indirectly or as components of larger issues in the region (e.g., poverty or status attainment research; Peters et al., 1986; Wilson et al., 1993). However, a starting point in conceptualizing the ecological context of Appalachian adolescents is to describe how the forces of (a) strong familism, (b) historic patterns of geographic and social seclusion, and (c) more recent economic exploitation by outside interests may have structured social patterns that some scholars have viewed as a unique cultural environment for the adolescents of the region. A much-debated point in the literature on Appalachia has centered around the extent to which these forces have shaped distinctive cultural patterns that have considerable impact on the social development of the region's children and adolescents (Keefe, 1992; Keefe, Reck, & Reck, 1983; Peters et al., 1986). Consequently, the subject of this chapter and the vast majority of existing information on Appalachian youth and families focuses on such rural populations who adapted to central and southern Appalachia in this distinctive, perhaps culturally specific, manner.

Early Historical Developments

Although Appalachian youth and families are predominately of Scotch-Irish, English, and German ancestry, this region is an amalgam of many cultures and sociocultural responses to their contextual circumstances (Batteau, 1979-1980; Klein, 1995). Besides the Native Americans who originally occupied this region, for example, considerable numbers of Dutch, French, southern European, and African populations were settling central and southern Appalachia by the late 1700s (Beaver, 1988; Elder, 1991). According to some Appalachian scholars, however, the original settlers from primarily western and northern European roots may have developed a regionally specific folk culture in response to the unique socioecological circumstances that confronted them (Keefe, 1992; Keefe et al., 1983).

There are several issues, stereotypes, misconceptions, and problems that have continued into the late 20th century, whose roots were established in the earlier history of Appalachia. Nevertheless, these historic themes, images, and characterizations must be understood before the contemporary experience of growing up in Appalachia can be accurately understood.

Isolation and political alliances. Several forces (some real and some invented) coalesced in the 19th century to accentuate the natural geographic and social isolation of Appalachia. Prior to the American Civil War, for example, Appalachia was relatively isolated from the communication and trade centers of the Eastern seaboard by its mountainous terrain. Additional sources of isolation were insufficient local government revenues, which led to the slower construction of roads, communication systems, and schools compared to other parts of the nation. The onset of the Civil war in the early 1860s ushered in a period of heightened deprivation, as well as even greater political and social isolation for Appalachia. Although not universal, mountain counties of the southern states tended to side with the Union instead of the Southern Confederacy (Salatino, 1995). Such developments contributed to the tendency for mountain counties of rural Appalachia to experience further political, social, and economic isolation from the larger society. After the nation's sectional strife ended, this "disloyalty" to the Southern cause was remembered by officials of neighboring Confederate counties, with the frequent result being that funding for schools and roads was allocated inequitably by majority politicians from nonmountain counties in most of southern Appalachian states except West Virginia (Beaver, 1988).

Deviance and pathology. Later in the 19th century, Appalachia was characterized more than could be justified as isolated, quaint, parochial, backward, violent, and dysfunctional. During the same time, many Northern Protestant churches followed the lead of writers of local color by instituting "home mission" fields in Appalachia staffed by well-meaning outsiders who "knew what was good for Appalachians." The reality of Appalachia, however, was not as alien or caricatured as the images conveyed by local color writers, missionaries, or well-intentioned but paternalistic national leaders of the era. Twentieth-century Appalachian society often has been portrayed in terms of stereotypic or pathological images. Specifically, Appalachian social life frequently is viewed as a "deviant subculture" whose problems owe to "physical isolation, depleted gene pools, pathological inbreeding, clan wars, hookworm, moonshining, and welfarism [rather] than to the nation's unceasing demands on the region for cheap labor, land, raw materials, and energy" (Whisnant, 1980, pp. xix-xx).

Environmental destruction. Forces external to the region also played major roles in shaping the economic circumstances faced by Appalachian youth and families as the region progressed through the 19th and entered the 20th century. Specifically, the region's great wealth of natural resources (minerals and timber) were discovered by outside industrial interests, and railroads unlocked the mountains for commerce and industrial development. Agents for coal, land, and railroad interests began buying mineral and land rights from Appalachian farmers whose financial circumstances were precarious. Through such acquisition agreements, Appalachian families not only lost their rights to minerals below the land but also relinquished surface rights, which precluded any residential and agricultural uses (Caudill, 1962; Eller, 1982). This control of resources by outside interests and the availability of cheap local labor were other factors that (a) attracted manufacturing interests to the mountain edge areas and (b) gave rise to company towns in southern Appalachia (Eller, 1978, 1982). The acquisition of land and resources by these outside corporations meant that external forces controlled local political processes, the management of local communities, and the provision of local services (Beaver, 1988; Childers, 1979; Gaventa, 1980). An important result was that many Appalachian families were compelled to leave their farms, move to the emergent company towns, and become increasingly influenced by outside forces.

Twentieth-Century Images

Contrasting with earlier images of isolation, political misalignment, backwardness, and deviance is a more recent alternative view that attributes the current socioeconomic problems experienced by Appalachian youth and families to a long history of exploitation, derogatory images conveyed, and discriminatory attitudes directed toward Appalachian social life. Between 1940 and 1970, 7 million people migrated from this region to Northern industrial centers in search of jobs with livable wages and benefits. This drain of human capital occurred mostly among the young, the best educated, and those seeking upward mobility. A sample outcome of such developments includes the fact that, between 1980 and 1990, Appalachian counties of Kentucky experienced more than an 18% decline in the number of resident children (Kentucky Kids Count Consortium, 1995). Another result has been that Appalachian families and their children are compelled frequently (usually for economic reasons) to live in other regions but have continued some of their traditional social, cultural, and familial patterns within these newer settings. Although hardships have resulted for many members of both transplanted families and those who remained in Appalachia, these migrations may have given rise to alternative means for "Appalachians in absentia" to affirm their family origins and bonds (e.g., frequent visits, telephoning relatives, and planning to retire near the home place; Rural and Appalachian Youth and Families Consortium [RAYFC], 1996).

Perhaps the most common 20th-century image of central and southern Appalachia is of an impoverished, backward, and forgotten segment of America through works such as Michael Harrington's *The Other America* (1962), which captured the attention of policy makers and social scientists alike. More recently, it has been argued that Appalachia and its people are marginalized from mainstream American life, a further means of underscoring the "differentness" of families and children from that region (RAYFC, 1996). From this perspective, Appalachia is seen as a domestic colony whose surplus population and abundant natural resources have been exported to support interests outside the region (Robertson & Shoffner, 1989). Appalachia has been defined increasingly as "America's Third World" (Lohmann, 1990), sharing common problems with other marginalized areas of North America (e.g., the inner cities; Rosenberg, 1979-1980); and elsewhere in the world, such as Wales, Northern Ireland, or Eastern Europe (Cécora, 1993; Couto, 1994; Day, 1987). Consequently, if elements of a unique culture have come to fruition in Appalachia, then a perspective worth considering is the view that these developments are partial products of (or at least reinforced by) the extended geographic isolation that previously existed and a "defense mechanism" against the later encroachments of outside interests.

In fact, contemporary Appalachia does suffer from severe economic distress, which has persisted over most of the current century. Even in the current decade, Appalachian families' average income ($15,816) is 83% of the national average. Poverty continues to be characteristic of Appalachia, but it remains unevenly distributed in severity throughout the region. For example, in the Appalachian areas of Kentucky, family income ($12,433) is only 65% of the national average, but it is even worse in McCreary County, Kentucky, where the average family income ($8,695) is even lower (46% of the national average for family income; ARC, 1994; Couto, 1994).

Familism in the Traditional Culture

Adolescent development in rural Appalachia is more readily understood by emphasizing the central importance of the family in terms of its "classical" or historic manifestations from past times. Among the pervasive influences of familism that continue today are the importance of family reputation and substantial loyalty to one's family, coupled with distrust for extrafamilial social institutions, such as the school, governmental authorities, and external agencies. Prior to World War II, the social organization in rural areas of southern Appalachia could be characterized more as collections of families living in the mountains rather than as a regional society (Beaver, 1988; Bryant, 1981; Hicks, 1992; Schwarzweller, 1970). In contrast to urban areas, where economic and political institutions were dominant, family life became the central form of Appalachian social organization. Because many residents of these isolated rural communities were members of overlapping kin groups, the lack of clearly defined boundaries between families and local communities was evident. Across generations, these "kinship communities," or interlocking networks of extended families, were symbolically associated with a particular locale (e.g., a mountain, a "holler," or a county) and rooted deeply in the land (Batteau, 1982; Beaver, 1988; Bryant, 1981; Hicks, 1992; Matthews, 1966).

Appalachian families were characterized by close interpersonal bonds within which adolescents and other family members were socialized. Relationships both within these families and their immediate communities were governed by systems of norms emphasizing collective success or failure through expectations such as "a person ought to stick up for their own kin" (i.e., family loyalty; see Beaver, 1986; Bryant, 1981; Hicks, 1992; Schwarzweller, 1970). Moreover, families functioned as agencies of social control and sought to prevent behavior that reflected badly on one's family name through such interpersonal mechanisms as gossip, ridicule, and ostracism (Keefe, 1988). An important consequence of traditional Appalachian familism for adolescents and other family members was a deep and abiding sense of continuity regarding their familial ancestry and association with a particular locale. Of paramount importance was an adolescent's family name (rather than social class) as a means of ascribing his or her social status (i.e., social prestige acquired at birth into a particular family). Specifically, kin groups often acquired notoriety for certain traits or attributes that were reputed to be shared by the members of particular families; these traits provided young people with a substantial part of their social identity within the community (Batteau, 1982; Beaver, 1986; Bryant, 1981; Hicks,

1992). Family reputations provided youth with family legacies for negative and positive attributes, such as being industrious or shiftless, ruthless or good-natured, dishonest or trustworthy (Batteau, 1982; Peters et al., 1986).

The complex and pervasive nature of Appalachian family life has spawned heated debates about the relative strengths and weakness of this intimate social system. Various deficit models have been proposed, with Appalachian familism being implicated as the source of many problematic psychosocial outcomes for adolescents and as excessive emotional dependency or enmeshment, diminished achievement motivation, and inhibited socioeconomic mobility (Group for the Advancement of Psychiatry, Committee on the Family, 1970; Mong, 1995; Weller, 1965). Related deficiencies for youth were identified also, including school phobia, extreme distrust of outsiders, and the inability to cope with forces of modernization from urban America (Ball, 1970; Looff, 1971). In contrast, the primary opposing view is more positive, with Appalachian families being portrayed as havens of security, sources of stability, and reservoirs of emotional support in times of crisis or stress (Brown & Schwarzweller, 1970; Dyk & Wilson, 1999; Hicks, 1992; Madsen, 1969; Stephenson, 1968; Wilson, Henry, & Peterson, 1997). Positive aspects of extended familism provide the resources of pride in one's heritage, a sense of having "roots," and a stable context that provides clear parameters for identity development (Keefe, 1988; Peters et al., 1986).

An unfortunate aspect of the existing scholarship on Appalachian social life is the tendency to use norms from the urban mainstream as the primary criteria for making judgments about the health or pathology of Appalachian familism. Rather than suffering from major deficits, however, the centrality of family ties in Appalachian society is reflective of existing variations in the extent to which these qualities are both prevalent and considered normative in different cultures. Specifically, the historic heritage of Appalachian society (as reflected in its family system) leans toward cultural patterns that emphasize the central role of "collectivism" (or relationship interdependence) rather than "individualism" (Kim, Triandis, Kagitcibasi, Choie, & Yoon, 1994; Peterson, 1995), in a manner similar to many other ethnic, minority, and religious groups, such as Hispanic, Asian, Irish-Catholic, Amish, Italian, and Mormon families. Many American minority groups share cultural patterns that tend to emphasize "collective" rather than "individualistic" beliefs and practices. Appalachian familism underscores the idea that individual welfare is best facilitated by fostering the interests of the group (or family) rather than by promoting characteristics of the larger society, such as self-interest, autonomy, and personal agency.

Given such cross-cultural diversity in emphasizing family connectedness versus individualism, it is clear that strong family ties per se are neither inherently beneficial nor inevitably problematic for adolescents and other family members. Instead, the essential issues involve (a) whether a particular family system has adapted itself to the surrounding social ecology and (b) the extent to which familial variation within a particular ethnic group has differential psychosocial consequences for its members. The central message, in this case, is that each family system should be judged in terms of its own historic heritage, physical circumstances, economic environment, and sociocultural context, rather than in terms of external criteria imposed from outside that group (e.g., the urban mainstream). In the case of Appalachian society, the historic pattern of geographic and cultural isolation helps to clarify the circumstances under which nuclear and extended family relationships became so central in the social life of rural mountain communities. The traditional folk culture of Appalachia, in its historic form, was adaptive for a geographically isolated region in which rural families attempted to create lifestyles consistent with self-sufficiency.

Traditional Culture and the Socialization of Adolescents

Besides the classic version of the Appalachian family as the most central social context, it is also important to acquire an historical understanding about the larger context of adolescent socialization in past times. Specifically, youth from rural Appalachia who experienced their years of adolescence prior to World War II were socialized within a context having limited ties to urban America. Rural Appalachian communities were essentially small networks of peers, neighbors, preachers, and, most importantly, family members (both nuclear and extended) who conveyed limited conceptions of the "outside world," coupled with a rather homogeneous set of attitudes and values to the young (Peters et al., 1986; Photiadis, 1977). As in most folk societies, informal communities were the primary means through which mountaineer culture was conveyed. Most of the indigenous socialization process was accomplished within tightly interconnected networks of churches, nuclear families, and extended kin members that comprised Appalachian communities, that is, details about family reputations, the importance of family ties, church standing, local folklore, the rich tradition of mountain music, aesthetic expressions (formal and folk art), and suspicions about "outsiders'" institutions, interests, and even ideas were learned in this fashion.

Religion and community churches played a central role in the socialization of Appalachian youth. The indigenous Christianity of Appalachia originated during the Great Revival on the Kentucky frontier from 1790 to 1810. Various perspectives (e.g., local church dogma and denominations) became steadfast sources of resistance to change and important mechanisms through which cultural isolation was reinforced (Boles, 1972; Humphrey, 1988). Adolescents were raised within very personal, conversion-oriented theologies, in which individuals were expected to demonstrate their Christian faith not by correct doctrine but through testimonials about their conversions and commitments to salvation. Central to the theology of Appalachian churches was the belief that the Bible serves as the "only true guide for faith and practice" and as a source of security, relief from anxiety, and an anchor for one's identity. A key socialization agent for the young was the homegrown, often unlettered preacher who often exhorted Appalachian youth to strive for salvation even while working to keep the spirit of revivalism alive and striving to convert those who were not yet saved (Humphrey, 1988).

The school was another social institution of considerable influence but one that often received ambivalent if not negative responses from Appalachian adolescents and their families. As sources of external urban influence, many aspects of educational institutions were viewed with suspicion by members of mountain communities (Keefe et al., 1983; Weller, 1965). Schools often have been portrayed by observers as fostering cultural conflict with traditional Appalachian society through efforts to reject the native folk culture, impose outside influences, and "acculturate" mountaineer youth into the dominant culture (Branscome, 1978; Keefe et al., 1983). Although most teachers within these schools originated from Appalachia, they often were viewed as considerably influenced by urban values, inclined to reject local culture, and likely to discourage students from using Appalachian society as the basis for identity development (Clark, 1974; Miller, 1977; Reck, Reck, & Keefe, 1993).

Compared to most other areas of the country, the disproportionate rates of lower academic achievement, higher drop-out rates, and lower percentages of youth who pursue advanced education may reflect the extent to which schools have failed to mesh effectively with Appalachian society (Caudill, 1962; Keefe, 1983; Wilson et al., 1993).

The adolescent peer group served as an arena within which Appalachian teenagers could develop aspects of their interpersonal identities, associate with the opposite gender, and develop some of the skills that prepared them for adulthood (Peters et al., 1986; Photiadis, 1977; Weller, 1965). Appalachian peer groups often were composed of kin or close friends with very similar cultural practices and family backgrounds and tended to complement rather than contradict adult society. The peer group was simply another aspect of close-knit communities and helped the young to attain adult status within the existing social system by reinforcing the attitudes, values, and behavior patterns of traditional Appalachian society. Courtship or dating, for example, was initiated within the peer group but monitored considerably by family members and extensively intertwined with family activities. A common courtship practice was for boys to visit girls and socialize together under the watchful eyes of family members (Beaver, 1986). Although fulfilling many of the same functions as youthful peer groups in the larger society (Brown, 1990), the social world of adolescent contemporaries in Appalachia was even more integrated with the adult world than was the case for urban norms.

An important outcome of strong familistic bonds and integrated communities was the tendency of Appalachian youth to become autonomous in a somewhat different manner than did youth from the urban middle class (Hicks, 1992; Peters et al., 1986). Although, for example, young couples were expected to establish their own dwellings separate from their families of orientation (similar to the urban middle class), they often did so in close proximity to parents. Moreover, deep personal involvements with family, obligations to kin, and high levels of value agreement with adults may have meant that Appalachian youth did not attain the same levels of cognitive, emotional, or behavioral autonomy experienced by adolescents outside Appalachia who were socialized for geographic mobility (Steinberg, 1990).

Despite being consistent with pervasive familism and the social atmosphere of rural Appalachia, this distinctive pattern of autonomy may not have been adaptive in reference to mainstream, urban culture, which underscored the importance of geographic mobility, individual self-interest, personal achievement, and flexible family ties, that is, youth were expected to remain geographically closer to their families and maintain stronger, more complicated interpersonal ties with kin than was the case for their urban contemporaries (Hicks, 1992; Peters et al., 1986).

Closely related to autonomy development, the identities of Appalachian youth were deeply rooted in close-knit mountain communities and generations of family history tied to the local area. Adolescent identities were shaped by rather uniform sets of values and attitudes to which the young were recurrently exposed within Appalachian families, churches, and communities. Family loyalty, obligations to kin, and religious consensus were pervasive orientations that Appalachian adolescents encountered on a daily basis. Combined with extensive emphasis on familism and devotion to the larger purpose of salvation, however, was the seemingly contradictory emphasis on egalitarianism or individuality, in which the refusal to obey peremptory orders and demands from others was the most common expression of this value (Hicks, 1992; Peters et al., 1986; Weller, 1965). Thus, Appalachian society also accommodated youthful individualism within a larger social context that reinforced subordination (i.e., conformity and connectedness) of the self to family and in reference to a higher power (Peterson, 1995).

Because of their membership in closely interconnected communities, Appalachian youth also were socialized to become person-oriented and to maintain effective social relationships with others (Matthews, 1966; Peters et al., 1986; Weller, 1965). Emphasis was placed on the "ethic of neutrality"—encouragement to assume a harmonious or noncompetitive approach in social relationships (Hicks, 1992). Expectations for social interaction with others included proscriptions against raising controversies, initiating conflicts, becoming aggressive, or exercising authority over others (Hicks, 1992). Family members were encouraged to manage conflict, talk things over, and save face, with the young being taught specifically to ignore objectional behavior and consciously to avoid controversial topics (Lewis, Kobak, & Johnson, 1978).

Several observers of Appalachian social life also have argued that an important socialization outcome for Appalachian mountaineer adolescents was the tendency to be fatalistic (or exhibit a high external locus of control) in their approaches to life (Ford, 1962; Peters et al., 1986; Polansky, Borgman, & DeSaix, 1972 ; Weller, 1965). Specifically, *fatalism* refers to feelings of powerlessness in the face of events that humans believe cannot be changed. Such a frame of reference involves the perception that outside forces beyond a person's influence are controlling his or her life. Fatalism often is discussed as an aspect of "culture of poverty" circumstances or as a component of evangelical religion that emphasizes placing one's fate in the hands of God. A common concern, however, is that fatalistic orientations are in conflict with the mainstream American values of success, individual achievement, and free will.

Considerable controversy has developed recently about the extent to which fatalism was a central component of Appalachian folk culture (Beaver, 1982; Lewis & Knipe, 1978; Peters et al., 1986; Weller, 1965; Wilson et al., 1997; Wilson & Peterson, 1988). Alternative interpretations, for example, tend to view fatalism as an adaptive response to special conditions faced by low-income Appalachian youth. Instead of a deficit impairing the adaptiveness of youth, fatalism or a sense of powerlessness may be reinterpreted as an appropriate response to immediate physical and social circumstances, which have long been criticized, dominated, and exploited by outside interests (e.g., mining industries, timber industries, external landowners, urban culture). According to this perspective, fatalism may be an adaptive mechanism for adolescents who must cope with rural environments in which economic opportunities are limited and powerful interests beyond the local area have substantial control over their own and their families' lives.

The best evidence also indicates that Appalachian families socialized their young to a large extent for traditional gender roles (Beaver, 1986; Fiene, 1988; Hennon & Photiadis, 1979; Wilson et al., 1993). As an adaptation to an economy previously based on self-sufficient agriculture, a division of labor based on gender differences evolved that was intended to foster family well-being consistent with demands of the immediate social and physical environment. Teenage boys, on the one hand, were socialized to assume roles in the "extradomestic" or public realm, such as raising cash crops, public work away from the home place, and associations with other men in community affairs (Beaver, 1986). Specific involvements of teenage boys included heavy farm chores, operating farm machinery, and tending livestock. In their spare time, boys were expected (especially by fathers) to be venturesome and were allowed to spend more time away from home than were girls (Hicks, 1992). Teenage girls, on the other hand, were socialized primarily for the domestic or familial realm involving primary responsibility for child-rearing, cleaning, food purchase, cooking, and gardening (Beaver, 1986; Hicks, 1992). Compared to boys, girls were monitored more closely and granted less freedom (Beaver, 1979; Hicks, 1992), with the resulting time spent at home functioning to foster strong bonds between mothers and daughters.

Therefore, an overall assessment might be that the traditional folk culture of Appalachia prepared adolescents for a geographically isolated region in which self-sufficiency (in the context of family and kin support) was the dominant economic endeavor. Adolescents who experienced this intimate social system often became members of integrated local communities characterized by strong familistic bonds, extended kinship, the importance of family name, religious commitment, traditional gender roles, and high levels of agreement with adult values. Only if measured by the inappropriate standards of outside social groups (e.g., urban, middle-class youth) can the social development of Appalachian youth be described in terms of deficit models.

Appalachia in Transition

In the decades since the mid-20th century, Appalachia has continued to be dominated by outside economic interests and to be misunderstood and subjugated by mainstream American culture (RAYFC, 1996). Like other regions of modern America, the pervasiveness of the print and electronic media, improvements in transportation, and the periodic movements of kin away from and back to the home place have increased the exposure of Appalachians to outside alternatives. Instead of being a parochial curiosity, contemporary Appalachia has become integrated into the larger society by television, national programming such as MTV, *Friends, The Drew Carey Show,* and *ER*; most aspects of American pop culture; plus the pervasive consumerism and materialism that stand at the center of the American value system. In addition to national electronic communications media and entertainment, modern superhighways, national retail franchises (e.g., Wal-Mart, Blockbuster Video, and Hardee's), and institutions invented and maintained by outsiders (e.g., Temporary Assistance for Needy Families, state boards of education, community colleges, the extension service, etc.) have guaranteed increased integration with the mainstream culture from outside the region.

Some observers of Appalachia argue that a process of "colonization" by outside interests has left the region with an underdeveloped infrastructure. Of particular concern are deficiencies in quality jobs that can provide adequate salaries and benefits for families and young people to support themselves. Most counties in central Appalachia, in fact, have had more than double the national rate of unemployment since the 1950s (Kentucky Kids Count Consortium, 1995; Lohmann, 1990; Robertson & Shoffner, 1989; Wilson, 1994). The passive acceptance and even fatalistic responses to such harsh circumstances have complicated further the economic and political plight of families and youth in the region (Gaventa, 1980).

Despite these pervasive pressures from the outside, aspects of the traditional folk culture continue to exist alongside urban mainstream alternatives. As a result, contemporary adolescents and their families appear to be faced with two systems of values, which are sometimes at odds with each other. Specifically, a traditional Appalachian worldview, on the one hand, emphasizes the rewards of stability and continuity, religious fundamentalism, historicity and localism, the centrality of family, family closeness, and kinship. Non-Appalachian, urban society, on the other hand, places premium value on secularism, individualism, diminished kinship ties, and the benefits of achievement through competition, materialism, and geographic mobility. Moreover, Appalachian families have been subjected to many of the same demographic trends as the larger society in the form of changes in family structure (i.e., high divorce rates and increased proportions of single-parent families) and periodic economic dislocations, which often become magnified in the region.

The reality of life for many families who remain in Appalachia, and for many who migrate, is continuing poverty or lower socioeconomic status (SES; Wilson, 1994), lower levels of educational and occupational attainment (Wilson et al., 1997), discrimination based on mountaineer speech patterns (Luhman, 1990), and devaluation of their cultural heritage by the mainstream urban society (RAYFC,

1996). Consequently, the path to adulthood is complicated for Appalachian adolescents by conflicting expectations from a variety of traditional and contemporary sources. Appalachian society is far more complex than either the ridiculous, comedic representations of *The Beverly Hillbillies* or the idyllic images of extended family households conveyed on *The Waltons*. Moreover, comedians such as Jeff Foxworthy do Appalachia's image a substantial disservice when they perpetuate the region's stereotype as a collective haven for rednecks.

Although Appalachian social life involves the complex interplay among lingering elements of the traditional folk culture and the powerful encroachment of urban influences, many of the problematic circumstances of Appalachian youth and their families are products of the widespread poverty and depressed socioeconomic conditions that characterize the region (Couto, 1994; Duncan & Lamborghini, 1994; Task Force on Persistent Poverty, 1993). Frequently cited family problems, such as domestic violence, marital disruption, and sexual abuse, are not unique to Appalachia and may, in part, have their origins in the stress and mental health problems associated with poverty (Dail, 1994). Moreover, the disproportionate levels of poverty in Appalachia are likely to produce relatively higher frequencies of such problems and to be more noticed by social workers and mental health professionals who service these populations. Such problems have not been shown, however, to be the consequences of Appalachian "culture" (or Hispanic, African American, or Anglo culture, for that matter), but, instead, they are more likely to result from disproportionate amounts of poverty in rural Appalachia (RAYFC, 1996).

The Socialization of Contemporary Appalachian Youth

The current status of Appalachian social life that serves as the context for youthful development can best be viewed as resulting from circumstances rooted in unique historical traditions and contemporary forces from the larger society. Adolescents and their families who are products of these complicated experiences will vary widely to include those who (a) remain marginalized, (b) identify in positive ways with aspects of the traditional culture, (c) recognize the importance of both traditional and contemporary cultures, or (d) are completely integrated into the mainstream values of the urban middle class. Migration out of Appalachia has led to a back-and-forth movement and exchange of ideas, which has contributed greatly to much broader views of the larger world and receptivity to influences from urban America.

Complicated influences from urban America have had considerable impact on both the contemporary socialization processes within Appalachian families and the current psychosocial outcomes developed by adolescents from that region. The first of these developments—the socialization values and practices used by Appalachian parents—are likely to range from those that are characteristic of urban America to those that remain fairly consistent with the traditional folk culture (RAYFC, 1996). Correspondingly, many Appalachian youth must adjust to the social expectations of these two worlds—with the one orientation (i.e., the traditional folk culture) emphasizing family closeness, kinship, obligation to kin, localism, and fundamentalist religion, and the second perspective (i.e., urban-contemporary) underscoring issues such as achievement, competition, geographic mobility, individualism, and secular values (Peters et al., 1986). Adolescents who range along this continuum from "traditional" to "contemporary" must accomplish this integration in various degrees from being "Appalachian-identified" at one end of this dimension, "biculturally identified" at the midpoint, and "urban-identified" at the opposite extreme.

Although urban patterns of socialization are undoubtedly more prevalent, observers of contemporary Appalachian youth and families continue to identify characteristic parenting styles that differ from patterns typical for much of mainstream America. Specifically, whereas the prototype of urban parenting styles often includes rational control, achievement pressure, independence granting, and support (i.e., authoritative parenting; see Baumrind, 1991; Peterson & Hahn, 1999), child-rearing typical of Appalachian parents has been variously characterized as highly indulgent and nurturant (Beaver, 1986; Egerton, 1983; Looff, 1971; Weller, 1965), as well as authoritarian (Dail, 1994) and physically punitive (Wiehe, 1990). Others have characterized Appalachian parenting as tending to foster family interdependence (Abbott, 1992) and as valuing obedience-conformity outcomes by the young rather than self-direction and autonomy (Peters & Peterson, 1988; RAYFC, 1996).

Child-rearing approaches of this kind, which seem to combine rigid control with nurturant acceptance, may reflect the characteristic family system of Appalachia, which emphasizes connectedness, interpersonal closeness, family loyalty, conformity to familial expectations, and continuing physical proximity. The greater tendency of Appalachian parents to use physical punishment might be rooted in fundamentalist religious beliefs that legitimize child-rearing approaches that reflect the biblical prescription "to spare the rod and spoil the child" (Wiehe, 1990). Another possibility, however, is that direct disciplinary approaches of this kind (i.e., obedience orientations and use of physical punishment) may not be a product of Appalachian culture but simply an outgrowth of the lower social status that is characteristic of many Appalachian parents (Peters & Peterson, 1988; Peterson & Peters, 1985), that is, child-rearing approaches that emphasize obedience to authority, arbitrary force, and rigid control tend to be more characteristic of parents from lower socioeconomic levels than of mothers and fathers from the middle class (Kohn, 1977; Peterson & Hahn, 1999; Peterson & Rollins, 1987). Consequently, much additional research is needed to identify the characteristic parenting styles of Appalachian parents, the cultural versus socioeconomic roots of such strategies, and the psychosocial consequences of these approaches.

Consistent with such changes in parent-adolescent relationships, the process of attaining autonomy in rural Appalachia appears to be somewhat of a compromise between both urban and traditional patterns (Peters et al., 1986; Peterson & Stivers, 1986a). Although it is increasingly apparent, even in urban America, that adolescent autonomy emerges within a context of close family bonds and continuing parental influence (Collins & Repinski, 1994; Grotevant & Cooper, 1986; Steinberg, 1990; Youniss & Smollar, 1985), it also appears that self-directedness by Appalachian youth is a function of family connectedness, even more so than in the urban middle class (Peterson, 1986; Peterson & Stivers, 1986a). Moreover, autonomy development within a context of relationship togetherness (i.e., within the context of Appalachian familism) contrasts markedly with classical accounts of adolescent development that view the emancipation process as one of separation, parent-adolescent conflict, and "storm and stress" (Blos, 1979; Freud, 1965).

This tendency to integrate both urban and traditional expectations means that progress toward autonomy remains somewhat different and perhaps more complex in rural Appalachia than in urban America (Peters et al., 1986). Alongside such traditional orientations as family loyalty, kinship ties, and localism, increased emphasis is now placed on individualism, achievement, success, and geographic mobility. Thus, Appalachian adolescents now must weigh complicated (and sometimes contradictory) pressures to maintain ties with their families of origin, fulfill obligations to extended kin, leave home to pursue an advanced education, and pursue geographic mobility to seek employment opportunities. As a result, Appalachian teenagers may become autonomous within the context of stronger family ties and more complicated circumstances than are typical of adolescents from the urban middle class (Peters et al., 1986).

Important social influences on adolescents that have diluted the pervasive impact of familism are both the changing nature of immediate social networks in Appalachian communities and the technological connections with urban America that have emerged in recent decades. For example, the homogeneity of the adolescent peer group, which existed earlier in the 20th century, has been increasingly diversified by the growing number of in-migrants from the larger society, the return of Appalachian youth from urban areas (whose families had out-migrated temporarily for economic opportunities), and the consolidation of rural schools. Such external influences have meant that values, attitudes, and lifestyles from urban America have had increasing influence on the lives of Appalachian youth. Of particular importance has been the increased availability of "youth culture" from the larger society, which conveys a wide array of youth-orientated celebrities, pop music, clothing styles, and cultural attitudes that provide alternatives to traditional Appalachian ways (Peters et al., 1986; Photiadis, 1977, 1980). One set of developments in particular—television and the mass media—has played a central role in the growth of urban influences. Exposure to the images and role models conveyed by the mass media has provided Appalachian adolescents with the raw materials for experimentation with lifestyles and behaviors that often differ from the traditional culture of the Appalachian mountains. The mass media (which increasingly include computer technology and the worldwide Internet) function as windows into worlds of alternative social values and behaviors that extend far beyond Appalachian teenagers' more restricted range of daily experiences in the past (Peters et al., 1986; Peterson, 1995; Peterson & Peters, 1983). An important result has been substantial declines in the uniformity of local values and decreases in parent-youth consensus that previously was based on the traditional folk culture of rural Appalachia.

A notable social mechanism that fosters adolescent autonomy is contact with a diversity of social agents outside both the family and the local Appalachian community. Many Appalachian adolescents seem to have struck a compromise in their social networks by remaining open to a complex pattern of influence from social agents originating both from urban America and from Appalachian society. Like the urban mainstream, therefore, Appalachian youth have expanded beyond the influences of nuclear families during the high school years and have identified increasingly with a more diverse array of significant others (e.g., peers and teachers) who influence their life plans (Peterson et al., 1986). Moreover, Appalachian adolescents seem to affirm their individuality by indicating more often than not that they have made marital and fertility decisions (i.e., number of children desired) by themselves, without the assistance of other social agents (Peterson & Stivers, 1986b; Wilson et al., 1993). These trends toward extrafamilial influences and greater individuality are tempered, however, by extraordinarily strong parental influences on educational and occupational decision making throughout the adolescent period of development (Wilson et al., 1993) and that substantial declines occur in the diversity of significant other choices during the period 2 to 4 years after high school graduation (Peters & Peterson, 1982). It appears that many Appalachian youth may experience their early 20s as a period of declining peer association, but one during which ties with nuclear family members are continued (Peterson & Stivers 1986b; Peterson et al., 1986). This persistence of rural family influences is further underscored by findings that indicate that close proximity to their place of birth and continued residence in rural areas were significant contributors to the life satisfaction of Appalachian youth (Wilson et al., 1997; Wilson & Peterson, 1988). Such patterns of parent versus peer association are not fundamentally different from those of urban adolescents (Brown, 1990), with perhaps the tendency being for Appalachian youth to lean a bit more toward parent and family influences.

Greater emphasis on urban patterns of autonomy also is consistent with more attention by Appalachian youth to the need for personal success and social mobility, that is, over the past several decades, Appalachian youth have been socialized increasingly to value status attainment (i.e., educational and occupational attainment) and to govern more of their behavior in the pursuit of social mobility (Otto, 1986; Sewell & Hauser, 1980; Wilson et al., 1993). The result has been that mainstream ideas about success have become more accepted but tempered by the realities of the Appalachian context and modified somewhat in terms of traditional mountaineer heritage (Wilson & Peterson, 1988).

Status attainment or social mobility, therefore, is a complex process that is deeply rooted within family socialization experiences, individual characteristics, and barriers to attainment within the Appalachian social context (Kerchoff, 1976; Wilson et al., 1997; Wilson et al., 1993). Family-of-origin predictors of attainment include available resources (e.g., money) for attainment that are based in the family's SES, attainment values consistent with the family's social class standing, and parents' aspirations and expectations that they communicate to their teenagers (Chapman, 1990). Individual factors that contribute to attainment include the adolescents' own aspirations and expectations for attainment and indicators of intellectual ability, such as IQ and academic achievement (Otto, 1986; Sewell & Hauser, 1980; Wilson et al., 1993).

Previous research has documented that Appalachian youth often have high educational and occupational aspirations early in adolescence but somewhat lower expectations about the realistic outcomes they can expect, both in terms of formal schooling and career outcomes (Kenkel, 1986b; Schiamberg, 1986; Wilson & Peterson, 1988). By late adolescence, however, youth from rural Appalachia often have adjusted their aspirations downward as reality testing has occurred. Thus, Appalachian youth often accept lower aspirations for attainment when barriers to social mobility are recognized, including (a) the necessity to leave the home place for economic opportunity, (b) the limited career options in Appalachia, (c) inadequate access to advanced education, and (d) limited family resources to support these endeavors (Kenkel, 1986b; Schiamberg, 1986). Additional factors that limit the opportunities of youth include widespread poverty in Appalachia (Stallmann & Johnson, 1996; Wilson, 1994), disproportionate exposure to role models who demonstrate low attainment, and inadequate information about educational and employment options (Peterson et al., 1986; Stallmann & Johnson, 1996; Wilson et al., 1993).

A study by Bickel (1989), for example, indicated that the tendencies for West Virginia youth to drop out of school disproportionately are based, in part, on rational decisions by adolescents that are shaped by the poor economic and employment opportunities they face. A similar study by Stallmann and Johnson (1996) reported that if the structure of the community does not reward education (e.g., no jobs or only service occupations are available), then students will drop out or not continue to higher education as a part of the decision to stay in the community. The consequences of such barriers include a complex combination of ambivalent or even negative attitudes toward social mobility (e.g., educational attainment) that continue to coexist with the growing recognition that success orientations are increasingly necessary (Wilson & Peterson, 1988). Moreover, the most frequently cited barriers to social mobility are the low levels of educational and occupational attainment, which are disproportionately characteristic of Appalachian youth even today (Bickel, 1989; Kenkel, 1986b; Wilson et al., 1993).

Despite the increased influence of attainment aspirations, formal education through high school (or beyond) does not occur as often and is not as essential for life satisfaction or as encouraged by parents as in the larger society (Wilson et al., 1997; Wilson & Peterson, 1988; Wilson et al., 1993). For example, whereas 54.8% of U.S. adults aged 25 years and over have no higher education, 77.1% of adults in central Appalachia aged 25 and over have no higher education (ARC, 1994). Furthermore, whereas 75.2% nationally have either a high school diploma or a GED, only 68.4% of Appalachians have these credentials, and only 53.3% have completed high school in Central Appalachia. Perhaps a more dramatic picture of family educational attainment histories is provided by comparing Appalachian counties to the non-Appalachian counties in the same states. For example, of those Kentucky adults aged 25 and over with eighth-grade or less education, the Appalachian portion of the state has 30.6% with eighth-grade or less education, whereas the non-Appalachian part of the state has only 14.5%. In a similar manner, the Appalachian sections of Virginia have a 25.2% rate compared to non-Appalachian Virginia, with a 9.8% rate (ARC, 1994). Compared to the 24.1% of adults in the nation who have not completed high school, the Appalachian areas of Kentucky and Virginia demonstrate much higher rates (48.5% and 43.6%, respectively). These high percentages stand in further contrast when compared to the respective figures for non-Appalachian areas of Kentucky and Virginia (30.3% and 23.1%. respectively).

A related set of circumstances is especially applicable to the life plans and status attainment possibilities of female adolescents from Appalachia (Egan, 1993; McCoy, 1993). Although family relationships in Appalachia have been subject to many of the same trends that fostered gender role change in the larger society (i.e., the increased entrance of women into the labor force, high divorce rates, growing numbers of mother-headed families, access to information in the mass media about women's issues), observers of social life in this region continue to report that attitudes toward the respective roles of men and women remain more traditional (or gender-role stereotyped) than they do in mainstream America (Beaver, 1986; Fiene, 1988; Wilson et al., 1993). As a result, many female adolescents continue to be socialized for the assumption of familial roles, domestic activities, and secondary jobs for supplementing family incomes. A frequent circumstance is that female adolescents view themselves as facing futures consisting mostly of blue-collar pursuits characterized by low wages, few or no benefits, few job alternatives, poor working conditions, arbitrary discipline, and an absence of career ladders (Beaver, 1986). Moreover, even when female adolescents do have high attainment aspirations, they tend disproportionately to select career lines that are traditionally stereotyped as "female endeavors," such as secretary, teacher, nurse, or social worker (Dunne, Elliott, & Carlsen, 1981; Kenkel, 1986a).

Appalachian youth also appear to cope with limited attainment possibilities by placing less importance on the objective circumstances of their lives (e.g., income, occupational prestige) and assigning priority to more subjective assessments, which allow more positive views of their circumstances. Despite objective conditions that might seem deficient by external standards, Appalachian adolescents maintain levels of self-concept and life satisfaction comparable to youth from the larger society who do not face such adversities (Barnes & Farrier, 1985; Reed & Kuipers, 1976; Shoffner, Boyd, & Ferris, 1986; Wilson & Peterson, 1988; Wilson et al., 1997; Wilson et al., 1993). Results of this kind underscore the importance of perspectives that are developed in specific cultural contexts rather than exclusive reliance on mainstream assumptions about objective attainment indicators as definitive benchmarks for a "successful or happy life." Many Appalachian adolescents appear to use high self-esteem as a personal coping resource for redefining their rather austere material circumstances of life in more positive terms. In fact, deficiencies in objective indicators might simply be viewed as reasonable "trade-offs" in exchange for subjectively defined assets such as proximity to kin, continued residence in a familiar rural environment, and more "realistic" attainment expectations, which are readjusted for the actual circumstances in their environments (Wilson & Peterson, 1988).

SUMMARY AND CONCLUSIONS

This chapter has proposed that an ecological perspective helps us to understand both the distinctive and complex circumstances of adolescents who originate in rural areas of southern Appalachia. Such an approach requires attention to the complicated interplay among social, economic, cultural, historic, geographic, and familial factors that shape the specific context of youthful development in the southern highlands. Themes such as external control of resources, initial geographic isolation followed by political and social ostracism, an historic emphasis on familism, elements of a diminishing folk culture, economic deprivation, the encroachment of urban values, and the current pervasiveness of American popular culture have combined to place at least bicultural if not multicultural pressures on Appalachian youth and their families.

Therefore, adolescents from Appalachia are faced with the complex tasks of coping with or balancing these forces during the processes of being socialized and making the transition to adulthood. Although demonstrating many "shades of gray" that typologies often fail to capture, for the sake of illustration, Appalachian youth might be classified in terms of three identity statuses—"Appalachian-identified," "urban-identified," and "biculturally identified" adolescents.

The first of these options, youth who are Appalachian-identified, encompasses those individuals (a fairly limited number) whose primary self-definitions involve having a continued affinity for residual aspects of the traditional folk culture. In the face of compelling mainstream influences, however, such an identity choice is likely to become increasingly difficult for many individuals to maintain.

Adolescents with Appalachian origins will find it much harder to turn their backs on the forces of change, which are conveyed so pervasively through the mass media, urban institutions, and the information superhighway (RAYFC, 1996).

The second of these options, becoming urban- (or mainstream-) identified, designates those young people who use the mass-produced culture of modern America as their primary reference point. Such an orientation is reminiscent of the circumstances faced by immigrant children of the second or third generations whose ethnic or traditional origins have been either consciously rejected or allowed to wither away. An identity of this kind is likely to be a comfortable choice for many adolescents, but a source of tension for those who continue to face (a) persisting expectations to perform family obligations, (b) pressures for more traditional patterns from previous generations, and (c) latent attractions for their rural origins that are difficult to recapture in later life.

The final option, becoming biculturally identified, involves either striking a balance between or integrating contemporary urban life-styles with the residual traditions of the Appalachian past. This option recognizes the need for both a sense of continuity and the acceptance of social change (RAYFC, 1996). Adolescents whose origins are Appalachian may find it comfortable to seek a reasonable balance among the recognized need to adapt to change, the importance of accommodating mainstream (urban) values, the security derived from their family heritage, and the richness of traditional folkways. Forging such a balance is a challenge shared by many adolescents whose origins lie within the ethnic-minority or subcultural communities of contemporary American society.

REFERENCES

Abbott, S. A. (1992). Holding on and pushing away: Comparative perspectives on an eastern Kentucky child-rearing practice. *Ethos, 20*, 33-65.

Appalachian Regional Commission. (1994). *General economic indicators: Appalachia and United States.* Washington, DC: Government Printing Office.

Ball, R. A. (1970). Poverty case: The analgesic subculture of the southern Appalachians. *American Sociological Review, 33*, 885-895.

Barnes, M. E., & Farrier, S. C. (1985). A longitudinal study of the self-concept of low-income youth. *Adolescence, 5*, 199-205.

Batteau, A. (1979-1980). Appalachia and the concept of culture: A theory of shared misunderstandings. *Appalachian Journal, 7,* 9-31.

Batteau, A. (1982). Mosbys and Broomseldge: The semantics of class in an Appalachian kinship system. *American Ethnologist, 9,* 445-466.

Baumrind, D. (1991). Effective parenting during the early adolescent transition. In P. A. Cowan & M. Hetherington (Eds.), *Family transitions* (pp. 111-163). Hillsdale, NJ: Lawrence Erlbaum.

Beaver, P. D. (1979). Hillbilly women, hillbilly men: Sex roles in rural-agricultural Appalachia. In S. Lord & C. P. Crowder (Eds.), *Appalachian educational module: The Appalachian women* (pp. 65-73). Newton, MA: Educational Development Corporation, WEEA Project.

Beaver, P. D. (1982). Appalachian families, land ownership, and public policy. In R. L Hall & C. B. Stack (Eds.), *Holding on to the land and the Lord: Kinship, ritual, land tenure, and social policy in the rural south* (pp. 146-154). Athens, GA: University of Georgia Press.

Beaver, P. (1986). *Rural community in the Appalachian south.* Lexington: University of Kentucky Press.

Beaver, P. (1988). Appalachian cultural systems, past and present. In S. E. Keefe (Ed.), *Appalachian mental health* (pp. 15-23). Lexington: University of Kentucky Press.

Belsky, J. (1981). Early human experiences: A family perspective. *Developmental Psychology, 17,* 3-23.

Belsky, J. (1984). The determinants of parenting: A process model. *Child Development, 55,* 83-96.

Bickel, R. (1989). Post-high school opportunities and high school completion rate in an Appalachian state: A near replication of Florida research. *Youth and Society, 21,* 61-84.

Blos, P. (1979). *The adolescent passage: Developmental issues.* New York: International Universities Press.

Boles, J. B. (1972). *The great revival, 1787-1805.* Lexington: University of Kentucky Press.

Branscome, J. G. (1978). Annihilating the hillbilly: The Appalachians' struggle with America's institutions. In H. M. Lewis, L. Johnson, & D. Askins (Eds.), *Colonialism in modern America: The Appalachian case* (pp. 211-227). Boone, NC: Appalachian Consortium Press.

Broderick, C. R. (1993). *Understanding family process: Basics of family systems theory.* Newbury Park, CA: Sage.

Bronfenbrenner, U. (1979). *The ecology of human development: Experiments by nature and design.* Cambridge, MA: Harvard University Press.

Bronfenbrenner, U. (1986). Ecology of the family as a context for human development: Research perspectives. *Developmental Psychology, 22,* 723-742.

Brown, B. B. (1990). Peer groups and peer cultures. In S. S. Feldman & G. R. Elliott (Eds.), *At the threshold: The developing adolescent* (pp. 171-196). Cambridge, MA: Harvard University Press.

Brown, D. L., & Schwarzweller, H. K. (1970). The Appalachian family. In J. D. Photiadis & H. K. Schwarzweller (Eds.), *Change in rural Appalachia: Implications for action programs* (pp. 85-98). Philadelphia: University of Pennsylvania Press.

Bryant, F. C. (1981). *We're all kin: A cultural study of a mountain neighborhood.* Knoxville: University of Tennessee Press.

104   ADOLESCENT DIVERSITY

Caudill, H. M. (1962). *Night comes to the Cumberlands*. Boston: Little, Brown.
Cécora, J. (Ed.). (1993). *Economic behavior of family households in an international context*. Bonn, Germany: Society for Agricultural Policy Research and Rural Sociology.
Chapman, T. W. (1990). The use of family systems interventions for the prevention of program dropouts: A practical approach. In S. Abbott (Ed.), *Proceedings from the 1990 Conference on Appalachia* (pp. 151-156). Lexington: University of Kentucky, Appalachian Center.
Childers, J. (1979). Absentee ownership of Harlan County. In S. Fisher (Ed.), *A landless people in a rural region: A reader on land ownership and property taxation in Appalachia* (pp. 81-92). New Market, TN: Highlands Research and Education Center.
Clark, M. (1974). Education and exploitation. In M. Clark, J. Branscome, & B. Snyder (Eds.), *Appalachian miseducation* (pp. 4-13). Huntington, WV: Appalachian Press.
Collins, W. A., & Repinski, S. J. (1994). Relationships during adolescence: Continuity and change in interpersonal perspective. In R. Montemayor, G. R. Adams, & T. E. Gullotta (Eds.), *Personal relationships during adolescence: Advances in adolescent development* (pp. 37-77). Thousand Oaks, CA: Sage.
Couto, R. (1994). *An American challenge: A report on economic trends and social issues in Appalachia*. Dubuque, IA: Kendall/Hunt.
Dail, P. (1994). The family environment and self-concept of rural Appalachian youth living in economic deprivation. *Family Perspectives, 28*, 125-138.
Day, G. (1987). The reconstruction of Wales and Appalachia: Development and regional identity. *Contemporary Wales: An Annual Review of Economic and Social Research, 1*, 73-89.
Duncan, C. M., & Lamborghini, N. (1994). Poverty and social context in remote rural communities. *Rural Sociology, 59*, 437-461.
Dunne, F., Elliott, R., & Carlsen, W. S. (1981). Sex differences in the educational and occupational aspirations of rural youth. *Journal of Vocational Behavior, 18*, 56-66.
Dyk, P., & Wilson, S. M. (1999). Family-based social capital considerations as predictors of attainment among Appalachian youth. *Sociological Inquiry, 69*, 477-503.
Egan, M. (1993). Appalachian women: The path from the "hollows" to higher education. *Affilia, 8*, 265-276.
Egerton, J. (1983). *Generations: An American family*. Lexington: University of Kentucky Press.
Elder, G. (1991). Life course. In E. F. Borgatta & M. L. Borgatta (Eds.), *The encyclopedia of sociology* (pp. 281-381). New York: Macmillan.
Eller, R. (1978). Industrialization and social change in Appalachia 1880-1930. In H. M. Lewis, L. Johnson, & D. Askins (Eds.), *Colonialism in modern America: The Appalachian case* (pp. 35-46). Boone, NC: Appalachian Consortium Press.
Eller, R. (1982). *Miners, millhands, and mountaineers*. Knoxville: University of Tennessee Press.
Fiene, J. I. (1988). Gender, class, and self-image. In S. E. Keefe (Ed.), *Appalachian mental health* (pp. 66-80). Lexington: University Press of Kentucky.
Ford, D. H., & Lerner, R. M. (1992). *Developmental systems theory: An integrative approach*. Newbury Park, CA: Sage.
Ford, T. R. (Ed.). (1962). *The southern Appalachian region: A survey*. Lexington: University of Kentucky Press.

Freud, A. (1965). *Normality and pathology in childhood.* New York: International Universities Press.

Gaventa, J. (1980). *Power and powerlessness: Quiescence and rebellion in an Appalachian valley.* Urbana: University of Illinois Press.

Grotevant, H. D., & Cooper, C. R. (1986). Individuation in family relationships: A perspective on individual differences in the development of identity and role-taking skill in adolescence. *Human Development, 29,* 82-100.

Group for the Advancement of Psychiatry, Committee on the Family. (1970). Integration and mal-integration in Spanish-American family patterns. In Group for the Advancement of Psychiatry (Eds.), *Treatment of families in conflict: The clinical study of family process* (pp. 281-288). New York: Science House.

Harrington, M. (1962). *The other America.* New York: Penguin.

Hennon, C. B., & Photiadis, J. (1979). The rural Appalachian low-income male: Changing role in a changing family. *The Family Coordinator, 46,* 608-615.

Hicks, G. L. (1992). *Appalachian valley.* Prospect Heights, IL: Waveland.

Humphrey, R. A. (1988). Religion in southern Appalachia. In S. E. Keefe (Ed.), *Appalachian mental health* (pp. 36-47). Lexington: University of Kentucky Press.

Keefe, S. E. (1983). Ethnic conflict in an Appalachian craft cooperative: On the application of structural ethnicity to mountaineers and outsiders. In B. M. Buxton, M. L. Crutchfield, W. E. Lightfoot, & J. P. Stewart (Eds.), *The Appalachian experience* (pp. 15-25). Boone, NC: Appalachian Consortium Press.

Keefe, S. E. (1988). Appalachian family ties. In S. E. Keefe (Ed.), *Appalachian mental health* (pp. 24-35). Lexington: University of Kentucky Press.

Keefe, S. E. (1992). Ethnic identity: The domain of perceptions of and attraction to ethnic groups and cultures. *Human Organization, 51,* 35-43.

Keefe, S. E., Reck, U. M. L., & Reck, G. G. (1983). Ethnicity and education in Southern Appalachia: A review. *Ethnic Groups, 5,* 199-226.

Kenkel, W. F. (1986a). Change and stability in the occupational plans of females. In S. M. Shoffner & W. F. Kenkel (Eds.), *On the way to adulthood: Changes and continuities in the life plans of low-income Southern youth* (Southern Cooperative Series Bulletin 320, Cooperative Regional Project S-126, pp. 79-106). Raleigh: North Carolina State University.

Kenkel, W. F. (1986b). Changes and continuities in the occupational plans of males. In S. M. Shoffner & W. F. Kenkel (Eds.), *On the way to adulthood: Changes and continuities in the life plans of low-income Southern youth* (Southern Cooperative Series Bulletin 320, Cooperative Regional Project S-126, pp. 57-78). Raleigh: North Carolina State University.

Kentucky Kids Count Consortium. (1995). *Kentucky's children: County data book, 1994.* Louisville: Kentucky Youth Advocates.

Kerchoff, A. C. (1976). The status attainment process: Socialization or allocation? *Social Forces, 55,* 368-381.

Kim, U., Triandis, H. C., Kagitcibasi, C., Choie, S., & Yoon, G. (1994). Introduction. In U. Kim, H. C. Triandis, C. Kagitcibasi, S. Choie, & G. Yoon (Eds.), *Individualism and collectivism* (pp. 1-16). Thousand Oaks, CA: Sage.

Klein, H. (1995). Urban Appalachian children in Northern schools: A study in diversity. *Young Children, 50,* 10-16.

Kohn, M. L. (1977). *Class and conformity: A study in values* (2nd ed.). Chicago: University of Chicago Press.

Lerner, R. M. (1991). Changing organism-context relations as the basic process of development: A developmental-contextual perspective. *Developmental Psychology, 27*, 27-32.

Lerner, R. M. (1995). *America's youth in crisis: Challenges and options for programs and policies.* Thousand Oaks, CA: Sage.

Lewis, H. M., & Knipe, E. E. (1978). The colonialism model: The Appalachian case. In H. M. Lewis, L. Johnson, & D. Askins (Eds.), *Colonialism in modern America: The Appalachian case* (pp. 9-31). Boone, NC: Appalachian Consortium Press.

Lewis, H. M., Kobak, S., & Johnson, L. (1978). Family, religion, and colonialism in central Appalachia. In H. M. Lewis, L. Johnson, & D. Askins (Eds.), *Colonialism in modern America: The Appalachian case* (pp. 113-139). Boone, NC: Appalachian Consortium Press.

Lohmann, R. A. (1990). Four perspectives on Appalachian culture and poverty. *Journal of the Appalachian Studies Association, 2*, 76-88.

Looff, D. (1971). *Appalachia's children: The challenge of mental health.* Lexington: University of Kentucky Press.

Luhman, R. (1990). Appalachian English stereotypes: Language attitudes in Kentucky. *Language in Society, 19*, 331-348.

Madsen, W. (1969). Mexican-American and Anglo-Americans. A comparative study of mental health in Texas. In S. C. Plog & R. B. Edgerton (Eds.), *Changing perspectives in mental illness* (pp. 217-241). New York: Holt, Rinehart & Winston.

Maloney, M. (1995, June). *Appalachian families and interventions.* Workshop presented at Brown County Counseling, Georgetown, OH.

Matthews, E. M. (1966). *Neighbor and kin: Life in a Tennessee ridge community.* Nashville, TN: Vanderbilt University Press.

McCoy, V. H. (1993). Appalachian women: Change in gender role expectations and ethnic identity. *International Journal of Group Tensions, 23*, 101-113.

Miller, J. (1977). Appalachian education: A critique and suggestions for reform. *Appalachian Journal, 5*, 13-22.

Mong, F. (1995, May). *Keynote address.* Presented at the Rural and Appalachian Youth and Their Families conference, Columbus, OH.

Obermiller, P. J., & Maloney, M. E. (1994). Looking for Appalachians in Pittsburgh: Seeking deliverance, finding the deer hunter. In K. M. Borman & P. J. Obermiller (Eds.), *From mountains to metropolis: Appalachian migrants in American cities* (pp. 13-24). Westport, CT: Bergin & Garvey.

Otto, L. B. (1986). Family influences on youth's occupational aspirations and achievements. In G. K. Leigh & G. W. Peterson (Eds.), *Adolescents in families* (pp. 226-255). Cincinnati, OH: South-Western.

Padilla, A. (Ed.). (1980). *Acculturation: Theory models and some new findings.* Boulder, CO: Westview.

Peters, D. F. , & Peterson, G. W. (1982). Important persons who influence the career decisions of rural Appalachian youth. *Tennessee Farm and Home Science, 123*, 22-25.

Peters, D. F., & Peterson, G. W. (1988). Adaptive socialization values of low-income Appalachian mothers. In S. E. Keefe (Ed.), *Appalachian mental health* (pp. 51-65). Lexington: University of Kentucky Press.

Peters, D. F., Wilson, S. M., & Peterson, G. W. (1986). Adolescents in rural Appalachian families. In G. K. Leigh & G. W. Peterson (Eds.), *Adolescents in families* (pp. 456-472). Cincinnati, OH: South-Western.

Peterson, G. W. (1986). Parent-youth power dimensions and the behavioral autonomy of adolescents. *Journal of Adolescent Research, 1*, 231-247.

Peterson, G. W. (1995). Autonomy and connectedness in families. In R. D. Day, K. Gilbert, B. H. Settles, & W. R. Burr (Eds.), *Research and theory in family science.* (pp. 20-41). Pacific Grove, CA: Brooks/Cole.

Peterson, G. W., & Hahn, D. (1999). Socializing parents and children in families. In S. K. Steinmetz & M. B. Sussman (Eds.), *Handbook of marriage and the family* (2nd ed., pp. 327-370). New York: Plenum.

Peterson, G. W., & Peters, D. F. (1983). Adolescents' construction of social reality: The impact of television and peers. *Youth and Society, 15*, 67-85.

Peterson, G. W., & Peters, D. F. (1985). The socialization values of low-income Appalachian White and rural Black mothers: A comparative study. *Journal of Comparative Family Studies, 16*, 75-91.

Peterson, G. W., & Rollins, B. C. (1987). Parent-child socialization. In M. B. Sussman & S. K. Steinmetz (Eds.), *Handbook of marriage and the family* (pp. 471-507). New York: Plenum.

Peterson, G. W., & Stivers, M. E. (1986a). Adolescents' behavioral autonomy and family connectedness in rural Appalachia. *Family Perspectives, 20*, 307-322.

Peterson, G. W., & Stivers, M. E. (1986b). Significant others for the life plans of low-income Black and White youth. In S. M. Shoffner & W. F. Kenkel (Eds.), *On the way to adulthood: Changes and continuities in the life plans of low-income southern youth* (Southern Cooperative Series Bulletin 320, Cooperative Regional Project S-126, pp. 125-143). Raleigh: North Carolina State University.

Peterson, G. W., Stivers, M. E., & Peters, D. F. (1986). Family versus nonfamily significant others for the career decisions of low-income youth. *Family Relations, 35*, 417-424.

Photiadis, J. D. (1977). *An overview of the processes of social transition in rural Appalachia.* Morgantown: West Virginia University, Office of Research and Development, Center for Extension and Continuing Education.

Photiadis, J. D. (1980). *The changing rural Appalachian community and low-income family: Implications for community development.* Morgantown: Center for Extension and Continuing Education.

Polansky, N. A., Borgman, R. D., & DeSaix, C. (1972). *Roots of futility.* San Francisco: Jossey-Bass.

Reck, U. M., Reck, G. G., & Keefe, S. (1993). Implications of teachers' perceptions of students in an Appalachian school system. *Journal of Research and Development in Education, 26*, 117-121.

Reed, H. M., & Kuipers, J. L. (1976). *Rural family functioning* (Bulletin 562). Knoxville: University of Tennessee, Agricultural Experiment Station.

Robertson, E. B., & Shoffner, S. M. (1989). Life satisfaction of young adults reared in low-income Appalachian families. *Lifestyles: Family and Economic Issues, 10*, 5-17.

Rosenberg, M. (1979-1980). Regional stereotype and folklore—Appalachia and Atlantic Canada. *Appalachian Journal, 7*, 46-50.

108   ADOLESCENT DIVERSITY

Rural and Appalachian Youth and Families Consortium. (1996). Parenting practices and interventions among marginalized families in Appalachia: Building on family strengths. *Family Relations, 45,* 387-396.

Salatino, A. J. (1995). *Will Appalachia finally overcome poverty?* Kuttawa, KY: McClanahan.

Schiamberg, L. B. (1986). Educational aspirations and expectations of rural, low-income youth. In S. M. Shoffner & W. F. Kenkel (Eds.), *On the way to adulthood: Changes and continuities in the life plans of low-income southern youth* (Southern Cooperative Series Bulletin 320, Cooperative Regional Project S-126, pp. 107-123). Raleigh: North Carolina State University.

Schwarzweller, H. (1970). Social change and the individual in rural Appalachia. In J. D. Photiadis & H. K. Schwarzweller (Eds.), *Change in rural Appalachia: Implications for action programs* (pp. 51-68). Philadelphia: University of Pennsylvania Press.

Sewell, W. H., & Hauser, R, M. (1980). The Wisconsin longitudinal study of social and psychological factors in aspirations and achievements. In A. C. Kerckhoff (Ed.), *Research in sociology of education and socialization* (Vol. 1, pp. 59-99). Greenwich, CT: JAI.

Shoffner, S. M., Boyd, J. C., & Ferris, M. C. (1986). Satisfaction with life conditions in early adulthood. In S. M. Shoffner & W. F. Kenkel (Eds.), *On the way to adulthood: Changes and continuities in the life plans of low-income southern youth* (Southern Cooperative Series Bulletin 320, Cooperative Regional Project S-126, pp. 145-161). Raleigh: North Carolina State University.

Stallmann, J. I., & Johnson, T. G. (1996). Community factors in secondary educational achievement in Appalachia. *Youth & Society, 27,* 469-484.

Steinberg, L. (1990). Autonomy, conflict, and harmony in the family relationship. In S. S. Feldman & F. R. Elliot (Eds.), *At the threshold: The developing adolescent* (pp. 255-276). Cambridge, MA: Harvard University Press.

Stephenson, J. B. (1968). *Shiloh: A mountain community.* Lexington: University of Kentucky Press.

Szapocznik, J., & Kurtines, W. (1980). Acculturation, biculturalism, and adjustment among Cuban Americans. In A. Padilla (Ed.), *Acculturation: Theory, methods, and some new findings* (pp. 134-160). Boulder, CO: Westview.

Task Force on Persistent Poverty. (1993). *Persistent poverty in rural America.* Boulder, CO: Westview.

Tribe, D. L. (1995, Summer). Celebrating Appalachian people. *Human Development and Family Life Bulletin, 1,* 4-5.

Weller, J. (1965). *Yesterday's people: Life in contemporary Appalachia.* Lexington: University of Kentucky Press.

Whisnant, P. E. (1980). *Modernizing the mountain: People, power, and planning in Appalachia.* New York: Burt Franklin.

Wiehe, V. R. (1990). Religious influence on parental attitudes toward the use of corporal punishment. *Journal of Family Violence, 5,* 173-186.

Wilson, S. M. (1994). Rural and Appalachian youth and their families. In P. McKenry & S. Gavazzi (Eds.), *Vision 2010: Families and adolescents* (pp. 38-39, 44). Minneapolis, MN: National Council on Family Relations.

Wilson, S. M., Henry, C. S., & Peterson, G. W. (1997). Life satisfaction among low-income, rural youth from Appalachia. *Journal of Adolescence, 20,* 443-459.

Wilson, S. M., & Peterson, G. W. (1988). Life satisfaction among young adults from rural families. *Family Relations, 37,* 84-91.

Wilson, S. M., Peterson, G. W., & Wilson, P. (1993). The process of educational and occupational attainment of adolescent girls from low-income, rural families. *Journal of Marriage and the Family, 55,* 158-175.

Youniss, J., & Smollar, J. (1985). *Adolescent relations with mothers, fathers, and friends.* Chicago: University of Chicago Press.

5. Indian Adolescence: Opportunity and Challenge

Fred Beauvais

Resiliency and adaptation in the face of adversity have been the hallmarks of success among American Indians for most of their existence as a people. In the distant past, most tribes were nomadic or seminomadic within geographic regions considered to be traditional homelands. With the coming of Europeans, there was a massive redistribution of tribes that continued for several centuries and abated only in the latter part of the last century with the imposition of the reservation system in the United States. The intervening time was marked by enormous year-to-year and even day-to-day changes in the sociopolitical, cultural, and physical environment. All these changes, of course, were accompanied by a great deal of stress, as Indian people encountered opposition and oppression. To survive, they had to adapt.

In many respects, this pattern of continual accommodation to changing and often stressful circumstances is reprised for Indian youth today as they negotiate the tasks of adolescent development. It is not uncommon for Indian adolescents to face the shifting requirements of multiple social and cultural systems as they grow up. They must adjust to the demands of both Indian culture and the White American culture. Family socialization may take place in the households of several different relatives or friends. Parents may be away for extended periods of time in a distant city pursuing employment, and an Indian adolescent may attend numerous schools before graduation. Added to this are the many differing cultural expectations that must be met as the young person interacts with members of different tribes during the various intertribal social gatherings that are common among Indian people. This complex set of changing sociocultural influences is often viewed as a hindrance to the competent development of Indian youth, and for some it does lead to stress and failure. But for those able to negotiate this variegated environment, it also can be an enriching process leading to a high degree of competence and stability.

The issues surrounding human development from a cross-cultural perspective are enormously complex and have received a great deal of attention from both an empirical and theoretical perspective. The majority of this effort, however, has been a search for "universals," that is, those processes and characteristics that are innate and describe people regardless of their environmental context (for a more extensive discussion, see Adamopoulos & Lonner, 1994). Although this approach has shed some light on cross-cultural development, it generally has been of limited explanatory use because it has ignored the importance of context. In contrast, this chapter focuses on context and proceeds from the perspective that adolescent development is largely a reflection of the sociocultural environment. Individuals have to meet the many demands for successful living imposed by the environment, and, in so doing, they move along a characteristic developmental path prescribed by those demands (Bronfenbrenner, 1979; Oetting, 1993; Tietjen, 1994). There are undoubtedly biologically determined imperatives that exist across sociocultural environments; however, the purpose of this chapter is to describe the external socialization forces encountered by Indian youth that shape their development.

Several caveats are in order in any discussion of "American Indians." First and foremost is the recognition that the collective term "American Indian" is used to represent an extremely diverse group of people. Unless this diversity is recognized, it is inappropriate to use this term in the characterization of individuals or individual tribes (Collins, 1996; Trimble, 1995). There are estimates of from 400 to 500 different tribal groups in the United States, each with its own history and cultural heritage. If one were to describe the developmental trajectory of individuals within any of these groups, the unique sociocultural conditions within each group would need to be considered. Furthermore, American Indian culture, as with any culture, is not static, nor does it change at the same pace or in the same direction among the various tribes or even among families within the same tribe. It is not uncommon in the literature on American Indians to come across an explication of a cultural belief or practice that may have been commonly followed in the distant past with the assumption that it still holds true today with the same meaning and intensity as it had historically. This leads to a distorted view of contemporary American Indian life. Furthermore, many Indian families have blended traditional customs with those of the larger Euro-American society (or, in the Southwest, with Hispano-American society) to create an amalgam that is difficult to dichotomize into "Indian" and "non-Indian." Within the general Indian community, tribal traditions have become blurred through intermarriage and the sharing of tribal customs. Thus, although the convention "American Indian" is used here, it must be kept in mind that the term describes a heterogeneous group of peoples existing along a continuum of both traditional and contemporary values and lifestyles.

A further complexity in describing Indian populations involves recent changes in demographic distribution (Snipp, 1989). Earlier in this century, most Indian people lived on reservations allotted by the government. The modern wage economy, along with concerted government attempts to "mainstream" Indian families, have resulted in the present pattern in which nearly half the Indian population in the United States lives off the reservation. Thus, today many Indian youth live in environments that more closely resemble those of non-Indian youth and experience the socializing influences of the larger society to a much greater degree than do those remaining on the reservation. Many of these families, however, still live in a complex, multicultural world because of the close ties they feel toward their homelands and the routine visits back to their reservation for extended periods of time, usually during periods of celebration of traditional feasts and dances and for healing ceremonies.

With these cautions in mind, there are a number of commonalities among the tribes that have a general impact on Indian adolescent development. The recent advances in communication, education, and travel have led to the emergence of a pan-Indian culture that has created a core of common conditions experienced by many Indian adolescents. Although it may seem inconsistent to talk about a general, pan-Indian culture and specific tribal differences, the situation in the United States provides an analogy. There is a broad, general culture in the United States with many shared elements, but there are also regional and community variations that have a strong impact on individuals. It is the broader dimensions of pan-Indian culture and development that are discussed here. They include the major socialization forces that have an impact on American Indian adolescents today and that can determine the developmental success or failure of many Indian youth.

Any attempt to summarize what is known about Indian adolescence leads to a certain frustration. A complete exposition reasonably should include both those factors leading to healthy development and that put youth at risk for dysfunction. However, the literature on this topic has a decidedly negative focus, and it is very difficult to find discussion of the strengths of Indian youth or of normal developmental factors. What empirical literature exists is virtually all focused on problem behavior; very few studies test or describe normative processes. What follows, then, necessarily and unfortunately paints a rather negative picture. The reader should keep this in mind and recognize that many Indian youth lead very healthy lives. From an academic perspective, however, we just do not know very much about successful Indian youth.

THE EMERGENCE OF ADOLESCENCE

Adolescence as a discrete life stage is a relatively recent phenomenon in Western culture. In the preindustrial world, most cultures did not recognize a developmental period occupying the decade between childhood and adulthood (Condon, 1990). Childhood was a period of learning and practicing those skills necessary to enter the adult world and contribute to the welfare of the family and community. When sufficient skills were developed, one entered adulthood. In many cultures, there were rituals to demarcate and announce this transition and, henceforth, one was expected to take his or her place fully within the adult world. Industrialization has been a factor in creating the period that we now label "adolescence." In an industrial society, there is need for a more extensive training period, and increased productivity makes it unnecessary for adolescents to contribute materially to the welfare of the family and community. In Western civilization, the emergence of this new developmental period has taken several centuries, and there has been an opportunity for society to develop rules, norms, and expectations for those in this stage of their lives (most notable for describing the dynamics of this period is Erikson, 1959). For Indian people, however, this evolutionary process has been sharply truncated: Tribes were required to move from a traditional "child to adult" pattern to a pattern that included adolescent development within a relatively short period of time. They have had little time to develop the social controls and expectations accompanying the period of adolescence. Many Indian youth, then, are subjected to the expectations of both tribal society with the sudden assumption of adult responsibilities and the "modern" world, in which these responsibilities are delayed. In some of the more pastoral tribes, for instance, a young man may be expected to take responsibility for the family livestock and at the same time be treated as a child by the contemporary school system. Likewise, young Indian women are expected to assume many of the responsibilities of rearing younger siblings within the family, yet they also are expected to attend school as dependent, not responsible, individuals. Even though some tribes retain their "rites of passage" ceremonies, their meaning has become ambiguous because the outside world will still treat those individuals who participate in these rites as adolescents rather than as full adults.

In those instances in which traditional tribal roles no longer exist, Indian youth are left with a great deal of free time and, given the rise of modern communications and mobility, are increasingly exposed to the adolescent culture of the larger society. Satellite television, in particular, has contributed to the rapid transmission of adolescent culture even into the far reaches of the northern frontier of America (Condon, 1990). Youth in even the remotest of villages are familiar with the substance and nuance of the lives of their counterparts in more developed areas, and it is no surprise that these youth will emulate what they see in the media, for better or for worse.

ECONOMIC AND
SOCIAL CONTEXT

There is little doubt that the physical environment has a great deal to do with one's ability to develop competently and to prosper. However, the unfortunate fact is that Indian youth exist in some of the most impoverished environments of this country. When the original treaties were signed, most tribes were allotted fairly extensive lands. For some tribes, these lands were on or near their traditional living areas and were relatively fruitful. Other tribes, however, were removed great distances to areas of little economic consequence (or so it seemed at the time). Subsequently, when natural resources were discovered on Indian lands, whether they were rich grazing and farming lands, minerals, or water, there were inexorable efforts to expropriate either the land or the resource. As a result of these historic and contemporary efforts, not surprisingly, American Indians have found themselves in a constant struggle for economic survival. These pressures have taken a strong toll on the socialization forces in many Indian communities and ultimately have had a deleterious effect on many Indian adolescents (Herdman & Behney, 1990).

Contemporary Conditions

The variation in the cultural landscape of Indian communities is mirrored by the demographic landscape (for a complete description, see Snipp, 1989). American Indians comprise a little less than 1% of the American population. One half of Indian people live on reservations, and the remainder are distributed across the country in a pattern similar to the general population, although there is a greater concentration in rural, nonreservation areas and in a few large cities. Reservations vary enormously in physical size and population from the largest (Navajo) of 25,000 square miles and 200,000 people to very small reservations of fewer than 100 people. Most reservations are rural with some very remote, although a substantial number of reservation residents are in routine contact with large urban population centers. The American Indian population is very young: The median age for the general U.S. population is 32.3; it is about 10 years younger for American Indians (Indian Health Service, 1994). This youthfulness makes the understanding of adolescence critical to the future of all tribes.

With the important exceptions of the cultural overlay and economic disadvantage, life for the average adolescent on a reservation has many similarities to that of other youth. Most Indian youth attend school, have nearly universal access to television and other media, and usually are in range of locations to "hang out" with other youth. School activities provide important opportunities for socialization and are similar in structure and function to nonreservation schools. Indian youth are extremely fond of and excel at athletics, which provides an important source of pride for many Indian young people. Employment opportunities are fairly limited, although in some of the more remote areas, adolescents contribute to family economic activities, such as livestock raising or the production and marketing of traditional art. Within the large, extended families, Indian youth take a greater role in caring for siblings, especially if the parents are working in the wage economy. Nearly three fourths of Indian adolescents are monolingual in English, with the remainder having some level of fluency in both English and their native language (Snipp, 1989). Many tribal elders are very concerned about the increasing loss of native speaking, particularly among their young people, because they believe that language is the primary carrier of culture.

Housing, although typically substandard, resembles that of other poor rural areas in the country. Health care and other social services are usually available, although typically not of the quality found in middle- or upper-class nonreservation areas. Transportation creates a number of problems because the infrastructure is not well developed, and the long distances traveled are especially troublesome during bad weather.

Generalizations, of course, cannot capture the gamut of living conditions for all Indian youth, nor do they reflect the more recent infusion of hope and energy seen in many Indian communities. Contemporary economic initiatives have improved living standards greatly for many Indian people, with better housing, education, and health and social services. In 1977, the federal government passed the Indian Self-Determination Act (Robbins, 1992), which allows tribes to manage many of their educational and social service functions without federal bureaucratic control. The Civil Rights movement of the 1960s and 1970s also provided Indian people with the sense that their culture has a legitimacy and they have a right to pursue life in accordance with their traditional beliefs. These changes hopefully will coalesce and provide Indian youth with a better quality of life than they have experienced in the past.

There is growing concern about the effects of environmental contamination on Indian lands, which most certainly affect the physical, social, and cultural development of Indian youth (Churchill & LaDuke, 1992). Because many Indian lands are remote and Indian people have relatively little political prominence, the effects of various types of pollution have been ignored. The extractive mineral industries have had a particularly damaging effect on the health of Indian people. Open-pit mining of coal, uranium, and other metals, often without standard containment practices, has been especially egregious in this regard. Added to this are the more recent impacts of air pollution by power plants, attempts to use reservations for the storage of nuclear waste materials, and the dumping of other hazardous materials. Without proper controls, the developmental and health effects of these activities are obvious. But, for Indian people there is another grievous burden. For most tribes, the land they occupy has a powerful spiritual meaning. Origin myths are tied directly to certain geographic areas that have been destroyed, and other locations exploited for natural resources have been used for hundreds of years for ceremonial purposes. The loss or degradation of these areas has had a profound effect on the tribes' sense of integrity and spiritual harmony, an effect that is passed on to the young through a lessening of the power of traditional beliefs, ceremonies, and their place in history.

Prejudice

It is difficult to specify the effects of prejudice on the developing sense of identity among Indian youth, yet it is clear that this is an onus that these youth share with other ethnic minorities. Through the 1950s and early 1960s, it was not uncommon for Indian parents to encourage their children to disavow their Indian heritage as a means of avoiding the effects of bias by the larger society. Many parents, especially in families living off the reservation, discouraged the use of native language in an effort to ensure that their children would speak fluent English and secure good jobs. Although this may have been motivated by genuine concern for the welfare of themselves and their children, it most certainly introduced a sense of ambivalence and ambiguity in the developmental process. Fortunately, this tendency is less common today and, in fact, there has been a strong resurgence in cultural pride in many Indian communities (Woodhead, 1996). It is not uncommon, for example, to find traditional dance, drum, and singing groups in Indian schools today. There is strong interest in traditional culture, and the elders of many tribes are taking an active role in this reawakening among Indian adolescents. There is little doubt that this emerging movement will have a positive effect on these young people as they attempt to define themselves and their place in society. Unfortunately, although these positive efforts exist within the tribes, Indian youth who venture out into the larger society are still confronted by powerful bias and stereotypes.

Family Environment

Indian family relationships are quite complex and may be puzzling to those more accustomed to the structure and function of nuclear families (LaFromboise & Low 1989; Redhorse, Lewis, Feit, & Decker, 1978). Indian youth, for example, may consider several people to be their parents. The biological parents are always in the picture, but the primary task of child-rearing may be assumed by a grandparent, aunt or uncle, or other close relatives; in some instances, this task may be taken on by nonfamily members. It is also common for Indian adolescents to spend extended periods of time living in the homes of close friends or to move between households casually. These arrangements are usually informal and rarely involve legal custody transactions. Cousins of varying degrees of separation, as well as same-aged aunts and uncles, may be viewed as brothers and sisters and may live within the same household. In the past, all these relationships were more systematically defined by clan structure, which included fairly strict rules regarding demeanor in the household, courtship, and marriage possibilities. Although much of this traditional structure may be ebbing in the face of the demands of modern economics and job requirements (see John, 1988), the legacy of an extended family composition and function remains and has a profound influence on the development of many Indian adolescents.

Indian family structure provides the Indian adolescent with both an extensive support system and a wide degree of freedom. There are numerous resources that can be called on in times of crisis or for advice when confronted with the normal issues of adolescence. Being a member of a tribe, as well as feeling close kinship with a wide range of people in the tribe, provides an Indian youth with a profound sense of acceptance and an enduring place of refuge. It is not uncommon for an Indian youth who may have been away from his or her reservation to have extremely strong feelings of wanting to return. This is especially powerful if a youth is experiencing difficulty or conflict while distant from family and friends.

The diffuse nature of Indian families and traditional beliefs regarding discipline create an interesting dilemma when considering how Indian adolescents relate to authority. In the past, the primary role of the natural parents was to provide the nurturance and sustenance needed for physical survival. Beyond that, parents rarely exerted control over the behavior of their children; discipline (or, more aptly put, guidance) was typically the responsibility of aunts and uncles and other members of the tribe (Gray & Cosgrove, 1985). Furthermore, punishment was a rare event, and the shaping of appropriate behavior was accomplished through the provision of strong role models and the giving of advice by relatives and respected elders. Adolescents were free to accept the advice or not, but were expected to endure the consequences if they ignored it. In those times when the tribal structure was fully intact, this system worked well. The Indian youth was motivated to assume his or her place among the adults of the tribe, and social sanctions provided strong constraints on behavior. Today, however, the demands of a wage economy and increased mobility have weakened the coherence of the traditional tribal structure, and, in many instances, those nonparental avenues of discipline and guidance are attenuated. When parents adhere to the traditional norm of noninterference in their child's behavior, the other means of control may be weak or absent. This clearly creates the possibility that Indian adolescents are left in many instances to engage in non-normative behavior without adequate controls or guidance.

For many decades, the adoption of Indian children by non-Indian parents was a common practice. In the middle part of this century, it was estimated that nearly one fourth of Indian youth were living in non-Indian families. The results of these adoptions were mixed. Some parents were able to solve the issues surrounding cross-cultural adoption effectively, but, unfortunately, many were not, resulting in a significant number of Indian youth with serious identity confusion. In their adolescent years, some of these youth embarked on a quest to rediscover their cultural roots and, depending on the support of their adopted families, were more or less successful in forging a blended identity. In the 1970s, however, tribes became seriously concerned about the many failures in this process and gained support for the passage of the Indian Child Welfare Act in 1978 (see Goodluck, 1993, for an extended analysis). This legislation gives tribes the sole authority over the adoption process, and, as a result, there are far fewer adoptions out of the tribe.

SCHOOL ENVIRONMENT

Legacy

Historically, the educational experience of American Indians has been painful, and, to a great extent, this legacy survives today. The initial efforts by the federal government to provide educational services for tribes (1600-1900) were largely motivated by official policy intended to supplant "savage" culture with "civilized" values, norms, language, and behaviors (Hirschfelder & de Montano, 1993). Although more recent educational policy has tempered these aims, vestiges remain. These stark and forceful efforts at cultural replacement quite clearly have left Indian people very guarded with respect to education (Robbins, 1991).

One of the more destructive effects of the federal government's attempts to provide education has been an erosion of the integrity of the Indian family and consequent problems for adolescent development (Attneave, 1979). For the greater part of the century, education has been provided through boarding schools administered by the Bureau of Indian Affairs. This typically required that Indian youth travel great distances to attend these schools and that they be separated from their families for 9 months out of every year or, in many instances, to be gone for several years at a time. Youth were placed in these schools as early as 5 years of age. Quite clearly, this had an extremely deleterious effect on the relationship between children and their parents. Normal family bonding was disrupted, and the personnel at the boarding schools were only able to provide a modicum of the nurturance needed for healthy development. Furthermore, because these schools were designed intentionally to foster non-Indian values and beliefs, they left Indian youth in a serious quandary regarding their allegiance to their traditional way of life. Discipline in the boarding schools was harsh and physical and was certainly at odds with that to which Indian youth were accustomed, creating great dissonance in their lives. The time spent at home during the summer was particularly awkward, as both Indian youth and their parents attempted to reach common ground in their belief and behavioral systems. To a large extent, parents were deprived of the opportunity to raise their children in a way that was culturally congruent. As Indian youth graduated from school and began their own families, it was difficult for them to decide which model of discipline was appropriate. Should they adhere to the traditional form of support, modeling, and advice, or should they use the punitive methods they experienced in the boarding school? In the face of this ambiguity, children were raised inconsistently, making bonding with the family very difficult. The result of the boarding school experience was several generations of disrupted family functioning and much uncertainty in Indian communities about the role and place of children in Indian culture.

The intent and operation of boarding schools has changed in recent years, and there has been a greater awareness of the developmental needs of Indian students. Goldstein (1974) demonstrated, for instance, that significant gains could be made in the intellectual, emotional, and physical development of Indian youth attending boarding schools if they were provided with sufficient staff who were trained to address the noneducational needs of the students. Furthermore, a majority of Indian youth are now attending public schools on the reservation and live at home with their families. Many of these public school systems have Indian members as superintendents and teachers and on the school board, and there is a concerted effort to bring cultural harmony back to the development of their youth. Until this harmony can be restored completely, Indian adolescents will continue to experience the cultural disjunction that the history of Indian education has engendered.

Although there is the recognition among most Indian people that education is the key to the future of their tribes, based on their own experiences, it is difficult to garner enthusiasm for the educational system. One result of this ambivalence is the relative lack of interaction between Indian parents and the schools (Joe, 1994). Indian parents are less likely to participate in school activities or to voice their opinions regarding school policy generally or as it applies to their children specifically. Although the situation is changing slowly, this lack of communication leaves Indian youth having to negotiate two social systems in which academic and behavioral expectations may be quite divergent.

Academic Motivation

The overall effect on Indian adolescents, then, is a lower investment in and skepticism about the educational process, resulting in generally depressed levels of school achievement (Snipp, 1989) and rates of school dropout that average 50% (Chavers, 1991). Although there is serious controversy over whether achievement testing may be culturally biased, the fact remains that achievement tests do predict success in the educational system, and their low attainment leaves many Indian youth at a serious disadvantage. To be sure, many Indian youth will espouse the value of education, yet their investment in the enterprise is not very high. For instance, in a recent unpublished study by the author, it was found that 82% of Indian high school students on one large reservation aspired to completion of a college education. However, despite this professed interest, recent numbers show that, compared to youth in general, a much smaller percentage of Indian youth will obtain a college degree (Kidwell, 1994). Clearly, there are serious impediments to achieving expressed educational goals. Although the barriers to college for Indian youth may include lack of financial resources and poor secondary school preparation, lack of confidence in the system is likely a strong component. Enthusiasm for schools is reduced further by the bleak prospect for employment on and near most reservations. Unemployment rates are exceedingly high, providing little incentive for completing school as a means of qualifying for future work. Indian students who are motivated to complete school must look off the reservation for employment opportunities. For many, this produces great reluctance, because it means separation from family, friends, and culture.

Indian adolescent behavior in the classroom often has been misinterpreted as indicative of low motivation and need for achievement (for a more complete description of Indian learning styles and classroom demeanor, see Hirschfelder & de Montano, 1993; Kleinfeld, 1994). Egalitarianism is a common value among Indian people and is expressed in the classroom as an unwillingness to put oneself above others or to call attention to oneself. Students may not volunteer answers or take the initiative in discussions for fear of being seen as boastful. Indian youth often emulate their elders in using a style wherein an opinion is not ventured until they feel they have all the information needed and have had a chance to consider all the implications of a situation; this usually results in a very much delayed response pattern. In a White American-oriented, competitive classroom, these behaviors can be taken as a sign of disinterest in academic tasks or as an unwillingness or inability to perform the expected work. Many Indian students also exhibit a strong deference to authority and will respond to reprimand or correction with silence and downcast eyes. This can be interpreted as lack of connection with the teacher, indifference to the learning situation, or even hostility.

The Future

There are definite signs that the educational process is improving for Indian youth. Since the mid-1970s, a number of government and tribal initiatives have addressed the issue of Indian involvement in education, resulting in greater community control and a renewed enthusiasm among Indian people for the benefits of education. Manifestations include progress for gifted and talented Indian youth (Robbins, 1991), the establishment of 24 Indian-controlled community colleges across the country (Hirschfelder & de Montano, 1993), the inclusion of Indian cultural teachings in tribally controlled elementary and secondary schools (Woodhead, 1996), and the development of Indian studies programs in numerous colleges across the country (Noriega, 1992). The intent of these and other similar efforts is to recast education in a way that is harmonious with the values and beliefs of Indian people and at the same time to enhance academic interest and success.

ASSESSMENT OF INDIVIDUAL TRAITS

There is a fairly extensive literature on psychological assessment of Indian youth, whether this be in the intellective-cognitive, personality, or psychopathology domains (for a complete listing of these efforts, see Trimble & Bagwell, 1995). There is good reason, however, to view the majority of this work with considerable skepticism; the problems are both conceptual and methodological (see especially Dauphinais & King, 1992; McShane & Berry, 1988). The majority of this work incorporates a distinct ethnocentric bias. The general paradigm has been to employ a wide range of assessment instruments with Indian youth and compare the outcomes with White youth, who are considered to be the standard. Typically, any deviation from the White standard is construed to be a deficit. In addition to using a faulty assumption of "normality," this research approach has led to an inaccurate and inappropriate negative description of Indian youth (Joe, 1994).

Psychometrically, there are a number of problems with most existing studies in that little or no attempt has been made to demonstrate equivalence across the constructs that are being measured, in the interpretation of the meaning of differences, or in the metric qualities of the results (see Berry, 1980, for an extended discussion of "equivalence" in cross-cultural assessment). A further problem lies in the contextual variables involved in psychological assessment. Rogoff and Chavajay (1995) argued that development is highly influenced by cultural experience and that tests developed in one cultural context will not accurately capture the intended qualities when administered in another context. As a practical example, most psychological tests are administered in a school or other formal setting, and, because Indian youth may be uneasy in these settings, their performance may suffer (LaFromboise & Low, 1989). Finally, the majority of studies involving assessment of Indian youth use a very small sample, may aggregate youth of culturally different backgrounds, and are rarely replicated. With a couple of exceptions described subsequently, the majority of the literature on psychological assessment of Indian youth is very weak, and it is very difficult to draw conclusions from the vast array of mixed and contradictory studies.

One area of consistency across a number of studies is the generally lower performance on intelligence measures for Indian youth with typically higher performance than verbal scores (McShane & Plas, 1984). In particular, some studies have found that spatial skills are better developed than verbal skills for Indian youth, thus purportedly accounting for the observation that Indian people excel in artistic areas. There is considerable debate, however, whether these findings actually speak to innate differences in potential or whether they reflect a cultural bias or educational deficit. The bulk of the opinion appears to reflect the bias and education interpretation based partly on the findings that less culture-bound tests of intelligence often reveal no differences between Indian and non-Indian youth (see, e.g., Dana, 1984). The observed variation in cognitive patterns, then, must not be overinterpreted and taken as evidence for innate differences and a lack of abstractive ability. The patterns are most likely a result of early experiences and do not preclude the full development of verbal skills that are requisite for formal educational settings. It has been unfortunate that Indian youth have been stereotyped and inordinately guided in the direction of more artistic endeavors when they are fully capable of developing other cognitive skills. Another common theme in the description of Indian youth is the supposition that they display a difference in cognitive style that has implications for teaching strategies. The argument is made that Indian children are visual learners and experience great difficulty in a verbally oriented classroom environment. As pervasive as this notion is, it has received very little experimental verification. Kleinfeld and Nelson (1991) took issue with the idea and, in a well-designed study, found that visual teaching strategies worked equally well with both Indian and non-Indian students of poor academic achievement. No differences were found for both Indian and non-Indian students who were doing well in school. Their conclusion was that the efficacy of a visual learning style was related to educational deficits and not cross-cultural differences. In sum, the measurement of individual traits among Indian adolescents is a very underdeveloped topic. Even where some consistency of findings occurs, there is little agreement as to the interpretation of the differences. Quite clearly, this is a fertile ground for research that could be of benefit to Indian youth and help to advance knowledge about cross-cultural differences in adolescent development.

PEER ENVIRONMENT

Reservations differ significantly from most of the United States in the living arrangements of the extended family. Reservations are almost exclusively rural, with families often living in geographically dispersed enclaves of relatives. These living arrangements result in Indian youth spending a considerable amount of time socializing with siblings; in Indian tradition, "siblings" is a rather loosely defined construct and may include what in the larger society are considered cousins (of varying degree) and in many instances same-aged aunts and uncles. This picture alters the composition of what is normally considered to be the "peer group" and restricts the range of socializing experiences of Indian youth. On the whole, there appears to be more socialization within the family for Indian youth and thus a greater opportunity for enculturation of traditional values. At the same time, however, there is also greater opportunity for the transmission of deviant norms within families that are marked by serious social problems.

Of course, the school situation and other social activities broaden the social milieu of Indian youth, as does the increasing availability of transportation. Increasingly, Indian adolescents are engaging in the types of activities usually associated with their non-Indian peers, including sports, school clubs, church groups, and a variety of civic activities, and thus they are not exclusively socialized with the family as they may have been historically. These activities are often in addition to the more traditional pursuits of dancing at pow-wows, singing in drum groups, and producing arts and crafts that are characteristic of their particular tribe. Indian youth certainly form "peer clusters" (Oetting & Beauvais, 1986) with nonfamily friends and are subject to the dynamics that are part of the adolescent process of individuation and separation from the family. These peer clusters serve the role of support and identity formation and are the arena in which it is decided what types of behavior are acceptable within the adolescent peer group. All too often, unfortunately, that behavior includes drug use (Beauvais, 1992, 1996) and other forms of deviance (Beauvais, Chavez, Oetting, Deffenbacher, & Cornell, 1996).

CULTURAL IDENTIFICATION

Perhaps the greatest challenge of Indian adolescents is learning to negotiate the different cultural expectations that are prevalent in their world. Most Indian adolescents, especially if they live on the reservation, are subjected to the daily demands of a strong, traditional cultural heritage. They are in constant contact with their grandparents, elders, and other family members who may hold very resolutely to traditional beliefs, behaviors, and language. In their presence, Indian youth are expected to understand and respond in culturally congruent ways. When in the school environment or perhaps in social situations off the reservation, the social expectations are very different and require a different set of social responses. An essential task of Indian adolescent development, then, is to learn to discriminate between the different sociocultural settings and to respond according to differing demands (LaFramboise & Rowe, 1983; Schinke, Orlandi, Botvin, & Gilchrist, 1988).

Past theoretical and empirical effort has focused on the purported stress that this discrimination task entails. The phrase "caught between two worlds" has been used often to describe this circumstance. Implied in this phrasing is the sense that people are being pulled between two cultures and are uncertain as to which cultural base should guide their behavior. This is often proffered as the reason that Indian youth exhibit higher levels of social deviance, such as substance abuse and dropping out of school. There is a fallacy in this analysis, however. The basis of the explanation is rooted in the belief that individuals have the capacity to meet the demands of only one cultural system at a time. If they attempt to adapt to the demands of another system, they will lose something from their original culture and in the transition will endure stress. The picture, in essence, is of a zero-sum game. If an Indian youth embraces the school classroom, for instance, he or she may be seen as giving up some "Indianness" because the school is not a part of traditional culture.

If this were the case, Indian youth would be in an untenable situation given the multiple cultural environments that they encounter. There is another perspective, however, that is more sanguine. Oetting and Beauvais (1990-1991) developed a theory of cultural identification that allows for simultaneous identification with two or more cultures in a way that does not diminish competency in either. An Indian youth from a very traditional background, for example, can embrace and adopt elements from the larger Euro-American culture, such as attending college, while still maintaining a strong identification with traditional Indian culture. Nothing need be lost. This model is very flexible in that it allows for an individual to be identified with cultures in any combination and still experience good adjustment. Alternatively, an individual may not identify with any culture (a condition of anomie), in which case there is a high probability of deviance because there is no underpinning of a value structure that guides behavior in accepted ways in any culture. Oetting and Beauvais (1990-1991) presented some intriguing evidence that Indian adolescents exhibiting strong identification with more than one culture may be among the most well-adjusted of individuals. These young people are able to perform competently in a wide variety of cultural environments and consequently are able to reap the rewards of both, leading to a more competent sense of self.

In one sense, this paradigm is idealistic because, in theory, it does not postulate that multiculturalism necessarily entails stress. Yet, we know from the descriptions of individuals who have managed to develop a multiple cultural identification that it is not always an easy road. Robbins (1991) very poignantly described the experiences of Indian adolescents with whom he worked in his programs for gifted and talented students. These students described the reactions they received from others in their tribe when they demonstrated academic excellence. There were not-so-subtle messages that these students "sold out" and rendered up their "Indianness" to succeed in the White world. There is obviously great conflict here because success in one realm of their lives elicits punishment from another. The pressure moves in the other direction also. Indian students in predominantly White schools are often encouraged to leave their traditional ways so that they can be successful in the White world. Although this was official policy during the early boarding school era for Indian students, it continues today in more subtle ways via "advice" from teachers and counselors. Oetting and Beauvais (1990-1991) pointed out that multicultural identity does not have to be stressful, and Robbins (1991) showed that there are situations that do include stress. Multicultural identification, per se, need not be stressful; rather, it becomes so when the messages from the social environment are intolerant. Much of this stress can be alleviated by a recognition that individuals are fully capable of identifying with and being successful in more than one cultural system.

MENTAL HEALTH AND TREATMENT

The concept of mental health is probably the most difficult to address from a cross-cultural perspective. The conditions, definitions, and descriptions of what constitute a "normal" mental status are highly saturated with cultural meaning. This most likely accounts for both the relative lack of research on this topic among Indian adolescents and the conflicting results in the research that is available (Dinges, Trimble, & Hollenbeck, 1979). Indian youth do show high rates of some behavior problems when compared to their non-Indian counterparts (e.g. school dropout, suicide, substance abuse). Possible sources for these differences are discussed subsequently and do not necessarily relate to mental health but rather are a function of socioeconomic conditions. Definitional problems multiply when the less-specifiable mental or emotional states are discussed. For example, numerous studies have reported that Indian youth suffer from low self-concept. The majority of these studies, however, rely on concepts and measures that have been developed in the majority culture, and an uncritical application to Indian youth may produce misleading results. Dinges et al. (1979) reviewed a number of studies that examined self-concept from an Indian perspective that found that the majority of Indian youth have a fairly good concept of self. Importantly, the criteria in these studies related mostly to how competent Indian youth felt in their ability to succeed within the Indian culture and thus were not biased by non-Indian constructs of self-concept.

In addition to conceptual issues surrounding cross-cultural assessment of mental health, there are measurement issues. Manson and his colleagues (Dick, Beals, Keane, & Manson, 1994; Manson, Ackerson, Dick, & Baron, 1990) engaged in a number of studies of depression among Indian adolescents and concluded that an uncritical application of standard measures of depression in this population will radically overestimate the prevalence of depression. Their work has led to recommendations regarding the use of different cutting scores for the clinical diagnosis of depression on standard measures to make them more applicable to Indian youth. It is clear that more of this type of work is necessary in other domains of mental health before good estimates of base rates are possible. Despite the difficulties in assessment, there are a handful of studies that indicate that self-reported feelings of depression among Indian youth are quite high and are cause for concern (Herdman & Behney, 1990). A similar conclusion is warranted for the presence of feelings of anxiety among Indian adolescents.

An enduring and very unfortunate circumstance among Indian youth is the high rate of suicide. Indian Health Service records for 1991 (Indian Health Service, 1994) list the rate for 15- to 24-year-old Indian youth at nearly three times that found among non-Indians of the same age (37.5/100,000 vs. 13.2/100,000). Even more dramatic is the differential between Indian males (63.3/100,000) and females (10.8/100,000) in that age group. A further departure from the general U.S. pattern is that suicides among Indians after the age of 44 decline, whereas they increase for non-Indians beyond that age, indicating that suicide is a much more serious problem among younger Indians. After reviewing the literature on Indian suicides, May (1990) discerned three patterns that characterize Indian suicides: There is a greater occurrence of cluster suicides, particularly among young males; suicide is more often associated with the use of alcohol; and violent suicides (via firearms and hanging) are more prevalent than among non-Indian populations. Clearly, there are enormous psychological and social pressures among young Indian males that are likely reflective of a very stressful environment.

Treatment of mental health problems among American Indian adolescents requires considerable openness and flexibility on the part of the non-Indian counselor (Attneave, 1982; Beauvais, 1977). The normal "templates" that guide therapy may not apply cross-culturally with American Indians (LaFromboise & Low, 1989; Trimble, Flemming, Beauvais, & Jumper-Thurman, 1996). Counselors need to listen carefully to understand the meaning of problems because they are embedded within the cultural matrix. An issue that is particularly pertinent to working with Indian adolescents is that of separation from the family and the development of an individual identity. From a non-Indian perspective, individuation and moving away from the family is the primary task of adolescence, and counseling with adolescents often involves assistance in this process. For Indian youth, however, individual identity is closely linked with that of the group, and it is important that a strong bond be maintained with the family and tribe, and in some instances even the clan (LaFromboise, Trimble, & Mohatt, 1990). A person is valued to the extent that he or she affiliates with and participates in all levels of the social structure. In this sense, it is inappropriate to put one's needs above those of the group; one's identity is more a function of the group than of the individual. Counselors may find themselves at odds with the needs of Indian youth and may even exacerbate existing problems if the therapeutic focus is on separation from these integral social structures.

In many Indian traditions, "mental illness" (actually, little or no distinction is made between physical and mental illness) results from events and forces outside the individual, and thus the usual therapeutic paradigm of internal examination, insight, and self-initiated behavior change may be inappropriate. The traditional cure for illness consists of ceremonies that call on spiritual forces to restore the harmony in the overall social structure that has become disrupted and has created problems for the individual. This realignment allows the individual to resume a healthy and productive life. Some counselors trained in the usual insight-oriented systems of psychotherapy often choose to work very closely with traditional healers to achieve a healing approach that is more congruent with the Indian view of the origins of illness.

Young Indian clients are likely to appear very passive in the therapeutic process, and verbalization will be minimal. Several reasons help explain this. First, any cross-cultural encounter is initially tentative, and the building of trust takes a great deal of time. This general tendency toward wariness is only heightened by the checkered relationship between Indians and non-Indians over the past several centuries. Second, an Indian youth coming for counseling is most likely looking for advice and may feel it is improper to be talking when listening is more appropriate. Finally, as in the school setting, most Indian youth will not venture forth with an opinion or statement until they are certain that they fully understand the situation. A non-Indian counselor typically will be quite surprised if they can sustain the patience and endure long periods of silence in counseling sessions. What at first appears to be passiveness and indifference actually is more a matter of intense reflection and trying to fit the therapeutic process into a coherent cultural framework.

SOCIAL PROBLEMS

The conditions and circumstances described thus far leave little doubt that Indian adolescents are confronted with serious challenges as they negotiate their entry into the adult world. This struggle is not without consequences. There is a considerable literature describing the extent of social deviance in this group of young people. Before summarizing these findings, however, several points of perspective are in order. In scrutinizing any particular subgroup of a population, it is relatively easy to chronicle all the ills that are present in the group and to describe all of the negative characteristics. It is probably as a result of training that most social scientists are problem-oriented and tend to focus on deviation from the norm. To the extent that this can lead to amelioration of problem behaviors by calling attention to areas of need, this is not a bad orientation. However, this perspective can serve to extend stereotypes and perhaps exacerbate the exact conditions it is intended to resolve. If serious levels of a problem are found in a group, there is a tendency to characterize the entire group as being aberrant, whereas, in fact, the majority of the group may be functioning quite well. This latter point is often lost in the discussion and creates a serious burden on those Indian youth who are competently striving to become successful adults.

Further problems lie in the definition of deviance across cultural boundaries, as illustrated by an example. Teenage pregnancy, especially among unmarried women, has been an area of social concern among a number of researchers. There is an underlying assumption that pregnancy at these early ages is indicative of a premature assumption of an adult role, is harmful to the development of young people, and is part of a more general pattern of deviance. Deyhle and Margonis (1995), however, in a study of dropping out of school among a group of Indian adolescents, found this assumption to be at odds with the cultural expectations of the tribe. In this study, a certain number of young Indian women had dropped out of school to give birth to and raise a child. Within the tribe, childbearing was seen as a valued role among women of any age, and these young women were fully accepted and supported in the tribe because of their pregnancy. These differing perspectives can create a real sense of ambivalence for the young women involved. On the one hand, they are seen as engaging in "precocious sexuality" and as being "school dropouts," terms with clear negative connotations; on the other hand, they were carrying out a role that is accepted and honored in the tribe.

Finally, most studies of American Indian social problems fail to make the distinction between ethnicity and socioeconomic status. For a host of reasons, many already discussed here, American Indian communities face serious economic problems, which in turn lead to a variety of social problems. In searching for explanations of the latter, it is common to ignore the economic factors and focus on purported cultural reasons. For example, it is not uncommon in the literature on alcohol problems among American Indians to attribute alcoholism to traditional religious practices (Leland, 1976). A popular conception is that the state of alcohol inebriation is a substitute for the seeking of visions that is practiced among a number of tribes as a means of obtaining spiritual guidance. Quite clearly, with the richness and variety of traditional Indian cultures, it is relatively easy to find such romantic and exotic post hoc explanations for any particular behavior. What is lost in the discussion is that these social ills are most likely a reflection of difficult social and economic circumstances that stress the social fabric and have very little to do with traditional beliefs or practices.

Bearing this in mind, the following is a brief summary of the literature on social problems among Indian adolescents. It is presented not as a description of all Indian youth; rather, it is intended to describe the social surround that most Indian youth experience. It is clear that many Indian youth are able to endure the problems that exist in their environment and develop as capable, productive adults.

Substance Abuse

Perhaps the area of greatest research interest among Indian adolescents has been that of alcohol and drug use and abuse. The most consistent record on substance abuse among Indian adolescents has been provided by Beauvais and Oetting and colleagues from a surveillance study that has been ongoing since 1975 (Beauvais, 1992, 1996; Beauvais, Oetting, Wolf, & Edwards, 1989). Over this period of time, rates of substance abuse among these youth have been found to be consistently much higher than among non-Indian youth across the country. Inquiry into the etiological factors reveals that Indian youth use drugs and alcohol for much the same reasons as do non-Indian youth, although, as discussed previously, the higher levels of use reflect a greater exposure to educational, social, and economic problems. Despite the overall similarity in these factors, there are some interesting differences that appear in the research that relate to Indian culture. For example, Indian youth are more responsive to family influences and less responsive to peer influences in their decisions to use or not use drugs and alcohol when compared to non-Indian youth (Swaim, Oetting, Jumper-Thurman, Beauvais, & Edwards, 1993). This is likely reflective of the centrality of the family in Indian culture and the living arrangements that force higher levels of interaction with same-aged relatives. The role of religion provides another example. For non-Indian youth, strong affiliation with religion serves as a protective factor against substance abuse; this relation is not found among Indian youth. To a great extent, this reflects differing conceptions of "religion" across cultures and thus becomes a methodological problem. For the most part, in non-

Indian culture, religion is seen as a fairly discrete and circumscribed social entity that has limited overlap with day-to-day life. Church activities, for instance, take place at specified times of the week and usually entail a different mind-set and demeanor than other social activities. Thus, when queried about their participation in "religious activities," non-Indian youth are able to describe their level of religious involvement with some accuracy. In Indian culture, however, religion or spirituality is much more woven into the daily social and cultural fabric, and questions about it as a distinct socializing force are difficult to answer in a consistent way, leading to low correlations. Therefore, the relation between "religion" and other social behaviors among Indian youth, such as substance use, remains unclear from a research perspective.

There is little question that substance abuse is disruptive to adolescent development and the levels found in many Indian communities have serious repercussions for both individuals and the very future of tribes themselves. Drug abuse interferes with socialization at the family and school levels and sharply curtails the ability to engage competently in the developmental tasks of adolescence. Indian youth face enough serious impediments as they approach adulthood, and the use of chemicals only exacerbates their problems. Use of drugs in adolescence sets the stage for lifelong patterns of disability and typically culminates in adult patterns of alcohol abuse. At the tribal level, attempts at economic development are hampered by a lack of both human and financial capital, and the loss of human potential due to chemicals is a serious barrier. In some smaller and remote villages, the problem is of such a magnitude that some have observed that entire communities may cease to exist as integral cultural units in the next century.

School Dropout

School dropout rates for Indian youth are extremely elusive. Estimates vary from 20% to 80%, with Chavers (1991) estimating an overall rate across tribes at 50%. This rate is probably high due to the fluidity in school enrollment and attendance in Indian communities. It is not uncommon for Indian youth to attend multiple schools in a given year while living with different relatives or families of friends. Furthermore, these schools may represent different jurisdictions— Bureau of Indian Affairs, public school districts, parochial schools, and tribally run schools. Record transfer across these jurisdictions is not always efficient, and many of the schools do not require previous school records before a student enrolls. When an Indian youth leaves a school and enrolls in another, the original school may list the youth as a dropout because they have no indication that enrollment has subsequently been taken. The result is that one student may be counted as a dropout a number of times in a year or between years. Despite this redundancy in figures, it is likely that the dropout rate for Indian adolescents is very high. Even for those youth who remain in school, the absentee rate is exceptionally high, resulting in lower overall levels of educational achievement (Bowker, 1992). The reasons for the latter vary but can include family obligations at home and difficulties with transportation; roads on many reservations are minimally maintained, and the remoteness of many Indian homes makes it difficult to reach schools during inclement weather.

Crime and Violence

The literature on crime and violence among Indian youth is not very complete, although what is available seems to indicate that Indian youth engage in these behaviors at least at the level of the larger society and possibly at somewhat higher levels. In looking at the adult Indian population statistics, Lee (1993) estimated that overall crime rates are twice as high as for the entire country. In a recent study (University of Minnesota Health Center, 1992), Indian youth reported the following rates of crime and violence: hit or beat someone up (40%), been in a group fight (25%), been knocked out (20%), vandalized (30%), shoplifted (25%), and stolen from parents (20%). These data would seem to indicate a serious problem for Indian youth. In a recent study, however, Beauvais et al. (1996) compared the rates of violence among school dropouts and students remaining in school across White Americans, Mexican Americans, and American Indian youth. As might be expected, school dropouts among all three groups exhibited higher rates of violent behavior than did students in school, but there were no differences across ethnic groups, with Indian dropouts showing levels of violence and victimization similar to those of other youth. Clearly, this is an understudied area that needs further investigation.

Although there has been recent concern in the general population about gang membership and gang violence, very little data are available about this phenomenon among Indian youth. The only published source of data comes from a study conducted several years ago among a large sample of Indian youth from across the country (University of Minnesota Health Center, 1992). Some level of gang involvement was reported by 15% of these youth; 5% indicated that they spent "a lot of time" in gang activities. These data, along with anecdotal evidence from tribal leaders and tribal police, indicate that gang problems may be emerging for Indian youth.

SUMMARY

American Indian adolescents are heirs to a rich and demonstrably viable heritage. Indian tribes have endured tremendous opposition and adversity in their struggle to survive as integral groups of people and have passed on this quality of hardiness to their young people. Indian youth have the advantages of an extended and nurturant family system, a cultural heritage that provides a solid sense of place in the world, and the opportunity to engage actively in and identify with multiple cultural systems. The latter may well confer an advantage, because it provides a wider range of options for becoming competent adults in a world in which technological advances are bringing together peoples of many cultural backgrounds. However, the rapidity with which sociocultural change has taken place in Indian tribes, as well as the lack of control they have been afforded over the process, have led to a number of problems that impede the healthy development of Indian adolescents. Poverty, inadequate and inappropriate educational systems, and a generally poor infrastructure in health care delivery systems, both physical and mental health, have placed inordinate stress on the family and other socialization structures. As a result, Indian youth face unusual pressures as they negotiate the tasks of adolescent development. Considerable research has chronicled the level and nature of the resulting dysfunctional patterns this has created for Indian youth. Unfortunately, this negative focus has done little to reveal the considerable strengths of Indian adolescents or to describe the parameters of successful development. The recent resurgence of interest in and promotion of traditional Indian values, identity, and ceremonies raise the hope that the vigor of Indian culture will provide the foundation for Indian youth as they blend the strengths of their people with the opportunities in the larger society.

REFERENCES

Adamopoulos, J., and Lonner, W. (1994). Absolutism, relativism and universalism in the study of human behavior. In W. Lonner & R. Malpass (Eds.), *Psychology and Culture* (pp. 129-134). Boston: Allyn & Bacon.

Attneave, C. (1979). The American Indian child. In J. Noshpitz (Ed.), *Basic handbook of psychiatry* (pp. 239-248). New York: Basic Books.

Attneave, C. (1982). American Indians and Alaska Native families: Emigrants in their own homeland. In M. McGoldrick, J. Pearce, & J. Giordano (Eds.), *Ethnicity and family therapy* (pp. 55-83). New York: Guilford.

Beauvais, F. (1977). Counseling psychology in a cross-cultural setting. *The Counseling Psychologist, 7*, 80-82.

Beauvais, F. (Ed.). (1992). Indian adolescent drug and alcohol use: Recent patterns and consequences [Special issue]. *American Indian and Alaska Native Mental Health Research, 5*(1).

Beauvais, F. (1996). Trends in drug use among American Indian students and dropouts, 1975-1994. *American Journal of Public Health, 186*, 1594-1598.

Beauvais, F., Oetting, E. R., Wolf, W., & Edwards, R. W. (1989). American Indian youth and drugs: 1975-1987—A continuing problem. *American Journal of Public Health, 79*, 634-636.

Beauvais, F. Chavez, E., Oetting, E., Deffenbacher, J., and Cornell, G. (1996). Drug use, violence and victimization among White American, Mexican American and American Indian dropouts, students with academic problems and students in good academic standing. *Journal of Counseling Psychology, 43*, 292-299.

Berry, J. (1980). Introduction to methodology. In H. Triandis & J. Berry (Eds.), *Handbook of cross-cultural psychology: Vol. 2. Methodology* (pp. 1-28). Boston: Allyn & Bacon.

Bowker, A. (1992, May). The American Indian female dropout. *Journal of American Indian Education, 31*, 3-20.

Bronfenbrenner, U. (1979). *The ecology of human development: Experiments by nature and design.* Cambridge, MA: Harvard University Press.

Chavers, D. (1991). Indian education: dealing with a disaster. *Principal, 70*, 28-29.

Churchill, W., & LaDuke, W. (1992). Native North America: The political economy of radioactive colonialism. In M. Jaimes (Ed.), *The state of Native America: Genocide, colonialization, and resistance* (pp. 241-266). Boston: South End.

Collins, R. L. (1996). The role of ethnic versus nonethnic sociocultural factors in substance abuse and misuse. *Substance Use and Misuse, 31*, 95-101.

Condon, R. (1990). The rise of adolescence; Social change and life stage dilemmas in the Central Canadian Arctic. *Human Organization, 49*, 266-279.

Dana, R. (1984). Intelligence testing of American Indian children: Sidesteps in quest of ethical practice. *White Cloud Journal, 3*, 35-43.

138   ADOLESCENT DIVERSITY

Dauphinais, P., & King, J. (1992). Psychological assessment with American Indian children. *Applied and Preventive Psychology, 1,* 97-110.

Deyhle, D., & Margonis, F. (1995). Navajo mothers and daughters: Schools, jobs and the family. *Anthropology and Education Quarterly, 26,* 135-167.

Dick, R., Beals, J., Keane, E., & Manson, S. (1994). Factorial structure of the CES-D among American Indian adolescents. *Journal of Adolescence, 17,* 73-79.

Dinges, N., Trimble, J., & Hollenbeck, A. (1979). American Indian adolescent socialization: A review of the literature. *Journal of Adolescence, 2,* 259-296.

Erikson, E. (1959). *Identity and the life cycle* (Psychological Issues Monograph No. 1). New York: International Universities Press.

Goldstein, G. (1974). The model dormitory. *Psychiatric Annals, 4,* 85-92.

Goodluck, C. (1993). Social services with Native Americans: Current status of the Indian Child Welfare Act. In H. McAdoo (Ed.), *Family ethnicity: Strength in diversity* (pp. 217-228). Newbury Park, CA: Sage.

Gray, E., & Cosgrove, J. (1985). Ethnocentric perceptions of childrearing practices in protective services. *Child Abuse and Neglect, 9,* 389-396.

Herdman, R., & Behney, C. (1990). *Indian adolescent mental health.* Washington, DC: Office of Technology Assessment, Congress of the United States.

Hirschfelder, A., & de Montano, K. M. (1993). *The Native American almanac: A portrait of Native America today.* Englewood Cliffs, NJ: Prentice Hall.

Indian Health Service. (1994). *Trends in Indian health.* Rockville, MD: Department of Health and Human Services.

Joe, J. (1994). Revaluing Native-American concepts of development and education. In P. Greenfield & R. Cocking (Eds.), *Cross-cultural roots of minority child development* (pp. 107-113). Hillsdale, NJ: Lawrence Erlbaum.

John, R. (1988). The Native American family. In C. Mindel, R. Habenstein, & R. Wright (Eds.), *Ethnic families in America: Patterns and variations* (pp. 325-366). New York: Elsevier North-Holland.

Kidwell, C. (1994). Higher education issues in Native American communities. In M. Justiz, R. Wilson, & L. Bjork (Eds.), *Minorities in higher education* (pp. 239-257). Phoenix, AZ: Oryx.

Kleinfeld, J. (1994). Learning styles and culture. In W. Lonner & R. Malpass (Eds.), *Psychology and culture* (pp. 151-156). Boston: Allyn & Bacon.

Kleinfeld, J., & Nelson, P. (1991). Adapting instruction to Native Americans' learning style. *Journal of Cross-Cultural Psychology, 22,* 273-282.

LaFromboise, T., & Low, K. (1989). American Indian children and adolescents. In J. Gibbs & L. Huang (Eds.), *Children of color: Psychological interventions with minority youth* (pp. 114-147). San Francisco: Jossey-Bass.

LaFromboise, T., & Rowe, W. (1983). Skills training for bicultural competence: Rationale and application. *Journal of Counseling Psychology, 30,* 589-595.

LaFromboise, T., Trimble, J., & Mohatt, G. V. (1990). Counseling intervention and American Indian tradition: An integrative approach. *Counseling Psychologist, 18,* 628-654.

Lee, N. (1993). Native American crime: The invisible tragedy. *Wicazo sa review, 9,* 8-13.

Leland, J. (1976). *Firewater myths: North American Indian drinking and alcohol addiction.* Rutgers, NJ: Rutgers Center of Alcohol Studies.

Manson, S., Ackerson, L., Dick, R., & Baron, A. (1990). Depressive symptoms among American Indian adolescents: Psychometric characteristics of the Center for

Epidemiologic Studies Depression Scale (CES-D). *Psychological Assessment, 2,* 231-237.

May, P. (1990). A bibliography on suicide and suicide attempts among American Indians and Alaska Natives. *OMEGA, 21,* 199-214.

McShane, D., & Berry, J. (1988). Native North Americans: Indian and Inuit abilities. In S. Irvine & J. Berry (Eds.), *Human abilities in cultural context* (pp. 385-426). New York: Cambridge University Press.

McShane, D., & Plas, J. (1984). The cognitive functioning of American Indian children: Moving from the WISC to the WISC-R. *School Psychology Review, 3,* 61-73.

Noriega, J. (1992). American Indian education in the United States: Indoctrination for subordination to colonialism. In M. Jaimes (Ed.), *The state of Native America: Genocide, colonialization and resistance* (pp. 371-402). Boston, MA: South End.

Oetting, E. R. (1993). Orthogonal cultural identification: Theoretical links between cultural identification and substance use. In M. De La Rosa & J. Adrados (Eds.), *Drug abuse among minority youth: Advances in research and methodology* (NIDA Research Monograph No. 130, pp. 32-56). Rockville, MD: National Institute on Drug Abuse.

Oetting, E. R., & Beauvais, F. (1986). Peer cluster theory: Drugs and the adolescent. *Journal of Counseling and Development, 65,,* 17-22.

Oetting, E. R., & Beauvais, F. (1990-1991). Orthogonal cultural identification theory: The cultural identification of minority adolescents. *International Journal of the Addictions, 25,* 655-685.

Redhorse, J., Lewis, R., Feit, M., & Decker, J. (1978). Family behavior of urban American Indians. *Social Casework, 59,,* 67-72.

Robbins, R. (1991 , October). American Indian gifted and talented students: Their problems and proposed solutions. *Journal of American Indian Education, 30,* 15-24.

Robbins, R. L. (1992). Self-determination & subordination: The past, present and future of American Indian governance. In M. Jaimes (Ed.), *The state of Native America: Genocide, colonization, and resistance.* Boston: South End Press.

Rogoff, B., & Chavajay, P. (1995). What's become of research on the cultural bias of cognitive development? *American Psychologist, 50,* 859-877.

Schinke, S., Orlandi, M., Botvin, G., & Gilchrist, L. (1988). Preventing substance abuse among American Indian adolescents: A bicultural competence skills approach. *Journal of Counseling Psychology, 35,* 87-90.

Snipp, C. (1989). *American Indians: The first of this land.* New York: Russell Sage Foundation.

Swaim, R., Oetting, E., Jumper-Thurman, P., Beauvais, F., & Edwards, R. (1993). American Indian adolescent drug use and socialization characteristics: A cross-cultural comparison. *Journal of Cross-Cultural Psychology, 24*(1), 53-70.

Tietjen, A. (1994). Children's social networks and social support in cultural context. In W. Lonner & R. Malpass (Eds.), *Psychology and culture* (pp. 101-106). Boston: Allyn & Bacon.

Trimble, J., & Bagwell, W. (Eds.). (1995). *North American Indians and Alaska Natives: Abstracts of the psychological and behavioral literature, 1967-1994.* Washington, DC: American Psychological Association.

Trimble, J. E. (1995). Toward an understanding of ethnicity and ethnic identity, and their relationship with drug use research. In G. J. Botvin, S. Schinke, &

M. A. Orlandi (Eds.), *Drug abuse prevention with multiethnic youth* (pp. 3-27). Thousand Oaks, CA: Sage.

Trimble, J., Flemming, C., Beauvais, F., & Jumper-Thurman, P. (1996). Essential cultural and social strategies for counseling Native American Indians. In P. Pedersen, J. Draguns, W. Lonner, & J. Trimble (Eds.), *Counseling across cultures* (pp. 177-209). Thousand Oaks, CA: Sage.

University of Minnesota Health Center. (1992). *The state of Native American youth health.* Minneapolis, MN: Division of General Pediatrics and Adolescent Health.

Woodhead, H. (Ed.). (1996). *Winds of renewal.* Alexandria, VA: Time-Life Books.

6. Healthy Adjustment in Mexican American and Other Hispanic Adolescents

Felipe Gonzales Castro
Gina R. Boyer
Hector G. Balcazar

What constitutes normal, healthy, and perhaps exceptional adjustment among youth confronted with life challenges imposed by two contrasting cultures? Similarly, what are the factors that promote healthy adjustment in Mexican American and other Hispanic adolescents? These two complex questions are examined in this chapter as they relate to the adjustment of Mexican American and other Hispanic youth, both native-born and immigrant. These youth include Mexican American-Chicano(a), Puerto Rican, Cuban, Dominican, Spanish American (youth from northern New Mexico), and other Hispanic/Latino youth.[1] Although our analysis has implications for this broad cross-section of U.S. Hispanic youth, our analysis focuses primarily on factors associated with adaptive adjustment in Mexican American-Chicano(a) youth from the Southwest (California, Colorado, Arizona, New Mexico, and Texas). We also touch on a third related question: How can we prevent psychological disorders (abnormal adjustment) and promote the development of personal and social competencies for normal and even exceptional adjustment among Mexican American and other Hispanic youth?

Mexican Americans are the largest subgroup in the United States. The Hispanic population was estimated to be 31.67 million as of October 1999 (U.S. Census Bureau, 1999). Census data for March 1988 indicated that the estimated total Hispanic population was 29.70 million, with 18.8 million Mexican Americans (63.3%), 3.15 million Puerto Ricans (10.6%), 1.26 million Cubans (4.2%), 4.29 million Central and South Americans (14.4%), and 2.2 million other Hispanics (7.4%; U.S. Census Bureau, 1997).

Mexican American and other Hispanic adolescents face the conventional challenges of adolescent adjustment as well as the challenges of adjustment in two distinct cultures. Issues involving culture conflict and the establishment of an ethnic identity present additional challenges for Mexican American adolescents, as compared to the usual challenges of adjustment faced during adolescence by White non-Hispanic adolescents. Given the limited research that addresses the "normal and healthy" adjustment of Hispanic adolescents, in this chapter we also move beyond extant findings and from a contemporary Hispanic perspective present an integrative framework on potential patterns of normal and exceptional adjustment in Mexican American and other Hispanic adolescents.

THE CHALLENGE OF IDENTITY FORMATION
FOR MEXICAN AMERICAN YOUTH

As a developmental challenge, at some point in their lives, Mexican American adolescents must cope with the cultural conflicts associated with ethnic identity formation. For some, but not all, the resolution to these conflicts prompts the development of a bilingual-bicultural identity. Furthermore, in late adolescence, youth should develop certain skills to begin exercising a socially sanctioned role, such as being a parent. With maturation in growth toward one or more social roles emerges a distinguishable "life trajectory" (Newcomb & Bentler, 1988). A life trajectory refers to a life course or direction taken by a youth in pursuit of a life dream or future goal, such as planning to go to college, becoming a doctor, or becoming a stay-at-home mother. The concept of a life trajectory is similar to the concept of "identity paths," which refers to patterns of identity formation that occur throughout adolescence (Frable, 1997), and it parallels the concept of "addiction careers," as described in longitudinal studies of heroin addicts (Anglin, Booth, Ryan, & Hser, 1988; Simpson & Sells, 1990). Here, it is recognized that all youth do not espouse specific aspirations and life goals and thus exhibit a life trajectory that remains undefined and lacking in direction. Indeed, youth who exhibit an "amotivational syndrome" exhibit no direction in life (Baumrind & Moselle, 1985). In contrast, other youth who exhibit a "problem behavior syndrome" (Jessor & Jessor, 1977) exhibit a core factor of "general deviance" (Jessor, 1993; Newcomb, 1995) and a distinct life trajectory directed toward legal problems and future incarceration. Unfortunately, at present, more evidence exists to aid in the identification of maladaptive life trajectories than in the identification of adaptive and exceptional life trajectories (Newcomb, 1995).

In adulthood, a person may have multiple social identities, such that the person's life trajectory and personal accomplishments (milestones reached) come to define a *composite personal identity*: family identity (e.g., mother), ethnic-cultural identity (e.g., Mexican American), gender identity (e.g., female), occupational identity (e.g., principal of Cesar Chavez Elementary School), religious identity (e.g., member of Queen of Peace Catholic Church), and so forth. A person may develop a rich personal identity as the product of adaptive function that facilitates goal-oriented growth. By contrast, the presence of psychiatric dysfunction that limits a youth's personal growth may yield a weak personal identity. In this context, it may be asked whether adolescents who lack progress along a life trajectory that leads to some social or occupational identity may exhibit a condition of risk for future maladjustment. Conversely, does the presence of an emerging life trajectory in an adolescent serve as a protective condition indicative of current and future healthy adjustment?

A recurring criterion in defining the presence of psychiatric disorder is the presence of impaired functioning in social, academic, occupational, or other life areas, as set out in the fourth edition of the *Diagnostic and Statistical Manual of Mental Disorders* (American Psychiatric Association [APA], 1994; Kazdin, 1993). Whether daily behavior becomes impaired is also related to the level of demand imposed by a person's major social or occupational role. As one example, a person with a doctorate who later is diagnosed with a personality disorder may exhibit impaired social and occupational function when working as a research chemist at a major pharmaceutical company, whereas that person may exhibit adequate social and occupational function in the less-demanding role of taxi driver (Oltmanns, Neale, & Davidson, 1988, pp. 112-127). Thus, normalcy in adaptive function must be defined in the context of the specific social and occupational demands imposed by the person's social role.

In general, poor adjustment in adults and adolescents is manifested by the presence of disruptive symptoms, such as chronic anxiety, depression, anger, or other dysphoric emotions (Wilson, Nathan, O'Leary, & Clark, 1996). Similarly, among preadolescent children, poor adjustment is indicated by the presence of symptomatology that impairs psychological and social function to levels that fall below adequate function for that child's developmental stage (Kazdin, 1993).

Generally, among children and adolescents, problems of aggression and lack of impulse control (e.g., oppositional defiant disorder, conduct disorder, attention deficit disorder) and problems of emotional distress (e.g., anxiety disorder, depression) are the major types of problem that reflect psychological abnormality and that interfere with normal adaptive development (APA, 1994). Adolescents who are free of these and related psychiatric problems are by definition "normal." However, for this population of "normal" youth, more research is needed to identify the factors that promote exceptional development, even in the face of adversity (Wilson et al., 1996). Moreover, the need is even more acute to identify the factors that promote exceptional development among Mexican American and other Hispanic youth (Felix-Ortiz & Newcomb, 1995).

Thus, identifying the presence of psychopathology in children may be challenging. However, identifying the cognitive, emotional, and behavioral determinants of *adaptive adjustment* and *exceptional adjustment* among children and youth presents a more difficult challenge. Doing so for Mexican American youth offers an even greater challenge, given the socioeconomic stressors and the dual-culture conflicts that confront many Mexican American youth. Generally, for Mexican American youth, adaptive and exceptional adjustment is the product of the youth's capacity to respond successfully to various developmental challenges with resilient coping responses and to do so with a minimum of symptoms, while also developing the skills for personal and social competence.

What Is Psychological Health?

Youth who exhibit the capacity to cope effectively with adverse life conditions, who rise above adversity, and who show adaptive growth are hypothesized to have developed some core of personal competencies that facilitates growth along a chosen life trajectory.

Although social and cultural variability exists regarding the characteristics of sound psychological health, some specific competencies associated with psychological health include (a) emotional stability that promotes the absence of chronic dysphoric emotions (e.g., anxiety, depression, anger); (b) a positive self-concept that includes high self-esteem and a strong personal identities; (c) an optimistic life outlook that includes aspirations for personal growth and a positive life dream along with the motivation to pursue it; (d) the capacity for adaptability-flexibility in adjusting to life's changes; (e) good reality testing, which involves having accurate perceptions of the environment, (f) good judgment, which involves the capacity to make adaptive decisions; (g) spirituality, which involves having a religious or spiritual connection with a higher power to cope at times with situations that one cannot control; (h) a health orientation, which involves active participation in maintaining one's own health (physical, psychological, and spiritual); (i) social competence for developing and nurturing rewarding social relationships with family, friends, and others; and (j) an orientation toward personal growth, which involves a quest for mastery and self-actualization (Meyer, 1999; Meyer & Osborne, 1996). Although exceptional children and youth appear to develop these capabilities as the result of a combination of genetic factors (e.g., temperament) and environmental factors (e.g., access to educational activities), a major factor in this growth is the guidance and emotional support provided by parents, family members, and other mentoring adults in collaborative efforts that build a youth's academic intelligence and emotional intelligence (Gardner, 1993).

These general criteria for psychological health would appear to apply to the healthy adjustment of Mexican American and other Hispanic youth, with the added emphasis that such youth are challenged to develop a positive self-concept, one that includes a maturing ethnic identity coupled with pride in asserting it. This capacity for assertiveness in the expression of one's own ethnic identity may well develop as a product of a strong positive self-concept that includes high self-esteem (Frable, 1997) and positive views of the self that exist in a multicultural orientation to life (Ramirez, 1991, 1999), in which the healthy Mexican American adolescent can express pride in his or her own ethnic identity, even in the face of criticism and ridicule from others. Here, more research is needed to identify the early sources that develop and nurture this psychological resilience that builds confidence in asserting with conviction and pride (Felix-Ortiz, Newcomb, & Myers, 1994) one's individuality and ethnic identity. In summary, a strong personal self-concept that includes high self-esteem may provide personal strength, a psychological resilience that helps the Mexican American youth explore his or her own background in a manner that fosters growth, and development of a strong ethnic identity (Phinney, 1993).

SOCIOECONOMIC CONTEXT
FOR MEXICAN AMERICAN YOUTH

From U.S. census data, a distinct social profile has emerged for Mexican Americans and other Hispanics. From 1980 to 1990, the U.S. Hispanic population grew by 53% from 14.6 million in 1980 to 22.3 million in 1990. In addition, U.S. census projections indicate that from 1995 to 2025, the U.S. Hispanic population will increase rapidly by 32 million, to a total of 54 million, which would constitute 44% of the 72 million persons who would add to the U.S. population by the year 2025 (Campbell, 1996). Hispanics are currently second to African Americans as the largest ethnic-racial population in the United States, although Hispanics are projected to become the largest ethnic-racial population in about the year 2005.

As a population, Hispanics exhibit a few noteworthy characteristics when compared to the mainstream U.S. White non-Hispanic population. Relative to that population, members of the Hispanic population are younger; have a lower educational attainment; and are more likely to be unemployed, earn less, and live in poverty (Aguirre-Molina & Molina, 1994; Del Pinal, 1997).

Also, relative to the White non-Hispanic population, the age distribution of the Hispanic population shows a higher proportion of children. In 1993, youth aged 5 to 19 in the White non-Hispanic population numbered 48.9 million, constituting 21.0% of that population. By contrast, Hispanic children and adolescents aged 5 to 19 numbered 7.3 million, constituting 27.4% of this population, and Mexican American children and adolescents aged 5 to 19 numbered 5.0 million, comprising 29.3% of the Mexican American population (U.S. Census Bureau, 1997).

Regarding the educational status of Hispanics, as compared to the White non-Hispanic population, Hispanics exhibit higher school drop-out rates and lower levels of educational attainment. Unfortunately, this trend has been evident for a few decades. In 1994, among White non-Hispanic adults aged 25 years and older, 84.9% had completed high school. This compares with high school completion rates of only 53.5% for Hispanics and only 46.7% for Mexican Americans (U.S. Census Bureau, 1997).

Regarding economic status, in 1994, the median household income for non-Hispanic Whites was $34,173. By contrast, the median household income for Hispanics was $22,879, and for Mexican Americans it was $23,992. Here, the proportion of families who live below the poverty line in 1992 was 9.6% for non-Hispanic Whites, as compared with 29.3% for Hispanics, and 30.1% for Mexican Americans (Montgomery, 1994).

As one favorable trend, the proportion of Hispanics who have obtained a higher education has increased between 1970 and 1990. The percentage of Hispanics who have completed high school or more increased from 32.1% in 1970, to 44.0% in 1980, to 49.8% in 1990. Similarly, the percentage of Hispanics who obtained a bachelor's degree or higher rose from 4.5% in 1970, to 7.6% in 1980, to 9.2% in 1990 (U.S. Census Bureau, 1997). By contrast, non-Hispanic Whites obtained bachelors' degrees in percentages of 10.8% in 1970, to 16.7% in 1980, to 21.2% in 1990 (U.S. Department of Commerce, 1993). Although this educational trend among Hispanics is a favorable one, the educational attainment of Hispanics still lagged behind that of non-Hispanic Whites during these three decades. These gains in educational attainment by Hispanics have generated a cohort of better-educated Hispanic young adults who have been able to enter the middle class. However, the children of these new middle-class Hispanics now face challenges that differ from those faced by their parents.

These census data suggest that Mexican American and other Hispanic youth, on average, still face difficult challenges that include coping with life in poverty, lower socioeconomic status, and limited educational success (Romo & Falbo, 1996). These demographic characteristics and trends have focused the attention of Hispanic leaders toward certain policy issues. From the perspective of social policy, the most salient contemporary concerns for Hispanics include the need for greater Hispanic political participation; and the need to improve the status of Hispanics in the areas of education, economic development, and leadership development (Enchautegui, 1995).

As a consequence of upward socioeconomic mobility among some Mexican Americans, for today's Mexican American child, new social conditions have emerged that create novel psychological and interpersonal challenges. Yet, despite being confronted by limited economic resources and having parents with low levels of education, many Mexican American youth express aspirations for upward social mobility that include the desire to enter high school, college, and the professional job market (Romo & Falbo, 1996). Moreover, despite the presence of challenges and barriers, some Mexican American adolescents exhibit early indications of exceptional adjustment, as they espouse high aspirations and exhibit psychological resilience, along with strong academic and social competencies. This chapter examines some of the factors that are associated with healthy and exceptional adjustment in Mexican American and other Hispanic adolescents.

GENERAL ISSUES IN CULTURALLY CONGRUENT DEFINITIONS OF HEALTH

Absolute "health" is a state of living that is difficult to define uniquely for all people, particularly as seen by the constructivist and cultural relativist perspectives. These perspectives assert that people construct their own conceptions of the world and attach their own meaning to environmental events. Accordingly, culturally diverse conceptions exist regarding the characteristics of "the good life" and the definitions of "normalcy" and "health" (Harwood, 1981; Schwandt, 1994). Epidemiologic studies have identified specific risk factors that are associated statistically with specific health and disease outcomes (Gordis, 1996; Yee et al., 1995), although the magnitude and effect of these risk factors can vary considerably in predicting health and illness outcomes in various ethnic populations (Vega, Zimmerman, Warheit, Apospori, & Gil, 1993). Moreover, identifying the predictors of psychological health is complicated by the diversity of views on the characteristics of "healthy" psychosocial adjustment (Dana, 1993; Harper & Lambert, 1994). Understanding and appreciating cultural variation in the interpretation of health requires *cultural competence*, the capacity to interpret social events accurately in the context of a given culture. It also involves skills in understanding the *cultural nuances* involved in distilling the meaning of a given behavior, as interpreted from the perspective of cultural "insiders" (Castro, 1998). Cultural competence in understanding cultural variability in the meaning of health and illness involves understanding minority persons "on their own terms," by developing a deeper understanding of their values, traditions, and customs (Orlandi, Weston, & Epstein, 1992). Thus, a valid and culturally competent case evaluation as needed for accurate diagnosis and treatment planning requires a systematic review of a youth's social, cultural, and environmental living conditions, because these influence thought and behavior and the interpretation of this thought and behavior as abnormal or dysfunctional (APA, 1994).

CONCERNS IN THE HEALTHY ADJUSTMENT OF MEXICAN-ORIGIN ADOLESCENTS

The challenges to healthy adjustment among Mexican American adolescents are compounded by the conflicts in identity formation that result from having a dual identity as a member of two cultural groups. These conflicts often prompt actions made under conditions that the Mexican American adolescent only partly understands. For example, many Mexican American youth are confronted with choices: (a) whether to identify with mainstream peers, with ethnic peers, or with both; (b) whether to learn to speak Spanish in addition to English; and (c) with which peer group to associate, although this may raise conflicts over loyalty to members of one's ethnic-racial group versus assimilating into the Anglo mainstream in part by attempting to join an Anglo peer group. In addition, in middle adolescence (ages 15-17; Grades 10-12), Hispanic youth may experience generational conflicts with their parents as the result of differing rates of acculturation that occur between youth and their parents (Szapocznik & Kurtines, 1989). Despite the challenges involved in adjusting to two cultures, a growing body of literature endorses the advantages of developing a bicultural identity and the benefits of developing *cultural flex*, which involve developing the skills to respond effectively in two distinct cultural environments (La Fromboise, Coleman, & Gerton, 1993; Ramirez, 1991).

ACCULTURATION, ASSIMILATION,
AND BICULTURALISM

For Mexican American youth, a major life challenge involves coping adaptively with the stressors of acculturation and assimilation. In its broadest context, *acculturation* refers to the acquisition of the skills needed to function effectively in a new environment. Under this broad conception, throughout adolescence, all youth acculturate to various new environments with varying degrees of success. For example, upon surpassing a milestone such as graduation from high school, a youth must "acculturate" to a new environment when going away to college. Similarly, migration to the United States from a Latin American country also prompts the need for an adolescent to learn several new skills and to rise above a "sense of relative depravation" experienced by some children of adult immigrants in the new country (Suarez-Orozco, 1997).

According to Berry (1980), the process of acculturation includes two different ways of adaptation to a different culture. The more extreme form of acculturation is *assimilation,* which involves abandoning one's own cultural identity in favor of adopting the identity of the new society. By contrast, Szapocznik and Kurtines (1989) noted that development in two cultures—*biculturation*—involves successfully integrating components of one's own culture with those of the dominant culture. Thus, to become *bicultural,* a youth must learn to communicate and negotiate in two different cultures, always cognizant of the "rules" involved in operating successfully in both cultural environments (Szapocznik & Kurtines, 1989).

Several studies have examined the effects of acculturation among Hispanic adolescents. These studies have examined the positive versus the negative effects of an exclusive alliance with one's own ethnic culture, that is, from being "culture-bound" in contrast to achieving a balance between involvement in one's own cultural group and with the larger society. These studies suggest that a degree of early assimilation followed by biculturation produces several more positive outcomes, as indicated by superior psychological adjustment (Gil, Vega, & Dimas, 1994; Moyerman & Forman, 1992; Rotheram-Borus, 1990; Szapocznik & Kurtines, 1989).

For example, Szapocznik and Kurtines (1989) examined the relation between biculturalism and personal adjustment among Cuban American students in junior high school. Teacher ratings indicated that scores on biculturalism predicted level of adjustment in these students. Additionally, when teachers were asked to select their best-adjusted and least-adjusted students, teacher ratings of adjustment were related significantly to levels of bicultural achievement and cultural involvement. The best-adjusted adolescents were also those who were higher in bicultural achievement, and they had a higher level of involvement with their own ethnic cultural group.

Gil et al. (1994) examined the relation of acculturation stress to personal adjustment among U.S.-born and foreign-born Hispanic adolescent boys. Their findings indicated that bicultural adolescents exhibited higher levels of adaptation relative to their peers who were not bicultural. The bicultural adolescents showed more positive self-images as well as positive views of their minority identity. Additionally, Gil et al. found that higher levels of family pride served as a buffer against the cumulative strains of acculturation.

A study by Rotheram-Borus (1990) examined the relation between a youth's choice of reference-group label and ethnic pride, value orientations, use of English, and perceptions of cross-ethnic contact and conflict. This study of 330 high school students from the New York City area observed that a majority (53.2%) of Hispanic adolescents, primarily Puerto Ricans, self-identified as bicultural instead of solely from one ethnic group or from the mainstream culture. When Rotherman-Borus examined separatist attitudes, ethnic pride, cross-ethnic contacts and conflicts, and the use of English, the bicultural adolescents exhibited an adaptive "blend of cultural norms and attitudes of different groups" (Rotheram-Borus, 1990, p. 1080). These results also suggest that local community norms can influence a youth's attitude toward ethnic identity: It may be easier for a youth in New York City, a multi-ethnic community, to endorse being bicultural than it is for a youth in a homogeneous White mainstream community.

The social and cultural norms that govern the culture of the local community, as well as family expectations, create conditions of social control that influence the behaviors of the children of that community, including their ethnic self-identification. However, youth who are raised in two cultural environments—home and school—often receive competing and at times conflicting messages on the behavior that is considered appropriate and desirable. For example, in a segregated two-culture community, a child may feel conflicted over whether to speak in English or in Spanish and, if able to speak both well, over which language is appropriate to speak in which situation. These conflicting and confusing situations intensify the social and psychological challenges to normal adjustment for bicultural adolescents.

Buriel, Calzada, and Vasquez (1983) examined the relation of a youth's integration into traditional Mexican culture in relation to academic achievement and social deviance. For Mexican American youth, Buriel et al. hypothesized that integration into traditional Mexican culture promotes healthier psychological adjustment and decreases the probability of delinquent behavior. Buriel et al. found support for this hypothesis, concluding that traditional Mexican culture has a protective effect that counters delinquency and fosters academic achievement. The researchers stated, "For Mexican Americans, integration in their traditional culture may be a prerequisite for healthy adjustment. . . . Mexican Americans may fare better if they maintain ties with their traditional culture while simultaneously incorporating aspects of the cultural mainstream" (p. 53).

From this perspective, Buriel et al. (1983) noted that traditional values among immigrant Mexicans include a high regard for academic achievement and strong social controls (discipline) that are based on strong religious and family values. A related value is cooperation, as opposed to competition, particularly when a child relates with members of his or her own culture. Some of these traditional value orientations may conflict with Anglo-American value orientations that emphasize individualism, competition, and direct confrontation in style of communication.

Some studies suggest that certain Hispanic adolescents tend to identify more strongly with traditional values (Black, Paz, & DeBlassie, 1991; Buriel et al., 1983; Ramirez, 1991), especially in the areas of gender roles, family structures, age, social status, and religion. For many Hispanic adolescents who are raised in conservative families, family messages about appropriate behavior may reinforce the value of accepting traditional values and roles in the context of their families. Yet, as a source of conflict, these youth also may be forced to adopt modernistic values in the academic environment or among peers from the mainstream culture.

In his examination of adjustment to distinct cultural environments, Ramirez (1991) examined the psychological aspects of *traditional* versus *modernistic* thinking in various ethnic cultures. Ramirez distinguished between *cultural styles* and *cognitive styles*. Cultural styles include variation in the dimension of traditionalism versus modernism, in which more traditionally oriented persons emphasize (a) distinct gender roles, (b) stronger level of identification with the family, (c) a strong sense of community involvement, (d) greater family loyalty and family identification, (e) a greater present-time orientation, (f) greater reverence for elders, (g) greater value of cultural traditions, and (h) greater value of spirituality and religion. Ramirez noted that rural environments are most commonly associated with traditional cultural orientations, and urban lifestyles usually reflect modernistic orientations to life (p. 18). This traditionalism has its roots in agrarian societies, in which survival of the group was dependent on mutual cooperation and on maintaining harmony in interpersonal relationships. In this system of sociocultural values, individuals judged to be most "intelligent" and "socially competent" were those who exhibited exceptional capabilities in relating well to others, in maintaining the community's social ties, and in leading in the promotion of cooperation between members of the group (Gardner, Kornhaber, & Krechevsky, 1993).

As differentiated from cultural styles, cognitive styles refer to a child's orientation to learning, which is categorized as either *field-sensitive* or *field-independent*. These two cognitive styles govern how a child relates to peers and teachers (Ramirez, 1991). A more field-sensitive child seeks affiliation with others and interacts in a collaborative manner. The field-sensitive cognitive style is congruent with a traditional worldview. By contrast, a field-independent child seeks to work independently of others and interacts in a more competitive manner. This field-independent cognitive style is congruent with a modernistic worldview. In this context, Ramirez (1991) and others (Buriel et al., 1983) indicated that the most successful children and adolescents are those who are flexible enough to move between both traditional and modernistic cultural environments by developing composite cognitive styles, which possess the capacity for cultural flex.

HISPANIC FAMILIES AND ETHNIC CULTURE

Within most, if not all, cultures, the family is the primary source of cultural transmission, the source that communicates values, beliefs, traditions, and practices that are passed along from elders to children (McGoldrick & Giordano, 1996). Among Mexican American and other Hispanic families (Mexican, Mexican American, Puerto Rican, Cuban families), variation exists regarding the level of parental conservative-traditionalism or liberal-modernism, used in child-rearing style and practices (Bernal & Shapiro, 1996; Falicov, 1982; Garcia-Prieto, 1996). Also, ethnic identity, as expressed in cultural pride in being "Mexican" or "Chicano," is a deeply ingrained quality in many of the more traditional Mexican American and other Hispanic families.

A family's Mexican cultural traditions and practices give family members their cultural identity and sense of belonging, based on a sense of *nosotros* (we-ness) that comes from having common values, beliefs, and traditions. For example, among Hispanics, Spanish as a romance language features emotional meanings not easily translated into English, such as the concept of *confianza* (a deep sense of trust and comfort with a special person). In many Hispanic families, orthodox Roman Catholic religious beliefs and a family's unique traditional practices all contribute to this sense of family unity, *familism*, which involves strong family identification, attachments, obligations, and loyalty (Marin, 1993). Issues of ethnic identity and whether one should maintain cultural identity are particularly salient for immigrant Mexican and other immigrant Hispanic families, as they cope with the stressors of adaptation to "the new culture" (Rogler, Cortes, & Malgady, 1991). Members of such families may compromise or even disavow their identity during the process of acculturation unless they resolve these cultural conflicts. A recurring conflict for many is the fear of being discriminated against by mainstream people during their struggle to develop a "hybrid" bilingual-bicultural identity as residents in a new country (McGoldrick, 1982).

Despite a common socialization provided by parents, within a given family siblings often vary in their level of identification with their ethnic or cultural heritage (McGoldrick, 1982). The younger siblings of an immigrant family typically retain less of the old cultural ways relative to their older siblings. Among Mexican American adolescents, this loss of cultural heritage and practices includes a loss of Spanish language usage and a loss of Mexican culture traditions during the process of acculturation. In the extreme case, this can involve a total assimilation into the U.S. mainstream culture that results in a youth's complete abandonment of ethnic-racial self-identification.

Regarding the process of acculturation, Szapocznik and Kurtines (1989) observed differential rates of acculturation between Cuban children and their parents, in which children typically were observed to acculturate at a faster rate. It appears that this differential in rates of acculturation between parents and their children is reflected by cultural and communication conflicts in the family. Although parenting style is a critical determinant of the parent-child relationship, traditional Mexican American parents who demand compliance with their more traditional cultural expectations may induce alienation and rebellion among some of their adolescent children, thus weakening the bond between parent and child. Consequently, as some of these youth become alienated from their parents, they may get involved with a peer group that engages in antisocial activities, including illicit drug use (Chavez, Edwards, & Oetting, 1989).

In the mainstream literature, risk factors for alcohol and other drug use among adolescents include three major types of factors: (a) a disrupted family system that includes high levels of family conflict and low youth bonding with their parents; (b) youth difficulties in school, including academic failure, alienation, and rebelliousness; and (c) youth associations with drug-using peers (Hawkins, Catalano, & Miller, 1992; Oetting & Beauvais, 1987). In a study of 6,760 White, Black, Cuban, and other Hispanic youth from sixth- and seventh-grade classes from Dade County, Florida, Vega et al. (1993) found risk factor profiles among the Cuban and other Hispanic youth that were similar to those observed in other studies. Specifically, they found that low family pride, family substance use, parental smoking, a youth's willingness to engage in non-normative behaviors, and perceptions of drug use by peers operated as significant risk factors for alcohol use. This same set of risk factors also operated as predictors of alcohol use among the White and Black youths in the Miami study, although the relative predictive weights of each of these risk factors differed for each of these four groups.

Vega (1990) reviewed the complex stressors that face many Mexican American and other Hispanic families as they adapt to economic marginality, labor market pressures, and physical relocation. Vega observed that relative to Anglo-American families, Mexican American families tend to have large kin networks that can include fictive kin (unrelated persons who serve as family members). In these networks, Mexican Americans visit relatives often, given their geographic proximity. Family bonding and their expectations of mutual support and aid from other family members also may foster this close relationship between various family members. The Hispanic tradition of *compadrazgo* (i.e., choosing godparents to oversee an infant's growth) creates close bonds between two families, within members of an extended family, or even between fictive kin. In the traditional Mexican culture that has strong Catholic values, the parents of an infant typically will choose reliable and trusted persons to serve as godparents, and this commitment is consummated during the infant's baptism. The mutual respect and affection that leads persons to be asked to serve as a *compadre* (godfather), or as a *comadre* (godmother) are based on the development of strong affective bonds. In this context of family closeness, in some Mexican American families problems are kept within the family, thus discouraging help-seeking outside the family and a reluctance to seek professional mental health services from sources outside the family (Keefe, Padilla, & Carlos, 1978).

In style of parental discipline, Hispanic family systems vary from being strongly "patriarchal families" that have a dominant father and emphasize distinct gender role separation, to more "egalitarian families," in which the father and mother share equally in family tasks and responsibilities. In the more traditional Mexican and Mexican American families, parents will emphasize obedience to their authority, more so than achievement. In some families, a child's conduct is acceptable as long as the child is obedient and respectful of his or her parents (Falicov, 1982, 1996). Nonetheless, in this context, one parent may criticize the more permissive parent for being an *alcahuete(a)*, that is, for being too lenient in discipline with the children. In contrast, the more permissive parent will argue that leniency that avoids imposing a harsh judgement sustains the strong interpersonal bonds and the sense of *confianza* between parent and child.

The remarkable closeness observed in many Mexican and other Hispanic families is a characteristic described as *familism* (Sabogal, Marin, & Otero-Sabogal, 1987). Familism refers to a "strong identification with and attachment to one's nuclear and extended families, and strong feelings of loyalty, reciprocity, and solidarity among members of the same family" (Marin & Marin, 1991, p. 13). There are other characteristic features in many Hispanic families. These include *personalismo,* the value ascribed to interpersonal relationships rather than to completing tasks; *simpatía,* the commitment to maintain harmonious social interactions and conflict avoidance; *dignidad,* the value ascribed to personal dignity; and *respeto,* the value ascribed to respect, with expectations that a person should show deference and respect to persons of higher stature and authority in the family and in the community. Another important feature of Hispanic families is *confianza.* This refers to a sense of trust, comfort, and security found in special relationships, in which a person feels a sense of closeness and intimacy with a special "persona de confianza" (Keefe et al., 1978). Children who have developed strong *respeto* (respect for elders, including their parents) avoid disrespecting their parents by openly disagreeing with them or by acting counter to their parents' wishes. This form of familial normative control can be a potent determinant of adolescent behavior and self-control among Mexican American and other Hispanic youth who have established strong affective bonds with their parents.

By contrast, the Anglo-American strategy of confrontation, openly revealing inconsistencies, or revealing contradictions in a person's behavior is typically disruptive in Mexican American and other Hispanic families, because such open confrontation often elicits tension and can strain interpersonal relationships. This is especially true among more traditional Mexican American families because confrontation often conflicts with the value of *simpatía,* which emphasizes deference to others for the sake of maintaining harmonious interpersonal relationships. Depending on how it is used, confrontation also may conflict with the expression of respect for one's elders. In this cultural context, acculturating Mexican American youth who begin to accept Anglo-American norms that include confrontation and the questioning of authority will experience considerable conflict when interacting with their more traditional Mexican American elders. These youth may believe that they are being assertive in expressing disagreements, whereas conservative elders may regard this behavior as brazen disrespect.

In summary, Mexican American and other Hispanic family systems are diverse, although several cultural practices, such as the practice of *compadrazgo* and the role of *respeto,* give these systems

their distinct cultural identity. Mexican American and other Hispanic youth who develop as exceptional individuals may do so
under particular conditions of support and nurturance from parents
and the extended family, despite living in impoverished neighborhoods. More research is needed to identify parental, familial, and
individual factors that promote adaptive and exceptional development of Mexican American and other Hispanic youth despite their
exposure to adverse social and economic conditions (Vega, 1990).

Sources of Cultural Conflict

As an aid to the analysis of salient cultural conflicts among Mexican American and other Hispanic youth, Table 6.1 presents contrasting value orientations in the idyllic Anglo-American and in the idyllic Mexican American culture, as these value orientations may
introduce cultural conflict in four lifestyle areas. For didactic purposes, and for simplicity, this table presents absolute differences
between the cultures, although it is recognized that any dual-culture
community will contain elements of both cultures represented
among the local families. For Mexican American and other Hispanic
adolescents, exposure to life events that introduce these competing
demands will elicit conflict and stress. It is postulated that adolescents who develop strong skills in adaptive coping will react con-
structively to these conflicts, at times on their own, but often with
the help of a confidant, family member, or friend. As these youth do
so, it is further postulated that they would develop a hybrid yet
more resilient bilingual-bicultural identity.

As indicated in Table 6.1, the idyllic Anglo-American and Mexican American cultures present contrasting *cultural prescripts,* cultural rules or regulations of conduct, "life shoulds" in the areas of:
Social Orientation, Family Orientation, Interpersonal Style, and
Expressive Style. As noted previously, for the purpose of clarity, the
summary in Table 6.1 simplifies the more complex value orientations and the nuances that exist in the two cultures (Locke, 1998); the
most salient aspects of these value orientations are presented here as
idyllic prototypical cultural features. Thus, Table 6.1 presents a cultural dialectic that contrasts the Anglo-American and Mexican
American cultures. In the area of social orientation, modernistic
Anglo-American culture, with its orientation toward progress and
technology, emphasizes and rewards individualism and competi-

Table 6.1 Sources of Cultural Conflict: Contrasting Value Orientations

Lifestyle Areas	Value Orientations	
	Anglo-American	Mexican American
Social orientation	Individualism	Collectivism
	Competition	Cooperation
Family orientation	Achievement-oriented (doing)	Family-oriented (*familism*) (being)
Interpersonal style	Precision in verbal expression	Focus on the relationship (*personalismo*)
	Confrontation	Social harmony (*simpatía*)
	Efficient task completion	Respect (*respeto*)
Expressive style	Rational, restrained	Affective, expressive

tion, whereas the traditional Mexican culture, with its agrarian origins, emphasizes and rewards collectivism (a focus on family needs over those of the individual) and mutual cooperation (Castro & Gutierres, 1997). Regarding family orientation, the Anglo-American culture emphasizes and rewards achievement and action to accomplish a task, whereas the Mexican culture emphasizes and rewards being with the family and maintaining harmonious social and family bonds.

In the area of interpersonal style, the Anglo-American culture emphasizes direct and specific communications (precision in verbal expression) that may include confrontation, and it emphasizes a task orientation and efficiency in task completion. By contrast, the Mexican culture emphasizes indirect and affective communications aimed at maintaining harmony in interpersonal relationships. Similarly, in the area of expressive style, the Anglo-American culture emphasizes rational, restrained forms of expression that involve precise logical thinking, whereas the Mexican culture also emphasizes affective forms of expression that involve interpersonal warmth and messages of support and affection.

These idyllic contrasts do not suggest that a value orientation observed in one culture does not appear or is entirely devalued in the opposing culture. Instead, these absolute contrasts highlight the more prominent and more strongly endorsed traits that exist in each distinct culture. Thus, Mexican American youth, who are exposed to events or issues that elicit these competing traits, expectations, and rewards, will experience the stressors of cultural conflict, and these conflicts will challenge the youth to respond effectively.

SOME THEORETICAL APPROACHES THAT RELATE TO ADOLESCENT ADJUSTMENT

This section examines three lines of research that relate to the social and psychological conflicts faced by Mexican American and other Hispanic youth, and it examines the skills that Mexican American adolescents may need to develop to cope adaptively with these conflicts.

Stage Theory Views of Adjustment

Ethnic identity development has been conceptualized as progressing through a series of stages (Phinney, 1989, 1990). In a study that examined ethnic identity development in three ethnic-racial groups and in Anglo-American 10th-grade students, Phinney (1989) found that the process of identity development was similar across ethnic-racial groups, although each ethnic-racial group also exhibited developmental patterns that were specific to members of that group. Phinney's study elaborated on Marcia's (1969, 1980) four theoretical stages of ethnic identity: (a) *diffuse identity,* the stage in which a youth does little to explore his or her own ethnic self-identity and has no clear understanding of the issues; (b) *foreclosed identity,* the stage in which a youth does little to explore his or her own ethnic self-identity although that youth develops an awareness of his or her ethnic identity; (c) *moratorium on identity,* the stage in which the youth explores his or her own ethnic identity and experiences confusion and ambivalence about it; and (d) *achieved identity,* the stage in which a youth develops a clear understanding and acceptance of his or her own ethnic identity. In her study, Phinney was able empirically to identify three distinct stages: (a) diffuse/ foreclosed identity, (b) moratorium on identity, and (c) achieved identity. She also observed that the highest levels of adaptive function, such as ego-identity and sense of mastery, occurred among youth who progressed to the stage of achieved identity.

Phinney noted that youth who are aware of their ethnic-racial identity but have not resolved their feelings about their ethnicity are the ones most likely to experience cultural conflicts. Furthermore, these identity conflicts are most likely to occur during the moratorium stage of ethnic identity development. Adolescents at this stage are more sensitive to any prejudice and discrimination. Often, at the moratorium stage of identification, anxiety and discomfort emerge when a youth is regarded as belonging to an "out-group" and thus as being "different" and perhaps "inferior" relative to youth from the "in-group," a mainstream reference group. If an adolescent at this stage assimilates these negative attitudes about being in the out-group, then that adolescent can develop self-doubt or self-hatred. Moreover, if these youth live in a disrupted family environment that is ravaged by poverty and fragmentation, then they may seek membership in a gang, which may serve as a "surrogate family" that provides nurturance and self-esteem (Morales, 1992). This quest for sources of acceptance and validation is especially important, as youth during early adolescence (ages 11-14, Grades 6-9) are remarkably self-conscious about their appearance and at times experience intense desires to belong.

One psychological cognitive response observed among some Mexican American youth who seek to overcome this state of negative self-appraisal (to reduce anxiety) is to disavow membership in their own ethnic group by identifying as a member of a mainstream social group (Castro, Proesholdbell, Abeita, & Rodriguez, 1999). This psychological maneuver, although adaptive in reducing anxiety and conflict in the short run, raises longer-term issues involving conflicts in self-concept unless the youth is successful in completely assimilating into mainstream cultural or social groups.

Unfortunately, many Mexican American youth who disavow their cultural heritage are still confronted by members of the majority culture with issues regarding their ethnic identity, especially if the Mexican American youth is dark-skinned (Betances, 1971). Youth with observable "minority" physical features are more likely to be confronted with questions about their ethnic identity, and they may feel strongly discriminated against when treated as a "minority person," regardless of the posture they take toward their ethnic identity. Moreover, their Mexican American peers who express pride in their ethnic identity and loyalty to the culture will criticize these assimilated adolescents as being psychologically weak or as "sellouts." For Mexican Americans and other Hispanics, attaining comfort with their concept of self is an important mental health issue. As noted previously, Phinney (1989) indicated that adolescents who establish an achieved identity tend to be more satisfied with themselves and with their concept of self relative to those who have not resolved the issues regarding their own ethnic-racial identity.

Peer Cluster and Social Bonding

Peer Cluster Theory (Oetting & Beauvais, 1987) is a "lifestyle theory" about youths' connections with family, school, and peers. It postulates that psychosocial factors, such as poverty, prejudice, family characteristics, and the characteristics of the community in which a youth lives, all interact with individual personality traits, needs, values, and beliefs to set the stage for illicit drug use or the avoidance of illicit drug use. By implication, the use of illicit drugs constitutes maladjustment, as it often precedes significant problems in social function (Newcomb & Bentler, 1988).

Within this context, Peer Cluster Theory proposes that a youth's connectedness or "bonding" with a specific group of adolescent peers will influence the development of adaptive or maladaptive adjustment (Oetting, 1992). Regarding this, a well-known Mexican cultural adage states, *"Dime con quien andas, y te digo quien eres,"* (Tell me with whom you associate, and I will tell you what kind of person you are). This adage underscores the influence of a person's affiliation with a certain peer or reference group on his or her identity and behaviors. Regarding social group membership and academic achievement, the achievement norms of the "peer crowd" with which a minority youth associates (e.g., "jocks," "populars," "brains," "nerds") serve as another source that strongly influences a youth's orientation to school and academic achievement (Steinberg, Dornbusch, & Brown, 1992).

Moreover, regarding the dynamics of group affiliation, membership in a group typically is governed by a balance of social forces involving the "push-pull" of two processes: (a) a youth's attraction to a given peer or reference group based on that youth's self-concept and life preferences, and (b) the reference group's acceptance of persons who conform to the group's norms and its rejection of persons who fail to conform to these norms. Moreover, the group's primary identity (e.g., drug users, athletes, religious groups, dancers) is further defined and shaped by the collective values and attitudes of its members (Oetting & Beauvais, 1987). Thus, a youth's peer involvement is initiated and maintained by that youth's loyalty to the group and by his or her conformity to the group's unique and perhaps deviant norms. For example, a youth's membership and standing in an athletic team involves conformity to that group's norms, whereas team leadership depends on performance on behaviors that are valued by the group, in this case behaviors that help the team win.

Unfortunately, rejection from a mainstream reference group may induce a strong sense of failure and lowered self-esteem for a Mexican American youth who seeks acceptance into a more established and perhaps a more prestigious "peer in-group." Rejection can communicate to the Mexican American youth that he or she is "different" or "inferior." Here, rejection may reflect the prejudicial or elitist values of members of the targeted reference group. At such times, the presence of a trustworthy person who can advise the adolescent and place the experience of rejection into perspective promotes psychological adjustment. As a Mexican American adolescent copes with challenges of adjustment and conformity to a mainstream culture, the evolving identity and the life trajectory of that youth will be shaped by the series of successful and unsuccessful efforts at membership in various reference groups within the minority and the majority cultures.

Emotional Intelligence

The concept of emotional intelligence is especially meaningful for youth from relational cultures like the Hispanic cultures. In their value system, these cultures place high value on the maintenance of strong interpersonal relationships (Gardner et al., 1993). Emotional intelligence is a meta-ability that involves the development of emotional and social competencies that are associated with successful social function. Emotional intelligence appears to operate above and beyond the influence of cognitive intelligence as measured by the IQ.

The major components of emotional intelligence are: (a) the capacity for self-control, (b) the capacity to motivate and guide one's own behavior, (c) the ability to defer gratification and to channel one's urges, and (d) the capacity for empathy and skills in listening to others and in taking another person's perspective (Goleman, 1995). These capacities are associated with strong personal character, self-discipline, and the capacity to work successfully with others. These elements of emotional intelligence parallel the five major dimensions of personality that are associated with effective leadership. These five dimensions are: (a) surgency—being assertive and socially gregarious, (b) emotional stability—being able to control and direct one's emotions, (c) conscientiousness—being responsible and hard-working, (d) agreeableness—being cooperative and good-natured, and (e) intelligence—being perceptive and capable of making sound decisions (Hogan, Curphy, & Hogan, 1994). The major components of emotional intelligence relate to the five dimensions of effective leadership in which these nine dimensions as a whole characterize a core personal competency for working effectively with people. High levels on these traits suggest a strong capacity to lead and mobilize members of a constituency and to procure resources in a manner that successfully accomplishes a specific goal that is valued by that constituency. By implication, a person with high levels of these traits would exhibit exceptional and healthy psychological adjustment, particularly as defined by that community of constituents.

Especially in relational cultures like the Hispanic cultures, exceptional skills at managing one's emotions and in motivating others to work on behalf of a group or community are important capabilities necessary for exercising strong community leadership. As an indication of the adaptive aspects of a youth's competence in working well with others, in a study involving American Indian adolescents, youth behaviors that reflect social competencies, that reflect community-mindedness, and that reflect involvement in traditional culture all identified a higher-order "positive behavior" factor (Mitchell & Beals, 1997). Given the importance of leadership development as a contemporary area of focus nationally among Hispanic community leaders, developing emotional intelligence skills among Mexican American and other Hispanic children and adolescents would appear as an emerging agenda of major importance in the educational development of Mexican American and other Hispanic youth.

Along these lines, regarding the adaptive benefits of skills for self-directed effort and for relating well with others, key elements of emotional intelligence that promote school readiness are (a) confidence—the child's belief in his or her own abilities, (b) curiosity—a child's interest in discovering new things, (c) intentionality—persistence in working toward a desired outcome, (d) self-control—the child's ability to modulate his or her actions in an age-appropriate manner, (e) relatedness—the child's ability to engage others, (f) the capacity to communicate and to share information with other children, and (g) cooperativeness—the child's ability to balance his or her needs with the needs of other children in the group (Goleman, 1995). These factors that describe "emotional literacy" as exhibited in rudimentary form among preschoolers serve as the foundation for effective scholastic and interpersonal development as children progress through school, and they appear important for continued social and academic success in adolescence.

IDENTIFYING PATTERNS OF HEALTHY ADJUSTMENT IN MEXICAN-ORIGIN ADOLESCENTS

The complex effects of the processes of acculturation and ethnic identity formation on the mental health of Mexican American and other Hispanic youth have been examined (Recio Adrados, 1993; Rogler et al., 1991). Table 6.2 presents a framework consisting of the dimensions and the skills for healthy adjustment that may occur among conventional youth and among youth who are challenged by demands from two distinct cultures. This table examines several criteria that serve as indicators of three distinct levels of function: abnormal (maladaptive), normal (adaptive), and exceptional (proficient) adjustment. The criteria on adjustment at these three levels of function are based on information from several sources (Goleman, 1995; Hawkins et al., 1992; Jessor & Jessor, 1977; Mitchell & Beals, 1997; Oetting, 1992; Phinney, 1989; Ramirez, 1991). Regarding these criteria, no child—no matter how well adjusted or maladjusted—will exhibit all of the traits of normal or abnormal development as shown in any given column of Table 6.2. However, assuming there are some shifts in these criteria due to the youth's age, in general, having a greater number of these traits increases the probability of exhibiting one of these three levels of adjustment.

For example, youth exhibiting abnormal (maladjusted) development would exhibit chronic dysphoric emotions, such as chronic anxiety, depression, or anger. They would exhibit a lack of empathic regard for others, impulsivity, a lack of future planning and problem-solving skills, and a lack of creative self-directed behavior; they would exhibit limited attachments to parents and to school and an attachment to deviant peers. These youth likely also would exhibit a lack of spiritual connectedness with a church or other culturally sanctioned spiritual group. Regarding culturally specific aspects of adjustment, abnormal Mexican American or other Hispanic youth likely would exhibit a lack of interest or dislike for their cultural heritage. They likely would exhibit an ethnic identity in the diffuse stage of development and exhibit a lack of cultural flex, a lack of interest in service to their community, and a lack of leadership skills.

By contrast, Mexican American and other Hispanic youth who exhibit normal (adaptive) development also could experience occasional dysphoria and symptomatology but would be able to cope adequately with a variety of stressors. These normal youth would exhibit some capacity for empathy; some capacity to delay gratification; the capacity for future time planning and problem solving; and sound attachments to parents, school, and peers. They also would exhibit a capacity for spiritual involvement. In addition, from a culturally specific perspective, these youth likely would express an interest in their cultural heritage, exhibit ethnic identity development in the moratorium on identity stage of ethnic identity formation, and exhibit some cultural flex, along with an interest in serving their community and in serving as a participant in leadership.

Beyond normalcy, for exceptional (proficient) adjustment, these youth may experience occasional dysphoria and symptomatology, although they also would exhibit the requisite coping skills to respond effectively to these stressors. Exceptionally adjusted Mexican American youth also would be likely to exhibit strong empathic skills, a strong capacity to delay gratification, a strong capacity to plan ahead and to engage in problem solving, and a strong interest in personal growth and creative development. It is likely that they would develop strong positive bonds with parents, school, and

Table 6.2 Dimensions of Healthy Adjustment: Some Skills and Capabilities

	Abnormal (maladaptive)	Normal (adaptive)	Exceptional (proficient)
CONVENTIONAL			
Emotionality	Frequent dysphoria and symptomatology: anxiety, depression, anger, etc.	Occasional dysphoria and symptomatology	Occasional dysphoria and symptomatology
Empathy	Lacking	Some capacity	Strong capacity
Self-Control	Impulsive	Some delay of gratification	Delays gratification
Planning	Lacking	Some	Strong skills
Problem solving	Lacking	Some	Strong skills
Creative Self-Directedness	Lack of interest in creative activities	Does some creative activities	Invests time and effort into creative activities
Attachments			
Parents	Neglect or parental rejection	Supportive attachments	Supportive attachments
School	Dislikes school	Likes school	Loves school
Peers	To deviant peers	To prosocial conventional peers	To prosocial conventional peers
Spirituality	Lacking	Some	Strong
CULTURALLY SPECIFIC			
Cultural heritage	Dislike of or lack of interest in heritage	Some interest in heritage	Strong appreciation for heritage
Ethnic identity	Diffuse stage of identity formation	Moratorium stage of identity formation	Achieved stage of identity formation
Cultural flex	No flex	Some flex	Strong flex; bicultural capabilities
Community interest	Lack of interest in service to community	Some interest	Strong interest in service to community
Leadership	Lack of leadership or antisocial behavior	Some leadership activity	Strong leadership activity

peers and a strong spiritual commitment to church or to other culturally sanctioned spiritual activities. Regarding culturally specific aspects of their development, exceptional Mexican American youth likely would exhibit a strong appreciation for their cultural heritage, ethnic identity development in the achieved identity stage, and strong cultural flex and bicultural capabilities. They likely also would exhibit a strong interest in serving their community and a strong interest in leadership.

SOME CONTEMPORARY CONCLUSIONS ON HEALTHY ADJUSTMENT IN MEXICAN AMERICAN YOUTH

In summary, healthy adolescent development among Mexican American adolescents may be regarded as a state of personal growth that primarily involves the acquisition of two types of skills: (a) skills for self-directed growth, and (b) skills to work effectively with others. From this skills perspective, and as indicated in Table 6.2, youth who live in a single cultural environment must develop a certain set of skills, whereas youth who are exposed to two or more cultural environments also must develop a broader set of skills that allow adaptive function in more than one cultural environment.

As an elaboration on Table 6.2, and from a different perspective, Table 6.3 presents a framework of skills and behaviors that would be needed for adaptive function in the Anglo-American and in the Mexican American cultures. From a skills perspective, Anglo-American youth and young adults who develop the noted skills in each of the domains (Growth and Maturation, Language, Achievement, Identity Formation, Family Relations, Social Relations, and Social Supports) in the Anglo-American column of Table 6.3 would be likely to function well and thus would be likely to succeed in the Anglo-American culture. Moreover, relative to youth and young adults who are not successful, youth and young adults who adapt successfully would be more likely to exhibit robust mental health and positive psychosocial outcomes. Some of these positive outcomes would include doing well in school; having a satisfying job or profession; and having a higher overall life satisfaction, a higher satisfaction with personal and social relations, and enhanced physical health.

Table 6.3 Skills and Behaviors for Adaptive Function in the Anglo-American and Mexican American Cultures

Skill Area	Anglo-American	Mexican American
		Behaviors
Growth and maturation	Developing individual self-directed capabilities	Relating harmoniously with family and friends
Language	English speaking and writing skills	Spanish speaking and writing skills
Achievement	Personal organization Future planning	Acculturation to Anglo-American culture via acquisition of skills for success in the mainstream culture
Identity formation	Developing capacities to discharge occupational or professional role	Developing capabilities to discharge occupational or professional role while still relating to Mexican culture and to own family
Family relations	Sound communication with parents Positive affective bonding with family	Sound communication with parents Positive affective bonding with parents Showing respect (*respeto*) for parents and elders
Social relations	Self-efficacy (confidence) in personal expression and task completion	Courteous conduct toward others in the community Genuine self in maintaining harmonious relations with other Latinos; humility relating with others (*personalismo*)
Social supports	Ability to communicate needs to others; to generate support Skills for obtaining tangible, instrumental, and affective support	Actions to maintain support from family and kin Responsiveness to family and kin rules, expectations and obligations Participation in traditional family celebrations (e.g., weddings, birthdays, baptisms, *quinceñeras*)

For each skills area under the Mexican American column, Table 6.3 presents the skills and behaviors for adaptive function in a traditional Mexican cultural environment. As evident in this comparative analysis, some distinct differences are evident regarding the specific skills and behaviors that would promote adaptive function in each of these two cultural environments. In a comparison of both cultures, clear differences are indicated on the benefits derived from skills directed at individualized self-direction; at speaking English effectively; at being organized, planful, and task-oriented—all specific skills favoring adaptive function in an Anglo-American environment. This contrasts with the benefits derived from skills involved in sensitivity to interpersonal relationships; speaking Spanish well; in being courteous, respectful, convivial, and family-oriented—skills and behaviors favoring adaptive function in a traditional Mexican cultural environment. Clearly, adolescents who participate in these two cultural environments, those evolving a bilingual-bicultural identity, are challenged to develop skills and behaviors that promote effective function in both cultural environments.

The framework presented here suggests that Mexican American youth evolving a bilingual-bicultural identity face a more complex challenge. They must negotiate successfully the demands from two distinct cultural environments by developing a broader repertoire of skills, as identified in Table 6.3. They also must be able to understand certain social and cultural cues and their nuances to respond appropriately in these two distinct cultural environments. Clearly, the challenge of developing a broader and more diverse repertoire of skills requires greater effort for Mexican American youths to become truly competent in two cultures. However, because of this, becoming truly bilingual-bicultural is expected to yield a more integrated and adaptive repertoire of personal competencies.

Despite the apparent benefits of a bilingual-bicultural identity, throughout adolescence and into adulthood, the "ethnic identity pathway" for developing an achieved bilingual-bicultural identity is also fraught with the challenges of coping with various cultural conflicts (Frable, 1997). Nevertheless, bilingual-bicultural adolescents who, with help from family and others, effectively negotiate the challenges of biculturalism may develop more robust mental health as compared with youths who have successfully negotiated conventional developmental conflicts in a single culture (Buriel et al., 1983; La Fromboise, Trimble, & Mohatt, 1990).

A significant challenge exists for bilingual-bicultural adolescents and young adults to develop broad skills and to establish a balance in the capacity to successfully negotiate the variety of aforementioned conflicts involved in coping with competing cultural expectations. Even into adulthood, this balance and the complete attainment of skills across all areas (growth and maturation, language, achievement, identity formation, etc.) are an ideal that few young persons will accomplish fully. By contrast, despite the inherent dynamic tension involved in the development of a true bicultural identity, adolescents who become more proficient bilingual-bicultural citizens would appear to be those who have coped successfully with the demands of two cultures and, in the process of coping and perhaps through adversity, have developed a unique hybrid identity, an identity characterized by a repertoire of more advanced proficiencies that reflect the healthiest levels of psychological, social, and cultural adjustment.

RESEARCH AND PREVENTION INTERVENTIONS WITH MEXICAN AMERICAN AND OTHER HISPANIC YOUTH

Future research with Mexican American and other Hispanic youth could examine various components of the framework as presented in this chapter. Such research with Mexican American youth and their families could be guided by two general questions: (a) What dimensions of healthy adjustment (both conventional and culturally specific) serve as the most important components of healthy adjustment? and (b) What skills and behaviors serve as the most important competencies for promoting healthy psychological adjustment? These questions are especially intriguing in the case of adolescents exposed from infancy to bilingual-bicultural environments and those who are developing the skills for participating in both cultural environments. What does the profile of adaptive function look like for these bilingual-bicultural youth when compared with that of the monolingual-monocultural youth?

In relation to these two research questions, future research on the adaptive adjustment of Mexican American youth could parallel the direction of research needed in the field of ethnic identity research. In that field, progressive and integrative research is needed that uses methods that allow the study of the complex interactions and multidimensional conditions that appear to operate in the development of a strong self-concept across time (Frable, 1997). To do so will require longitudinal studies that offer a process-oriented examination of various ethnic identity pathways.

Similarly, in studying the healthy adjustment of Mexican American youth, longitudinal studies using a process-oriented approach would examine youths' life trajectories as they are influenced by social pressures toward acculturation and assimilation. Here, integrative research designs that use qualitative approaches, coupled with multivariate quantitative approaches, would be useful to examine the process of identity formation as it affects psychological adjustment across time. Furthermore, the process of identity formation and psychological adjustment likely does not develop in a linear fashion. For this reason also, longitudinal designs, multivariate methods, and integrative (qualitative-quantitative) research designs (Denizen & Lincoln, 1994; Miles & Huberman, 1994) will aid in fully examining and understanding these processes and the complex relations that likely exist between ethnic identity formation, parental support, the effects of peer influences, and life aspirations, as factors that foster abnormality, normal development, or exceptional development in Mexican American and other Hispanic youth.

As an example of the competencies of the bilingual-bicultural person that may promote robust psychological health, the bilingual-bicultural person may be able to cope effectively with cultural conflicts and to reconcile apparent paradoxes, as the result of developing the capacity for cultural flex (Ramirez, 1999). With the capacity for cultural flex, these bilingual-bicultural youth may thus exhibit the capacity to be self-directed yet family-oriented, to speak English and Spanish, and to be organized for future planning yet able to relate harmoniously with family members who are present-time-oriented. Moreover, these youth may exhibit self-efficacy in completing tasks yet also relate well to traditional-conservative elders. These youth also may attain success in school yet also maintain participation in traditional family celebrations and contribute to the local community.

More research is also needed that examines a variety of cultural factors, such as traditionalism, because these factors may promote adaptive development. Future research is needed that examines the potential protective effects of ethnic pride and bilingual-bicultural skills development on youth adaptive development (Castro & Gutierres, 1997; Ramirez, 1999). Current data are suggestive of the benefits of developing bicultural competencies (Felix-Ortiz & Newcomb, 1995). However, the effects are not always positive, and it is not clearly known that bicultural competencies or strong cultural involvements are truly protective against abnormal adjustment and supportive of exceptional adjustment. By contrast, are there psychological costs or liabilities that accompany the development of a bicultural identity?

Similarly, future research should examine the multiple influences of the local community on the development of ethnic identification and pride and on adaptive adjustment. In a multilevel analysis, such research could examine the community, familial, parental, and individual factors that may promote healthy adjustment in Mexican American and other Hispanic youths. Again, a process-related perspective can improve our understanding of adaptive adjustment by offering a close analysis of the types of cultural conflict faced by various Mexican American youth and by information on the manner in which these youth resolve such conflicts and advance toward greater psychological adjustment. Much intriguing and useful work that contributes significantly to the literature on psychological adjustment can be conducted in the years to come by the study of the healthy psychological adjustment of Mexican American and other Hispanic youth.

NOTE

1. We use the term "Mexican American" in a broad sense when referring to youth of Mexican origin who represent the entire range of acculturation levels. These include youth who are native-born U.S. citizens and persons who may self-identify either as Mexican Americans or as Chicanos. These may include immigrant Mexican youth who typically would self-identify as Mexicans (*Mexicanos*). We recognize that, generally, Mexicans when they are recent immigrants to the United States tend to be unacculturated (low level of acculturation) and may self-identify as Mexicans, whereas Mexican Americans and Chicanos are typically high in level of acculturation, exhibiting some level of bilingual-bicultural traits

(medium in level of acculturation), or they may be primarily English-speaking and mainly oriented toward the mainstream culture (high acculturation).

REFERENCES

Aguirre-Molina, M., & Molina, C. (1994). Latino populations: Who are they? In C. W. Molina & M. Aguirre-Molina (Eds.), *Latino health in the US: A growing challenge* (pp. 3-22). Washington, DC: American Public Health Association.

American Psychiatric Association. (1994). *Diagnostic and statistical manual of mental disorders* (4th ed.). Washington, DC: Author.

Anglin, M. D., Booth, M. W., Ryan, T. M., & Hser, Y. (1988). Ethnic differences in narcotics addiction: II. Chicano and Anglo addiction career patterns. *International Journal of the Addictions, 23,* 1011-1027.

Baumrind, D., & Moselle, K. A. (1985). A developmental perspective on adolescent drug use. *Advances in Alcohol and Substance Use, 5,* 41-67.

Bernal, G., & Shapiro, E. (1996). Cuban families. In M. McGoldrick, J. Giordano, & J. K. Pearce (Eds.), *Ethnicity and family therapy* (2nd ed., pp. 155-168). New York: Guilford.

Berry, J. W. (1980). Acculturation as adaptation. In A. M. Padilla (Ed.), *Acculturation: Theory, models, and some new findings* (pp. 139-159). Boulder, CO: Westview.

Betances, S. (1971). Puerto Rican youth. *The Rican, 1,* 4-13.

Black, C., Paz, H., & DeBlassie, R. R. (1991). Counseling the Hispanic male adolescent. *Adolescence, 26,* 223-232.

Buriel, R., Calzada, S., & Vasquez, R. (1983). The relationship of traditional Mexican American culture to adjustment and delinquency among three generations of Mexican American male adolescents. *Hispanic Journal of Behavioral Sciences, 4,* 41-55.

Campbell, P. R. (1996). *Population projections for states by age, sex, race and Hispanic origin: 1995 to 2025* (U.S. Bureau of the Census, Population Division PPL-47). Washington, DC: U.S. Department of Commerce.

Castro, F. G. (1998). Cultural competence training in clinical psychology: Assessment, clinical intervention, and research. In A. S. Bellack & M. Hersen (Eds.), *Comprehensive clinical psychology: Sociocultural and individual differences* (Vol. 10, pp. 127-140). Elmsford, NY: Pergamon.

Castro, F. G., & Gutierres, S. (1997). Drug and alcohol use among rural Mexican Americans. In E. B. Robertson, Z. Sloboda, G. M. Boyd, L. Beatty, & N. J. Kozel (Eds.), *Rural substance abuse: State of knowledge and issues* (NIDA Research Monograph No. 168, pp. 498-533). Rockville, MD: National Institute on Drug Abuse.

Castro, F. G., Proesholdbell, R. J., Abeita, L., & Rodriguez, D. (1999). Ethnic and cultural minority groups. In B. S. McCrady & E. E. Epstein (Eds.), *Addictions: A comprehensive guidebook* (pp. 499-526). New York: Oxford University Press.

Chavez, E. L., Edwards, R., & Oetting, E. R. (1989). Mexican American and White American school dropouts' drug use, health status, and involvement in violence. *Public Health Reports, 104,* 594-604.

Dana, R. H. (1993). *Multicultural assessment perspectives for professional psychology.* Boston: Allyn & Bacon.

Del Pinal, G. (1997). *The Hispanic population.* Retrieved January 1998 from the World Wide Web: www.census.gov/population/sociodemo/race/hispanic

Denizen, N. K., & Lincoln, Y. S. (1994). *Handbook of qualitative research.* Thousand Oaks, CA: Sage.

Enchautegui, M. E. (1995). *Policy implications of Latino poverty.* Washington, DC: Urban Institute.

Falicov, C. J. (1982). Mexican families. In M. McGoldrick, J. K. Pearce, & J. Giordano (Eds.), *Ethnicity and family therapy* (pp. 134-163). New York: Guilford.

Falicov, C. J. (1996). Mexican families. In M. McGoldrick, J. Giordano, & J. K. Pearce (Eds.), *Ethnicity and family therapy* (2nd ed., pp. 169-182). New York: Guilford.

Felix-Ortiz, M., & Newcomb, M. D. (1995). Cultural identity and drug use among Latino and Latina adolescents. In G. J. Botvin, S. Schinke, & M. A. Orlandi (Eds.), *Drug abuse prevention with multiethnic youth* (pp. 147-165). Thousand Oaks, CA: Sage.

Felix-Ortiz, M., Newcomb, M. D., & Myers, H. (1994). A multidimensional measure of cultural identity for Latino and Latina adolescents. *Hispanic Journal of Behavioral Sciences, 16,* 99-115.

Frable, D. E. S. (1997). Gender, racial, ethnic, sexual, and class identities. *Annual Review of Psychology, 48,* 139-162.

Garcia-Prieto, N. (1996). Puerto Rican families. In M. McGoldrick, J. Giordano, & J. K. Pearce (Eds.), *Ethnicity and family therapy* (2nd ed., pp. 183-199). New York: Guilford.

Gardner, H. (1993). *Multiple intelligences: The theory in practice.* New York: Basic Books.

Gardner, H., Kornhaber, M., & Krechevsky, M. (1993). Engaging intelligence. In H. Gardner (Ed.), *Multiple intelligences: The theory in practice* (pp. 231-248). New York: Basic Books.

Gil, A.G., Vega, W. A., & Dimas, J. M. (1994). Acculturative stress and personal adjustment among Hispanic adolescent boys. *Journal of Community Psychology, 22,* 43-54.

Goleman, D. (1995). *Emotional intelligence.* New York: Bantam.

Gordis, L. (1996). *Epidemiology.* Philadelphia: W. B. Saunders.

Harper, A. C., & Lambert, L. J. (1994). *The health of populations: An introduction* (2nd ed.). New York: Springer.

Harwood, A. (1981). *Ethnicity and medical care.* Cambridge, MA: Harvard University Press.

Hawkins, J. D., Catalano, R. F., & Miller, J. Y. (1992). Risk and protective factors for alcohol and other drug problems in adolescence and early adulthood: Implications for substance abuse prevention. *Psychological Bulletin, 112,* 64-105.

Hogan, R., Curphy, G. J., & Hogan, J. (1994). What we know about leadership: Effectiveness and personality. *American Psychologist, 49,* 493-504.

Jessor, R. (1993). Successful adolescent development among youth in high-risk settings. *American Psychologist, 48,* 117-126.

Jessor, R., & Jessor, S. (1977). *Problem behavior and psychosocial development.* New York: Academic Press.

Kazdin, A. E. (1993). Adolescent mental health: Prevention and treatment programs. *American Psychologist, 48,* 127-141.

Keefe, S. E., Padilla, A. M., & Carlos, M. L. (1978). The Mexican American extended family as an emotional support system. In J. M. Casas & S. E. Keefe (Eds.), *Family and mental health in the Mexican American community* (pp. 49-67). Berkeley: University of California Press.

La Fromboise, T., Coleman, H. L. K., & Gerton, J. (1993). Psychological impact of biculturalism: Evidence and theory. *Psychological Bulletin, 114*, 395-412.

La Fromboise, T. D., Trimble, J. E., & Mohatt, G. V. (1990). Counseling intervention and American Indian tradition: An integrative approach. *The Counseling Psychologist, 18*, 628-654.

Locke, D. C. (1998). *Increasing multicultural understanding: A comprehensive model* (2nd ed.). Thousand Oaks, CA: Sage.

Marcia, J. (1969). Development and validation of ego-identity status. *Journal of Personality and Social Psychology, 3*, 551-558.

Marcia, J. (1980). Identity in adolescence. In J. Adelson (Ed.), *Handbook of adolescent psychology* (pp. 159-187). New York: John Wiley.

Marin, G. (1993). Influence of acculturation on familism and self-identification among Hispanics. In M. E. Bernal & G. P. Knight (Eds.), *Ethnic identity: Formation and transmission among Hispanics and other minorities* (pp. 181-196). Albany: State University of New York Press.

Marin, G., & Marin, B.V. (1991). *Research with Hispanic populations*. Newbury Park, CA: Sage.

McGoldrick, M. (1982). Ethnicity and family therapy: An overview. In M. McGoldrick, J. K. Pearce, & J. Giordano (Eds.), *Ethnicity and family therapy* (pp. 3-30). New York: Guilford.

McGoldrick, M. & Giordano, J. (1996). Overview: Ethnicity and family therapy. In M. McGoldrick, J. Giordano, & J. K. Pearce (Eds.), *Ethnicity and family therapy* (2nd ed., pp. 1-12). New York: Guilford.

Meyer, R. G. (1999). *Case studies in abnormal behavior* (4th ed.). Boston: Allyn & Bacon.

Meyer, R. G., & Osborne, Y. H. (1996). *Case studies in abnormal behavior* (3rd ed.). Boston: Allyn & Bacon.

Miles, M. B., & Huberman, A. M. (1994). *Qualitative data analysis: An expanded sourcebook* (2nd ed.). Thousand Oaks, CA: Sage.

Mitchell, C. M., & Beals, J. (1997). The structure of problem and positive behavior among American Indian adolescents: Gender and community differences. *American Journal of Community Psychology, 25*, 257-288.

Montgomery, P. A. (1994). *The Hispanic population in the United States: March 1993* (Current Population Reports, Series P20-475). Washington DC: U.S. Census Bureau.

Morales, A. (1992). Therapy with Latino gang members. In L. A. Vargas & J. D. Koss-Chiono (Eds.), *Working with culture: Psychotherapy interventions with ethnic minority children and adolescents* (pp. 129-154). San Francisco, CA: Jossey-Bass.

Moyerman, D. R., & Forman, B. D. (1992). Acculturation and adjustment: A meta-analytic study. *Hispanic Journal of Behavioral Sciences, 14*, 163-200.

Newcomb, M. D. (1995). Drug use etiology among ethnic minority adolescents. In G. J. Botvin, S. Schinke, & M. A. Orlandi (Eds.), *Drug abuse prevention with multiethnic youth.* (pp. 105-129). Thousand Oaks, CA: Sage.

Newcomb, M. D., & Bentler, P. M. (1988). *Consequences of adolescent drug use: Impact on the lives of young adults*. Newbury Park, CA: Sage.

Oetting, E. R. (1992). Planning programs for prevention of deviant behavior: A psychosocial model. *Drugs and Society, 6,* 313-344.

Oetting, E. R., & Beauvais, F. (1987). Peer Cluster Theory, socialization characteristics, and adolescent drug use: A path analysis. *Journal of Counseling Psychology, 34,* 205-213.

Oltmanns, T. F., Neale, J. M., & Davidson, G. C. (1988). *Case studies in abnormal psychology* (2nd ed.). New York: John Wiley.

Orlandi, M. A., Weston, R., & Epstein, L. G. (1992). *Cultural competence for evaluators.* Rockville, MD: Office of Substance Abuse Prevention.

Phinney, J. S. (1989). Stages of ethnic identity development in minority group adolescents. *Journal of Early Adolescence, 9,* 34-49.

Phinney, J. S. (1990). Ethnic identity in adolescents and adults: Review of research. *Psychological Bulletin, 108,* 499-514.

Phinney, J. S. (1993). A three-stage model of ethnic identity development in adolescence. In M. E. Bernal & G. P. Knight (Eds.), *Ethnic identity: Formation and transmission among Hispanics and other minorities* (pp. 61-79). Albany: State University of New York Press.

Ramirez, M. (1991). *Psychotherapy and counseling with minorities: A cognitive approach to individual and cultural differences.* Elmsford, NY: Pergamon.

Ramirez, M. (1999). *Multicultural psychotherapy: An approach to individual and cultural differences* (2nd ed.). Boston: Allyn & Bacon.

Recio Adrados, J. (1993). Acculturation: The broader view—Theoretical framework of the acculturation scales. In M. R. De la Rosa & J. L. Recio Adrados (Eds.), *Drug abuse among minority youth: Advances in research and methodology* (NIDA Research Monograph No. 130, pp. 57-78). Rockville, MD: National Institute on Drug Abuse.

Rogler, L. H., Cortes, D. E., & Malgady, R. G. (1991). Acculturation and mental health status among Hispanics: Convergence and new directions for research. *American Psychologist, 46,* 585-597.

Romo, H. D., & Falbo, T. (1996). *Latino high school graduation: Defying the odds.* Austin: University of Texas Press.

Rotheram-Borus, M. J. (1990). Adolescents' reference-group choices, self-esteem, and adjustment. *Journal of Personality and Social Psychology, 59,* 1075-1081.

Sabogal, J., Marin, G., & Otero-Sabogal, R. (1987). Hispanic familism and acculturation: What changes and what doesn't? *Hispanic Journal of Behavioral Sciences, 9,* 397-412.

Schwandt, T. A. (1994). Constructivist, interpretist approaches to American inquiry. In N. K. Denzin & Y. S. Lincoln (Eds.), *Handbook of qualitative research* (pp. 118-137). Thousand Oaks, CA: Sage.

Simpson, D. D., & Sells, S. B. (1990). *Opioid addiction and treatment: A 12-year follow-up.* Malabar, FL: Krieger.

Steinberg, L., Dornbusch, S. M., & Brown, B. B. (1992). Ethnic differences in adolescent achievement: An ecological perspective. *American Psychologist, 47,* 723-729.

Suarez-Orozco, M. M. (1997). The cultural psychology of immigration. In A. Ugalde & G. Cardenas (Eds.), *Health and social services among international labor migrants: A comparative perspective* (pp. 131-149). Austin, TX: Center for Mexican American Studies.

Szapocznik, J., & Kurtines, W. M. (1989). *Breakthroughs in family therapy with drug abusing and problem youth.* New York: Springer.

U.S. Census Bureau. (1997). *March 1994 CPS: Age of population by ethnicity.* Retrieved January 1998 from the World Wide Web: www.census.gov/population/ www.sociodemo/hispanic/html

U.S. Census Bureau. (1999). Retrieved December, 1999 from the World Wide Web: www.census.gov/population/estimates/nation/intfile3-1.txt

U.S. Department of Commerce. (1993). *We the American . . . Hispanics.* Washington, DC: Author.

Vega, W.A. (1990). Hispanic families in the 1980s: A decade of research. *Journal of Marriage and the Family, 52,* 1015-1024.

Vega, W. A., Zimmerman, R. S., Warheit, G. J., Apospori, E., & Gil, A. G. (1993). Risk factors for early adolescent drug use in four ethnic and racial groups. *American Journal of Public Health, 83,* 185-189.

Wilson, G. T., Nathan, P. E., O'Leary, K. D., & Clark, L. A. (1996). *Abnormal psychology: Integrating perspectives.* Boston: Allyn & Bacon.

Yee, B. W. K., Castro, F. G., Hammond, W. R., John, R., Wyatt, G. E., & Yung, B. R. (1995). Panel IV: Risk taking and abusive behaviors among ethnic minorities. *Health Psychology, 14,* 622-631.

7. Asian American Adolescents: A Research Review to Dispel the Model Minority Myth

Frederick T. L. Leong
Ruth K. Chao
Erin E. Hardin

Between 1980 and 1990, Asian Americans, including Pacific Islanders, were the fastest-growing ethnic minority group in the United
States, growing at a rate of 95%, nearly double that of Hispanic
Americans, the next fastest-growing group, more than triple that of
Native American, Eskimo, and Aleuts, and more than seven times
the growth rate of African Americans. According to a projection by
the U.S. Department of Commerce, the number of Asian Americans
will grow from 7 million to more than 40 million by the year 2050
(Gall & Gall, 1993). In addition, there is a larger proportion of adolescents among Asian Americans. According to the 1991 current population reports, adolescents 15 to 19 years of age constituted 6.8% of
the total U.S. population but constituted 8.3% of the Asian American
Pacific Islander population (Gall & Gall, 1993). This fact, combined
with the rapid growth rate of the Asian American population, indicates that research on the development of Asian American adolescents is becoming especially crucial.

DISPELLING THE
MODEL MINORITY MYTH

More than 25 years ago, Kitano and Sue (1973) introduced the concept of Asian Americans as the "model minority" to the social sciences in the *Journal of Social Issues*. In the introduction to the special

issue on Asian Americans, the authors noted that Asian Americans are perceived as a nonoppressed minority and therefore are overlooked in terms of research attention and aid. Implicit in the view of Asian Americans as model minorities who have overcome prejudice and oppression is the idea that the lack of success in other minority groups stems from their own personal shortcomings or lack of hard work, rather than from the shortcomings of society.

Kitano and Sue (1973) noted the relative lack of research on Asian Americans, stemming from lack of interest in this group and difficulty in obtaining adequate samples, especially of nonstudent populations. The authors also noted that although Asians have made strides in American society, they continue to face more subtle forms of prejudice and discrimination, along with higher expectations for success. In an article in the special issue, Sue and Kitano (1973) traced the historical development of different stereotypes of Asian Americans that eventually ended up in the stereotype of Asian Americans as the model minority. However, as pointed out by many scholars and researchers (e.g., Kitano & Sue, 1973; Sue & Kitano, 1973; Takaki, 1989) this notion of Asian Americans being the successful model minority is inaccurate and misleading.

This characterization of Asian Americans has come to be referred to as the "model minority myth," in which Asian Americans are stereotyped as the most successful minority who have so effectively adapted to life in the United States. This myth ignores the bimodal distribution in many Asian American communities where there are successful Asian Americans as well as Asian Americans living at the poverty level and working in "sweat shops." It also overlooks the distribution of severe mental illnesses and major adjustment difficulties among many Asian Americans.

The perpetuation of this model minority myth, as opposed to a realistic portrait of the Asian American community, creates many additional problems: (a) It pits Asian Americans against other ethnic minority groups, (b) it presents a false and inaccurate picture of the economic and social success of Asian Americans as more pervasive than it really is, (c) it sets up unrealistic expectations and standards for Asian Americans who have to live up to this image of the "Super Minority" (Ramirez, 1986), (d) it discourages researchers from studying the problems and adjustment difficulties of Asian Americans because funding agencies are more likely to pay for research on the more disadvantaged minorities, and (e) it encourages policy-makers to overlook the special needs and concerns of Asian Americans in terms of funding and distribution of resources.

The purpose of this chapter is to dispel the model minority myth by providing a critical review of the research and emerging theoretical issues related to the development of Asian American adolescents. By countering the model minority myth, this review presents a more realistic and accurate portrait of Asian American adolescents. To achieve this goal, we organized the chapter into three sections representing the three major areas of research most applicable to the model minority myth evident in the literature. These areas are: (a) academic achievement, (b) ethnic identity, and (c) psychological adjustment. In each of these areas, we present a more realistic and complex picture of the Asian American adolescent than is currently available due to the model minority myth, which seems to have currency even among social scientists due to its pervasiveness (e.g., see Takaki, 1989).

ACADEMIC ACHIEVEMENT OF ASIAN AMERICAN ADOLESCENTS

One of the most enduring features of the model minority stereotype is the notion that Asian Americans do better academically than other racial and ethnic groups in the United States. Interview (Lee, 1994, 1996; Matute-Bianchi, 1986) and empirical (Kao, 1995) data show that, more often than other students, Asian American youth are viewed as good students by peers and teachers. Moreover, Asian American youth are aware of being judged by this stereotype. As a group, Asian Americans do, indeed, have higher grade point averages (e.g., Kao, 1995), SAT-math scores (e.g., Reglin & Adams, 1990), and general achievement scores (e.g., Peng & Wright, 1994) than do all other groups in the United States. Even after accounting for differences due to parents' level of education and socioeconomic status (SES), Asian American adolescents outperform their peers (e.g., Kao, 1995).

An obvious question, then, is what leads to these differences in academic achievement between Asian American adolescents and other groups. Several different theoretical perspectives have been invoked to explain the high achievement of this group. Some focus on cultural differences, whereas others look more broadly to the social context and speculate on how Asian Americans' minority status may influence achievement. Guided by these theories, empirical research has focused on differences in educational values, attainment, and aspirations; effort and time use; and parental involvement to explain the patterns of achievement observed among Asian American adolescents. Nearly all this research, however, has perpetuated the model minority stereotype by focusing only on explanations for high achievement. Low-achieving Asian American adolescents are absent in most of the literature, as are discussions of the implications of this stereotype for all Asian American adolescents.

Theories of Success

In the 1980s, when popular magazines throughout the United States were portraying Asian American students as "whiz kids" ("The New Whiz Kids," 1987), researchers tended to focus on cultural differences in attempting to explain the differences in achievement. The cultural explanation attributes the academic success of Asian Americans to "Asian" values and characteristics, such as highly valuing education and inducing guilt over parental sacrifices (see Sue & Okazaki, 1990, for a discussion of the cultural explanation). Some researchers have attributed Asian American academic success partially to family structure. For example, children from intact families tend to do better in school, and Asian Americans are more likely to come from intact families (Kao, 1995). Schneider & Lee (1990) also suggested that "the quiet, industrious, disciplined, and orderly behaviors emphasized in East Asian cultures are rewarded at school" (p. 374). Although these attributions often may be valid, the cultural explanation is limited because it largely ignores environmental factors. For example, attributing academic achievement solely to Asian cultural values fails to explain the occurrence of low achievement among students in Asian countries, where Asian values are presumably strongest (Lee, 1996).

Theories combining cultural and environmental factors are potentially more explanatory. To account for differences in achievement among minority groups in the United States, Ogbu (1987, 1989) distinguished between voluntary and involuntary minorities. Unlike most other minorities, who historically became part of the United States through slavery (e.g., African Americans) or colonization (e.g., Native Americans), Asian Americans are voluntary minorities because they chose to come to this country and therefore perceive themselves as guests. Although both types of minorities face discrimination, Ogbu argued that voluntary minorities, who perceive themselves as guests, are willing to "play by the rules" of the host society. Because education is a respected avenue to success in White, middle-class society, Asian Americans see education as a way to overcome prejudice and achieve success. On the other hand, involuntary minorities expect discrimination and limited opportunities regardless of their education, perceive the school system as a tool of White middle-class society, and therefore reject education as a route to success. This so-called cultural-ecological theory accounts well for differences in academic achievement between Asian Americans and other minorities, but it does not explain as well the superior achievement of Asian Americans compared to Whites.

One explanation is provided by Sue and Okazaki's (1990) theory of relative functionalism. They argued that Asian Americans experience and perceive limited mobility in many areas, especially those in which success does not rely heavily on education, such as sports, politics, and entertainment. Asian Americans thus see education as the only route to success. Consistent with this hypothesis, Asian American students and their parents believe more strongly than do others in the value of education and its importance for getting a good job (Steinberg, Dornbusch, & Brown, 1992). Asian American adolescents also tend to hold significantly higher standards for acceptable grades and achievement than do their White peers (Chen & Stevenson, 1995; Huang & Waxman, 1995).

Consistent with Sue and Okazaki's (1990) relative functionalism hypothesis, Asian Americans as adults are overrepresented in education-dependent math and science occupations (Hsia, 1988). Asian American parents and students, as well as their teachers, reported in interviews that Asian Americans are better suited for jobs that do not emphasize language skills (Lee, 1994, 1996; Schneider & Lee, 1990). One student interviewed, for example, "explained that his mother had counseled him against a career that would require public speaking because he has a Chinese accent. Thus, while [he] would like to be a lawyer or politician, he says that he plans to be an engineer" (Lee, 1994, p. 419). The student's mother felt that a career in law, which depends not only on educational achievement but also on speaking skills, was not open to him. She encouraged him to focus his efforts on a more education-dependent

career, engineering, in which she felt he had more chances for success. "Education is increasingly functional as a means for mobility
when other avenues are blocked" (Sue & Okazaki, 1990, p. 917).
Because Asian Americans likely perceive school as relatively more
functional than do other groups, this theory argues, they perform
better in school.

Educational Aspirations and Attainment

To the extent that Asian Americans perceive education as more
functional than do others, one would expect Asian Americans to
have higher educational aspirations and to be more educated.
Empirical evidence is consistent with these expectations. Kao (1995)
used data from the National Education Longitudinal Study of 1988
(NELS:88), a national sample of 24,599 eighth graders, including
1,527 Asians. She reported that 43% of Asian American students
aspired to postgraduate education, compared to 25% of White
students. For both groups, the students' own goals were similar to
those their parents had for them: 47% of Asian American parents
wanted their children to pursue postgraduate education, as opposed
to 20% of White parents. Kao examined within-group differences
by comparing eight Asian subgroups: Chinese, Filipino, Japanese,
Korean, Southeast Asian (Vietnamese, Laotian, etc.), Pacific Islander
(Samoan, Guamanian, etc.), South Asian (Indian, Pakistani, etc.),
and West Asian (Iranian, Turkish, etc.). Asian American parents and
students of all eight subgroups had significantly higher educational aspirations than did their White counterparts.

Given these high goals, it is not surprising that Asian Americans
are in fact more educated than are other groups. Kao (1995) and
Peng and Wright (1994), using the NELS:88 data, found that, on
average, Asian American parents were significantly more educated
than White parents. Six of the eight subgroups examined by Kao
(1995) had higher mean educational levels than did Whites; Pacific
Islander parents had comparable levels, and Southeast Asian parents had significantly lower levels. Kao suggested the latter finding
is likely due to the more recent immigration of Southeast Asians
compared to other Asian groups.

Obviously, Asian Americans' superior educational achievement,
aspirations, and attainment are well established. The cultural explanation theory, Ogbu's (1987, 1989) cultural-ecological theory, and

Sue and Okazaki's (1990) relative functionalism theory have all been offered to explain these differences. However, the question of what day-to-day factors actually lead to these differences remains. Numerous researchers have investigated specific behavioral and environmental factors that may contribute to the differential academic success of Asian American adolescents.

Factors Contributing to Success

Effort and time use. Asian American high school students are more likely than are Whites to attribute academic success to effort than to ability (Chen & Stevenson, 1995). Consistent with this belief in effort and their educational goals, Asian Americans work harder at academics than do other students. Asian American youth spend more time studying (Chen & Stevenson, 1995; Huang & Waxman, 1995). According to one report, Asian American 11th graders studied for nearly 20 hours a week, whereas Whites studied for only about 14 hours (Chen & Stevenson, 1995). Asian Americans also tend to spend more time in educational activities such as private tutoring and music lessons (Kao, 1995; Peng & Wright, 1994).

Not surprisingly, Asian American adolescents spend less time on nonacademic activities. For instance, they are less likely than White students to date or hold part-time jobs (Chen & Stevenson, 1995; Reglin & Adams, 1990). Asian American parents also encourage their children to focus on school. They are more likely than White parents to limit time spent watching television and to have rules about maintaining grades (Kao, 1995), and they are less likely to have rules about performing household chores (Kao, 1995; Lee, 1994, 1996). As one middle school student explained, "My parents . . . are happiest when I study a lot. That's the only thing they want me to do" (Schneider & Lee, 1990, p. 37).

Parental involvement. Schneider and Lee (1990) found that more Asian American parents had tutored their sixth- and seventh-grade children when they were in preschool and the elementary grades. Nearly 60% of the Asian parents, but only 16% of the White parents, reported having taught their children basic math, reading, and writing skills before kindergarten. Moreover, 80% of the Asian parents had given their children homework during the primary grades when homework was usually not assigned; only 13% of the White parents had provided such extra work.

Surprisingly, Asian American parents are less likely than other parents to be involved in their children's later schooling (Kao, 1995; Steinberg et al., 1992). For example, 38% of the Asian high school students in the sample of Reglin and Adams (1990) said their parents showed "no interest" in their homework, compared to only 3% of the non-Asian students. However, another study found that Asian American middle school students reported significantly higher levels of parental praise and support than White students (Pang, 1991).

Kao (1995) reported evidence for the greater commitment to education shown by Asian American than White parents. Although average incomes were comparable for the two groups, Asian American parents were more likely to have started saving money for college. Of those parents who had begun saving, Asian American parents had saved more and planned to save more by the time their children graduated from high school than had White parents. Although more White students had their own room, more Asian American students had their own place to study. Asian Americans also were more likely than Whites to have a personal computer in their home. Filipinos, having an average income comparable to that of Whites, were the only subgroup that was not more likely to have a computer; Southeast Asians, whose average income was less than two thirds that of Whites, were still more likely to have a computer.

When these factors are considered, differences in achievement between Asian Americans and other groups are reduced or eliminated. For example, when Chen and Stevenson (1995) accounted for time use (e.g., holding a part-time job), attitudes toward mathematics, and perceived value of education, mathematics achievement between Asian American and Caucasian American students was comparable. Similarly, Kao (1995) found that when differences due to level of educational aspiration were accounted for, math test scores differed only among those with the highest aspirations. In another analysis, she found SES, household structure, and resources accounted for differences in math and reading test scores. In other words, regardless of race, students who have high aspirations; work hard at school; have parents who value education; and have sufficient resources, such as their own place to study, do better in school. As a group, Asian Americans are more likely to have these behaviors, values, and resources, which likely explains their higher achievement.

This consistently high level of achievement among Asian Americans as a group is perhaps the most striking feature of the model minority stereotype, and it is, most would argue, positive. Although the outcome may indeed be positive, we must consider the motivation. If Asian American adolescents are excelling in school because they fear it is their only hope for success in a discriminatory society, or if they are sacrificing pursuit of their true interests because they believe their opportunities are limited, the model minority image cannot be seen as positive.

The model minority stereotype characterizes all Asian Americans as successful superachievers. Although many Asian American adolescents do exhibit very high levels of academic achievement, there are certainly many who do not. In her ethnographic study of high school students, Lee (1994, 1996) found that Asian American students with average achievement reported being made to feel as if their performance was actually low because they were not meeting model minority expectations. Below-average students were reluctant to seek help for academic problems because they felt ashamed for not living up to the stereotype's standards; their academic performance likely suffered even further. Even high-performing Asian Americans felt pressure to live up to the model minority stereotype, as seen in one student's words:

> I used to go into classes, and if you don't do that well in math or science, the teacher is like, "What are you? Some kind of mutant Asian? You don't do well in math." . . . I also find that a lot of my friends become upset if they're not good students. . . . I don't think it's right for them to have to feel defensive. . . . And for people who are doing well, it's just like, "Oh, they (Asians) didn't have to work for it. . . . They're just made that way." (Lee, 1994, p. 426)

These statements indicate that the model minority stereotype leads many to believe that academic achievement is somehow part of an Asian American adolescent's ethnic identity. Students who do not achieve at expected levels may be seen, in this student's words, as "mutant Asians." Although it may seem absurd that low academic achievement would make one "less" Asian, Asian American students in several studies (e.g., Lee, 1994, 1996; Matute-Bianchi, 1986) felt that the model minority stereotype affected the development and stability of their ethnic identities.

ETHNIC IDENTITY OF
ASIAN AMERICAN ADOLESCENTS

The study of ethnic identity for Asian American adolescents also provides some compelling evidence for questioning the model minority myth. Contrary to the stereotype of Asian Americans as successfully and easily assimilated into American society, many Asian American adolescents seem to face great difficulties or challenges with their ethnic identity. These challenges involve both the developmental progression of their identity and their patterns of acculturation and adaptation to the larger dominant culture.

Based on these two areas of challenge (developmental progression and acculturation), two theoretical approaches to the study of Asian Americans' ethnic identity are prominent: ethnic identity formation theory and acculturation theory. The following review of the research on ethnic identity is organized around these two theoretical approaches. The first approach, ethnic identity formation theory, has a more developmental focus, in that it looks at individual change and originally was based on ego identity formation theories. The second approach, acculturation theory, is a more conflict-based perspective that assumes that two cultural groups in continuous contact with one another necessarily lead to changes in the cultural values, attitudes, and behaviors of their members. Of particular concern for this perspective is the extent to which ethnic identity is maintained when an ethnic minority group is in continuous contact with the dominant group. The relation between ethnic identity and psychological adjustment and self-esteem, addressed in the last part of this section, more specifically conveys the challenges Asian American adolescents experience regarding their ethnic identification.

Ethnic Identity Formation

The formation of ethnic identity generally is regarded as a process that is similar to ego identity formation. Marcia (1966) derived four ego identity statuses based on Erikson's (1968) theories of adolescence as a period of exploration and experimentation that eventually leads to decision making and commitment. The first status involves an individual who has not engaged in exploration nor made a commitment and so is said to be "diffuse." An individual who has made a commitment but without engaging in exploration is said to be in the "foreclosed" status, whereas an individual who is in the process of exploration but has not made a commitment is in the "moratorium" status. Finally, an individual who has both completed an exploration process and also has made a commitment is in the "achieved" status.

Phinney (1990) proposed a three-stage progression of ethnic identity formation that reflects Marcia's (1966) ego identity statuses: an unexamined ethnic identity phase, an exploration phase, and, finally, commitment to an ethnic identity. Phinney holds that the diffused and foreclosed statuses from Marcia are similar to each other. With foreclosure, individuals either have accepted the ethnic attitudes or identification of their parents or they have accepted the majority culture's values and attitudes, whereas in the diffuse status, the adolescent may not have been exposed to ethnic identity issues. In both the diffuse and foreclosed states, the adolescent has not examined his or her ethnic identity and is therefore in Phinney's "unexamined" first stage. In the second stage, similar to Marcia's moratorium stage, individuals begin exploring their ethnic identity. This exploration may be triggered by a significant "awakening" experience around their ethnicity that often is followed by an "intense process of immersion in one's own culture through activities such as reading, talking to people, going to ethnic museums, and participating actively in cultural events" (pp. 502-503). Through this process, Phinney argued, individuals come to a deeper understanding of what their ethnic identity means to them. This culminates in the third stage of ethnic identity development, the achievement or internalization of ethnic identity.

Findings for Asian Americans: Comparisons across ethnic groups. In cross-minority group comparisons of 10th-grade students, Phinney (1989) found that the percentages of other ethnic groups in each stage were quite similar to the percentages of Asian Americans— 57.1% in the diffused-foreclosed stage, 21.4% in the moratorium stage, and 21.4% in the achieved stage. In other studies, Asian Americans were also similar to other minority adolescents in their ethnic identity achievement (i.e., whether they have made an ethnic identity decision or commitment), although they were less involved in ethnic identity exploration than were Blacks or Mexican Americans (Phinney & Alipuria, 1990; Phinney, Chavira, & Williamson, 1992). Asian Americans also were more identified with American ideals than were African Americans, but not more than Latinos or Whites (Phinney et al., 1992). Thus, Asian American adolescents appear to come to some final decision making or commitment regarding their ethnic identity, although they may differ from other minority groups in terms of greater acceptance of the dominant group.

A stage model specific to Asian Americans. Atkinson, Morten, & Sue (1983) developed a model of ethnic identity formation specific to Asian Americans that is based on clinical experience. This model is also a stage theory framework, in that there is a sequential progression in which individuals experience specific conflicts that must be resolved to move to the next stage. The first stage involves the notion of conformity; the second stage involves dissonance, confusion, and conflict over the dominant culture's system and an awareness of one's own cultural system; then a resistance and immersion period is followed by a period of introspection or questioning of both the minority and majority cultures; finally, individuals achieve a synergy of articulation and awareness that involves the resolution of conflicts in previous stages and the development of a cultural identity. This complex sequence, based on clinical experience with Asian Americans, emphasizes the many conflicts experienced as the adolescents negotiated the development of their ethnic identity. Clearly, ethnic identity development is not an easy process for many Asian Americans, contrary to the model minority image of Asian Americans as easily adjusted to American society.

Although this model differs from other stage models by being specifically applicable to Asian Americans and by focusing more on conflict, emphasis on stage theories for capturing ethnic identity formation has fallen under heavy criticism by some researchers as being too linear and not recognizing the multidimensional nature of ethnic identity (Phinney, 1990; Yeh & Huang, 1996).

Biculturalism and Acculturation Theory

The second theoretical framework, acculturation theory, is similar to Atkinson et al.'s (1983) theory in its emphasis on a conflict model of ethnic identity. Both theories assume there will be an apparent conflict for ethnic minorities because of being part of two different cultural systems—the minority group to which they belong and the majority or dominant group. According to some other conflict-based theories (e.g., social identity theory; see Phinney, 1990), members of low-status groups often seek to improve their status by leaving their own group to pass as members of the dominant group. However, other researchers have argued that much of the research relying on social identity theories has been rather myopic and ethnocentric, in that it has failed to recognize other strategies adopted by minority group members.

Acculturation theory assumes cultural conflict based on the notion of "cultural contact," that is, when two or more groups are in contact with one another, potential acculturative changes involving cultural attitudes, values, and behavior naturally occur. Phinney (1990) pointed out that although the terms "ethnic identity" and "acculturation" are often used synonymously, ethnic identity is an aspect of acculturation that is concerned with how individuals feel about or relate to their own ethnic group as part of the larger majority or dominant society. Acculturation theory, then, is concerned with the extent to which ethnic identity is maintained when an ethnic group is in continuous contact with the dominant group.

Previously, these acculturative changes were recognized as falling on only one continuum, involving identification with the ethnic group at one end and identification with the dominant group at the other (Phinney, 1990). More recently, however, there is the recognition of these identifications as separate aspects, so that an individual can be both ethnically identified as well as identified or acculturated with the dominant group. Individuals with this dual identification are labeled "bicultural." Based on this two-dimensional model, then, there would be three other possibilities besides the bicultural identity: "assimilated," when identification with the dominant group is strong but identification with the ethnic group is weak; "ethnically identified," when identification with the ethnic group is strong but identification with the dominant group is weak; or "marginal," the last possibility, when identification with both groups is weak.

Other categorizations based on acculturation theory have been developed for Asian Americans, such as Sue and Sue's (1971) three distinctions: traditionalist, marginalist, and Asian American. Traditionalists are individuals who typically are foreign-born or first-generation immigrants who prize the cultural values of their parents and socialize only with members of their ethnic group. A marginalist, on the other hand, rejects Asian values in favor of assimilating into American culture. These individuals typically only associate with Whites. The third group, those labeled "Asian American," have achieved a balance in their identity by feeling pride in their ethnic group while at the same time combining the values of the dominant group.

Across-group comparisons by ethnic group and generation of immigration. The research does not appear to be very conclusive regarding the ethnic identifications of Asian American adolescents in comparison with other ethnic minorities. Asian American adolescents tended to identify themselves as "assimilated" more often than did other ethnic minority groups, but they were not different from other ethnic minority groups in the identifications involving "bicultural" or "strongly ethnic" (Phinney et al., 1992; Rotheram-Borus, 1990).

Phinney's (1990) review of generational differences in ethnic identity emphasized a general decline in ethnic group identification in later generations. Interestingly, the studies Phinney cited that contradicted this trend all involved Asian Americans. For instance, Wooden, Leon, and Toshima (1988) found no differences in ethnic identifications among 112 sansei and yonsei (i.e., third- and fourth-generation, respectively) Japanese American adolescents. In another study by Rosenthal and Feldman (1992a) involving first- and second-generation Chinese adolescents in the United States and Australia, the authors found that in both countries, first-generation Chinese were different from second-generation in ethnic identification and engagement and knowledge of ethnic practices, but not in terms of the importance of maintaining these practices and the value ascribed to their ethnic origin. In reference to another study of Chinese Americans by Ting-Toomey (1981), Phinney (1990) pointed out that change in ethnic identity may involve a more "cyclical process," whereby ethnicity becomes more important, especially by the third- or fourth-generation descendants of immigrants.

In two other studies, Feldman and Rosenthal and their colleagues found that acculturation occurred very slowly and differed across domains at different rates and times (Feldman, Mont-Reynaud, & Rosenthal, 1992; Feldman & Rosenthal, 1990). Feldman and Rosenthal (1990) examined the acculturation of autonomy expectations among Chinese high school students residing in Hong Kong, the United States, and Australia. Acculturation did not occur evenly and equally for all domains of autonomy. For example, the first- and second-generation Chinese had age expectations for certain activities, such as heterosexual dating behaviors and more deviant behaviors, that were more similar to those of their Hong Kong Chinese counterparts, whereas expectations for other behaviors, such as staying home alone when sick and choosing which TV programs to watch, were more similar to their White counterparts. The areas in which acculturation was more evident may have been related to the changed living situations and the parents allowing the adolescents to partake in valued Western culture. Reasons for the areas of slower acculturation are probably associated with fewer peer relationships among the Chinese students.

In the other study of acculturation among Asian American adolescents, Feldman et al. (1992) examined the extent to which there is acculturation of values across two generations of Chinese youth in the United States and Australia. Using the same seven groups of participants as the previous study (i.e., first- and second-generation Chinese Americans and Chinese Australians, native-born Hong Kong Chinese, and White Americans and Australians), acculturation of values was evident. The largest acculturative differences were found between Hong Kong and first-generation youth. First-generation Chinese living in the West differed from their Hong Kong counterparts in that they placed less value on tradition and the family as a unit and more value on success. There were modest differences between the first- and the second-generation Chinese, with first-generation youth placing slightly more value on the importance of the family as a residential unit.

Ethnic Identity and Psychological Adjustment

Ethnic identification and relation to self-esteem. Research on ethnic-minority adolescents is beginning to find links between ethnic identification and levels of self-esteem. Key questions regarding ethnic identity revolve around whether being more ethnically identified is related to better psychological adjustment and self-esteem or if it is possible to hold negative views about one's ethnic group and yet still have a strong self-esteem. In Phinney's (1990) review, three of the studies suggested positive effects with stronger ethnic identification, and an additional four revealed no relation to various measures of adjustment. A number of the studies were conducted with Blacks, a few with Mexican Americans, and others with ethnic Whites. In a more recent study that included Asian Americans, degree of ethnic identification was positively related to self-esteem for their sample overall, but for Asian Americans only, it was not related to self-esteem (Phinney, DuPont, Espinosa, Revill, & Sanders, 1994).

Stage model framework and relation to self-esteem. Other studies examined self-esteem in relation to the stage model of ethnic identity. Phinney and her colleagues (Phinney & Alipuria, 1990; Phinney & Chavira, 1992) found that in the overall samples, those in the last stage of achieved ethnic identity appear to have higher self-esteem and self-concept than those in other statuses. Furthermore, this relation seems to hold up over time, with achieved identity predicting self-esteem 3 years later. In studies that provided analyses by ethnic group, for Asian Americans there was no relation between the search or moratorium stage and self-esteem, but the achieved stage was positively and significantly related to self-esteem. However, in additional analyses looking at gender differences among Asian Americans, this relation was significant only among Asian American males and not females (Phinney & Alipuria, 1990). Studies that have looked at both ethnic and gender differences in global self-esteem (e.g., Rosenberg's Self-Esteem Scale, 1965) report that Asian American females score the lowest of any of the ethnic-gender groups (Dukes & Martinez, 1994; Martinez & Dukes, 1991). Perhaps evaluations of the self involving global qualities are problematic for Asian Americans, particularly for females, in that they are more self-effacing.

Conflicts with ethnic identity among Asian American adolescents. In explaining some of the potential identity conflicts for Asian Americans, Spencer and Markstrom-Adams (1990) described a pattern of possible "identification with the aggressor," consistent with social identity theory, that may be associated with the high out-group marriage rate of some Asian American groups such as the Japanese. Although this may represent a rather extreme interpretation of the assimilation pattern of Asian Americans, a number of studies seem to indicate that Asian American adolescents may experience more conflicting attitudes and feelings around their ethnic identification than other minority groups. Rotheram-Borus (1990) found Asian American high school students, in contrast to Blacks and Hispanics, reported significantly less ethnic pride.

Asian Americans also reported significantly less cross-ethnic contact than did other groups, associating more with their own ethnic group (Rosenthal & Feldman, 1992b; Rotheram-Borus, 1990). In a study assessing satisfaction with their own ethnicity, Phinney (1989) found that significantly more Asian Americans said they would prefer to be White than did Blacks or Hispanics. However, in a study looking at the impact of parenting style on ethnic pride, such pride was positively predicted among Chinese high school students in the United States and Canada by parental warmth, control, and autonomy-promoting (Rosenthal & Feldman, 1992b). This additional parental or familial support may be necessary for Asian American adolescents to develop a positive sense of their ethnic identity, because adolescents seem to perceive their own ethnic group as lacking a political presence or as having less power than other groups (Rotheram-Borus, 1990).

Asian Americans also had different perceptions regarding the issues important to the resolution of their ethnic identity. They were more concerned about the pressures to achieve in school, especially related to the quotas set by colleges that create more difficulty for them to get into a good college. According to Spencer and Markstrom-Adams (1990), and consistent with the previous review, Asian Americans typically have supported an assimilation pattern that heavily emphasizes "the academic prowess of its youth, which may be accompanied by significant stress" (p. 302).

PSYCHOLOGICAL ADJUSTMENT AMONG ASIAN AMERICAN ADOLESCENTS

One of the negative consequences of the model minority myth is the creation of a parallel myth that all or most Asian Americans are psychologically well adjusted and free from mental health problems because they are so successful in the United States. As the research summarized previously indicates, this is not true. Asian American adolescents experience conflict in resolving their ethnic identities and stress from trying to meet academic expectations. They tend to have less pride in their ethnic group than other minority adolescents, and Asian American females have exhibited lower self-esteem than any other group. Research on adult samples of Asian Americans has demonstrated that Asian Americans have the same and sometimes higher levels of mental health problems relative to adult White European Americans (e.g., see Sue & Morishima, 1982; Uba, 1994).

In this section of the chapter, we review articles related to the mental health and psychological adjustment of Asian American adolescents to dispel these myths. Instead of assuming that Asian Americans have few or no mental health problems, we examine two main questions that often are raised by this literature: (a) Do Asian American adolescents experience the same rate of mental health problems as do White American adolescents? and (b) Do Asian American adolescents experience any unique psychological adjustment issues or mental health problems due to their cultural differences?

Nature and Type of Psychological
Adjustment Problems

Regarding the two questions, Chang, Morrisey, and Koplewicz (1995) examined the prevalence of psychiatric symptoms among Chinese American youth in relation to their psychological adjustment. They used Achenbach's (1981) Child Behavior Checklist (CBCL) to estimate the prevalence of different symptomatology and determine the impact of acculturation on these symptoms. They pointed out that this was a significant question, because Chinese Americans have been shown to underuse mental health services, and it is unknown whether this reflects less psychopathology among Chinese Americans or just an avoidance of mental health services. A Chinese version of the CBCL and a 10-item questionnaire on education, occupation, years in the United States, adjustment, and ethnic patterns of socialization were completed by a parent or guardian of Chinese American children attending a Chinese school in New York City. The children had a mean age of 11.2 years, with a range of age 5 to age 17. Forty-one percent were boys. Fifty-one percent of the respondents were mothers, 38% fathers, and 11% were other family members. The results from this sample were compared to American CBCL norms.

It was found that the Chinese American children's total problem, internalizing, externalizing, total competence, activities, and social scores were lower than American norms across both different age and gender groupings. As with existing studies, favorable adjustment, as rated by parents, was correlated significantly with lower total problem and internalizing scores for the Chinese American sample. Recent immigrants (6%) did not have higher symptom scores. Using a crude operationalization of acculturation (i.e., father's and mother's occupation and child's number of years in the United States), no significant relation was found between acculturation and adjustment. However, extrapolating from the cross-sectional data, it appears as if girls can adjust better over time than boys in the United States.

The authors also compared the data to norms from China. They found no significant differences in total problem, internalizing, or externalizing scores between the Chinese American children and the Chinese norm groups. On the other hand, the Chinese American boys, as compared to the Chinese norm group, did score significantly higher on the withdrawn, anxious-depressed, thought problems, aggressive behavior, and social problems scales. The authors interpreted these findings to reflect the higher expectations of the Chinese American parents for their children to maintain a cultural identity and traditional Chinese values and customs.

It appears that there is some cross-cultural generalizability to Achenbach's (1981) model and assessment of adjustment problems, because Chinese American children with higher scores on the CBCL were found to have more adjustment difficulties. The other major finding, that Chinese American children have lower scores than the norm group, needs to be interpreted with more caution. The authors observed that the lower scores of the Chinese American children may be due to temperamental differences, underreporting by the respondents, or cultural intolerance of misbehavior. This interpretation highlights the important issue of cultural validity in assessment of mental health problems for Asian American adolescents. Finally, the authors cautioned against overgeneralizing the findings, because the survey was not conducted among randomly selected students from various schools representing different demographics, varied adjustment levels, or years of acculturation.

In a second study on psychiatric problems, Kim and Chun (1993) examined ethnic differences in psychiatric diagnosis among Asian

American adolescents. The authors pointed out that even as children's mental health has become a more prominent issue in the nation's policy agenda, very little is known about the distribution of mental health problems among ethnic-minority children, especially Asian Americans. According to Kim and Chun, previous research has indicated that Asian American adolescents tended to underuse community mental health services, probably because of the differences in accessibility to appropriate resources, language proficiency, culture, and attitudes toward mental health problems and treatment. These contextual differences also may be reflected in the types of mental problems of Asian and Caucasian adolescents. The purpose of their study was to examine the racial differences between Asian and Caucasian adolescents and the ethnic differences among Asian groups in psychiatric diagnosis. Gender differences were also to be examined.

The authors used an archival data set from the Los Angeles County Department of Mental Health representing data collected between 1983 and 1988 by trained therapists and professionals using the third edition of the *Diagnostic and Statistical Manual of Mental Disorders* (American Psychiatric Association, 1980). Using this data set, a subsample of 529 Asian American males and 425 Asian American females was drawn. A matched sample of 576 White American males and 471 White American females was also drawn. The Asian American groups were separated into Chinese, Japanese, Korean, Filipino, Vietnamese, and other Asians (Southeast Asians and Pacific Islanders). Each client's data included client information (age, gender, income, ethnicity), therapist information, type of treatment received, and service provider information.

Gender differences were found in both of the Asian American and White American samples. For Asian Americans, males were diagnosed more often with conduct disorder and nonpsychiatric disorder, and females were diagnosed more often with affective disorder and major depression. For White Americans, a greater proportion of males was found to be diagnosed with conduct disorder than of females. Significant ethnic differences also were found, in which a greater proportion of Asian American males was diagnosed with conduct disorder, and a greater proportion of White males was diagnosed with affective disorder. Asian American females were diagnosed more often with major depression and nonpsychiatric disorder, and White females were diagnosed more often with adjustment and conduct disorder. Thus, more ethnic differences were found in the female group than in the male group, and the non-psychiatric disorder was the only shared difference between males and females.

In addition to finding gender differences, Kim and Chun's (1993) study confirmed the presence of ethnic differences in psychiatric diagnosis. They found that Asian American adolescents were more frequently diagnosed with nonpsychiatric disorder than White American adolescents. This may be due to the fact that the Vietnamese were very often diagnosed with this category. Cultural norms of behavior fostered in Asian societies also were speculated to contribute to this difference.

The differences in diagnosis among various Asian American subgroups indicated the heterogeneity of the Asian American population. Chinese and Japanese seemed very similar in presenting their mental problems, in that they were comparable in the percentages of people represented in each of the six diagnoses, with no significant difference on any of the diagnoses. Similarly, Koreans and Vietnamese showed a diagnostic picture that was somewhat different from other Asian groups, in that they were more often diagnosed with nonpsychiatric disorder. Differences in ethnic heritage and language as well as degree of migrational stress and level of acculturation were speculated to explain the differences in diagnosis. Japanese and Chinese, who have longer histories in the United States, may share more in common than Korean and Vietnamese, who are mainly recent immigrants and refugees and have experienced more war stress. Thus, it is very important to keep in mind that newer immigrants may be subject to more pervasive and chronic stressors, which, in turn, can influence diagnosis.

Other major implications of this study are the need to increase the cultural sensitivity in the provision of mental health services for Asian American adolescents and the need to increase the accuracy of psychiatric diagnoses. Cultural sensitivity can be increased by hiring more bicultural-bilingual therapists and by designing culturally sensitive assessment tools. Accurate psychiatric diagnosis is also very important, in that it not only warrants investigation but also helps to determine the course of psychiatric treatment and prognosis of clients.

In the third study examining the psychological adjustment of Asian American adolescents, Lorenzo, Pakiz, Reinherz, and Frost

(1995) compared the emotional and behavioral problems of Asian American adolescents to a group of White American adolescents. The authors pointed out that despite the commonly held belief that Asian Americans can easily assimilate and adapt to a new society, many of them also are experiencing psychological problems and various dysfunctions. The idea that Asian Americans are well adjusted is further strengthened by research focusing on the high level of academic achievement among Asian American adolescents, which tends to mask the stressors experienced by Asian American adolescents brought on by this pressure toward achievement, as discussed previously. Asian American adolescents also suffer from the confusion of adapting to the Western value of individualism while being taught the Asian value of collectivism at home. Based on these observations, the authors formulated the following research questions: (a) What are the psychosocial, behavioral, and academic functioning and social supports of Asian American adolescents, and how do these compare to White American adolescents? and (b) What are the specific mental health problems of the Asian American adolescents, and do they differ significantly from those of their White American counterparts?

The sample of Asian American adolescents used in this study included 99 Asian American students. The mean age of the sample was 14.5 years. One third were born in the United States, and the rest were divided evenly between groups that had been in this country for less than 5 years, less than 10 years, and more than 11 years. Seventy percent were born in China and Hong Kong, and 21% were born in Vietnam. Standardized questionnaires to assess social support and academic and psychosocial functioning were administered to the sample primarily in the English language (Chinese or Vietnamese where necessary).

When compared to the White adolescents, the Asian American adolescents lived in lower-middle-class communities, and most of their parents worked in the service industry. About 80% of the Asian American adolescents lived with both parents, compared to only 70% of White adolescents. Among the Asian American sample, 13 households had single mothers, and 4 had guardians. There were more Asian American households that had grandmothers, grandfathers, aunts, and uncles living with them. In terms of psychosocial functioning and social support, the Asian American adolescents were found to have lower self-concepts regarding happiness, lack of anxiety, popularity, and physical appearance. They had less delinquent and aggressive behavior than their White counterparts. On the other hand, they were more withdrawn, anxious, depressed, and had more social problems. The Asian American students also were found to be less satisfied with social support in the areas of assistance, advice, positive feedback, and availability of people in whom to confide.

In terms of school performance, the Asian American adolescents did much better than their White American counterparts but received less praise from their parents. With regard to school behavior, the Asian American adolescents were less involved in school functions and were also less likely to disrupt class and generally misbehave. They also had fewer close friends and fewer role models. Seventy-four percent of White adolescents identified adult role models, with most being a parental figure, whereas only 52% of the Asian American adolescents reported having role models, the majority of whom were teachers.

In one of only a few studies of mental health that focused on the Korean American subgroup, Park (1995) investigated the special needs and concerns of Korean American students by using a survey questionnaire. Park sought to determine if there is a significant number of Korean American students who are educationally at risk and in need of special services beyond a regular education. As pointed out by the author, this study is important because of the rapid increase of Asian American immigrants into the United States, especially in California. According to the California Department of Education, 54% of students enrolled in public school were reported to be members of non-White racial-ethnic groups, and approximately 8% of these were Asian. Because of the language barriers and cultural differences, Korean American students and their families may experience problems at home and school. To develop a working relationship with parents or teachers, there must be an understanding of these students' thoughts and feelings about various aspects of their lives. The research questions for the study were (a) How do the Korean American students feel about living in the United States? (b) How do they feel about themselves and their parents? (c) How do they feel about their schools, friends, and life opportunities? and (d) What are their special concerns or needs? The participants were 207 Korean Americans from across the state of California. They ranged from Grade 2 to freshman year of college, with Grades 7 through 12 being predominant (85%). The survey questionnaire consisted of 30 yes-no-sometimes type questions and 18 incomplete sentences that related to self-image, feelings about school, relationship with parents, and their needs and concerns. They were distributed at selected churches on Sunday with the help of Sunday school teachers.

In analyzing the results, Park (1995) observed that the majority of Korean American students appeared to be well adjusted to life in the United States and content with school, family life, and friends. On the other hand, there were some who experienced difficulty with schoolwork and learning. Also, one third had difficulty with English. The findings among the parents and students' wishes for their parents resulted in answers typical of most teenagers, with the exception of two items. They concerned the limited English proficiency of the parents and the feeling that the adolescents were loved by their parents. Two other interesting findings were that the majority of students thought that taking drugs was bad, but 51% said that their peers do use drugs. The other interesting finding was the fact that 90% of the students wished to know more about their Korean culture.

Park (1995) concluded that there is a great need for educational programs and services for the parents of these students to learn more about the United States educational system, philosophy, curriculum, and to improve their English. Examples of services would be community-based English training programs and volunteer programs such as mentoring. There is also a need for programs that would teach Korean language and culture to the students. Of course, the current study was limited by the fact that the participants were exclusively from church-attending families, and the results may have been affected by socioeconomic factors, religious upbringing, and/or family value system of such a restricted sample.

CONCLUSION

This chapter has reviewed the literature on Asian American adolescent development in three major areas: academic achievement, ethnic development, and psychological adjustment. In all three areas, the literature does not entirely support the model minority perspective, namely, that Asian American adolescents are highly successful and evidence few, if any, problems in school, identity development, or psychological adjustment.

In terms of academic achievement, Asian American adolescents do, on average, outperform their peers in all other ethnic groups. This well-established academic success among Asian Americans as a group would seem to support the model minority myth. However, the research reviewed indicated that this stereotype is misleading and often detrimental. It is misleading because it implies that Asian Americans have succeeded in overcoming discrimination and that all Asian Americans are superachievers. On the contrary, it seems likely that the academic achievement of this group does not reflect the absence of discrimination but rather is a response to continued societal prejudice, both real and perceived. The model minority myth is detrimental because it ignores the heterogeneity of this group and sets up unrealistic expectations for success. In school, Asian American adolescents do not succeed easily, as the model minority myth suggests. Rather, most work harder than their peers, many feel that their career opportunities are limited, and nearly all experience pressure to conform to the model minority standards.

Regarding the development of Asian American adolescents' ethnic identities, there is some clear evidence that Asian American adolescents may face more challenges in the development of their ethnic identification that are not evident for other ethnic-minority youngsters. The findings regarding these adolescents' ethnic identification provide further support for the need to dispel or counter the stereotypes of Asian Americans as the model minority. Specifically, Asian American adolescents have been found to experience more conflicting attitudes and feelings around their ethnic identification than other minority groups. Compared to other ethnic minority groups, Asian Americans appear to have less pride in their ethnic group, are less satisfied with their own ethnicity, and tend not to associate with other ethnic groups. Although evidence is conflicting, Asian Americans also may be somewhat more assimilationist in their ethnic identification than are other ethnic groups. All these findings are contrary to the model minority image of Asian American adolescents as successfully and easily adjusted to their minority status in the United States.

Similarly, the literature on the psychological adjustment of Asian American adolescents revealed that they exhibited either similar or lower levels of psychological adjustment than their White

European counterparts. Rather than supporting the model minority myth, the picture that emerges is a rather complex one worthy of continued and systematic research. For example, one study found that although Chinese Americans exhibited better adjustment than their White counterparts, Chinese American males evidenced poorer adjustment in several areas compared to Chinese norms (Chang et al., 1995). Kim and Chun (1993) found significant ethnic differences in psychiatric diagnoses between Asian American and White adolescents. Furthermore, psychological adjustment was found to be significantly moderated by ethnic identity and acculturation processes. In general, the model minority myth was once again unsupported by empirical studies because Asian American adolescents seem to have same or higher levels of psychological adjustment problems as White European American adolescents.

Sue and Kitano (1973) argued that the model minority image of Asian Americans was a myth, yet, more than 25 years later, the stereotype remains. To dispel this myth, we have critically examined the current literature on Asian American adolescents. By portraying Asian American adolescents as uniformly successful and well-adjusted, the model minority myth has discouraged researchers from investigating the challenges they face. Emphasizing the diversity among Asian American adolescents rather than the differences between them and other groups will allow us to begin to construct a more realistic understanding of the unique and complex factors affecting the development of Asian American adolescents.

REFERENCES

Achenbach, T. (1981). *Child Behavior Checklist.* Burlington, VT: University Associates in Psychiatry.

American Psychiatric Association. (1980). *Diagnostic and statistical manual of mental disorders* (3rd ed.). Washington, DC: Author.

Atkinson, D. R., Morten, G. & Sue, D. (1983). *Counseling American minorities.* Dubuque, IA: William C. Brown.

Chang, L., Morrisey, R. F., & Koplewicz, H. S. (1995). Prevalence of psychiatric symptoms and their relation to adjustment among Chinese American youth. *Journal of the American Academy of Child and Adolescent Psychiatry, 34,* 91-99.

Chen, C. & Stevenson, H. W. (1995). Motivation and mathematics achievement: A comparative study of Asian-American, Caucasian-American, and East Asian high school students. *Child Development, 66,* 1215-1234.

Dukes, R. L., & Martinez, R. (1994). The impact of ethgender on self-esteem among adolescents. *Adolescence, 29,* 105-115.

Erikson, E. (1968). *Identity: Youth and crisis.* New York: Norton.

Feldman, S. S., Mont-Reynaud, R., & Rosenthal, D. A. (1992). When East moves West: The acculturation of values of Chinese adolescents in the US and Australia. *Journal of Research on Adolescence, 2,* 147-173.

Feldman, S. S., & Rosenthal, D. A. (1990). The acculturation of autonomy expectations in Chinese high schoolers residing in two Western nations. *International Journal of Psychology, 25,* 259-281.

Gall, S. B., and Gall, P. L. (Eds.). (1993). *Statistical record of Asian Americans.* Detroit, MI: Gale Research.

Hsia, J. (1988). *Asian Americans in higher education and at work.* Hillsdale, NJ: Lawrence Erlbaum.

Huang, S. L., & Waxman, H. C. (1995). Motivation and learning-environment differences between Asian-American and White middle school students in mathematics. *Journal of Research and Development in Education, 28,* 208-219.

Kao, G. (1995). Asian Americans as model minorities? A look at their academic performance. *American Journal of Education, 103,* 121-159.

Kim, L. S., & Chun, C. A. (1993). Ethnic differences in psychiatric diagnosis among Asian American adolescents. *Journal of Nervous and Mental Disease, 181,* 612-617.

Kitano, H. H. L., & Sue, S. (1973). The model minorities. *Journal of Social Issues, 29,* 1-9.

Lee, S. J. (1994). Behind the model minority stereotype: Voices of high- and low-achieving Asian American students. *Anthropology and Education Quarterly, 25,* 413-429.

Lee, S. J. (1996). *Unraveling the "model minority" stereotype: Listening to Asian American youth.* New York: Teachers College Press.

Lorenzo, M. K., Pakiz, B., Reinherz, H. Z., & Frost, A. (1995). Emotional and behavioral problems of Asian American adolescents: A comparative study. *Child and Adolescent Social Work Journal, 12,* 197-212.

Marcia, J. (1966). Development and validation of ego-identity status. *Journal of Personality and Social Psychology, 3,* 551-558.

Martinez, R., & Dukes, R. L. (1991). Ethnic and gender differences in self-esteem. *Youth and Society, 32,* 318-338.

Matute-Bianchi, M. E. (1986). Ethnic identities and patterns of success and failure among Mexican-descent and Japanese-American students in a California high school: An ethnographic analysis. *American Journal of Education, 95,* 233-255.

The new whiz kids. (1987, August 31). *Time,* 42-51.

Ogbu, J. U. (1987). Variability in school performance: A problem in search of an explanation. *Anthropology and Education Quarterly, 18,* 312-334.

Ogbu, J. U. (1989). The individual in collective adaptation: A framework for focusing on academic underperformance and dropping out among involuntary minorities. In L. Weis, E. Farrar, & H. G. Petrie (Eds.), *Dropouts from school: Issues, dilemmas, and solutions* (pp. 181-204). Albany: State University of New York Press.

Pang, V. O. (1991). The relationships of test anxiety and math achievement to parental values in Asian-American and European-American middle school students. *Journal of Research and Development in Education, 24,* 1-10.

Park, E. J. (1995). Voices of Korean-American students. *Adolescence, 30,* 945-953.

Peng, S. S., & Wright, D. (1994). Explanation of academic achievement of Asian American students. *Journal of Educational Research, 87,* 346-352.

Phinney, J. S. (1989). Stages of ethnic identity development in minority group adolescents. *Journal of Early Adolescence, 9,* 34-49.

Phinney, J. S. (1990). Ethnic identity in adolescents and adults: A review of research. *Psychological Bulletin, 108,* 499-514.

Phinney, J. S., & Alipuria, L. L. (1990). Ethnic identity in college students from four ethnic groups. *Journal of Adolescence, 13,* 171-183.

Phinney, J. S., & Chavira, V. (1992). Ethnic identity and self-esteem: An exploratory longitudinal study. *Journal of Adolescence, 15,* 271-281.

Phinney, J. S., Chavira, V., & Williamson, L. (1992). Acculturation attitudes and self-esteem among high school and college students. *Youth and Society, 23,* 299-312.

Phinney, J. S., DuPont, S., Espinosa, C., Revill, J., & Sanders, K. (1994). Ethnic identity and American identification among ethnic minority youths. In A. M. Bouvy, F. J. R. van de Vijver, P. Boski, & P. G. Schmitz (Eds.), *Journeys into cross-cultural psychology* (pp. 167-183). Amsterdam: Swets & Zeitlinger.

Ramirez, A. (1986, November 24). America's super minority. *Fortune,* 148-149, 152, 156, 160.

Reglin, G. L., & Adams, D. R. (1990). Why Asian-American high school students have higher grade point averages and SAT scores than other high school students. *High School Journal, 73,* 143-149.

Rosenberg, M. (1965). *Society and the adolescent self-image.* Princeton, NJ: Princeton Univ. Press.

Rosenthal, D. A., & Feldman, S. S. (1992a). The nature and stability of ethnic identity in Chinese youth: Effects of length of residence in two cultural contexts. *Journal of Cross Cultural Psychology, 23,* 214-227.

Rosenthal, D. A., & Feldman, S. S. (1992b). The relationship between parenting behaviour and ethnic identity in Chinese American and Chinese-Australian adolescents. *International Journal of Psychology, 27(1),* 19-31.

Rotheram-Borus, M. J. (1990). Adolescents' reference-group choices, self-esteem, and adjustment. *Journal of Personality and Social Psychology, 59,* 1075-1081.

Schneider, B., & Lee, Y. (1990). A model for academic success: The school and home environment of East Asian students. *Anthropology and Education Quarterly, 21,* 358-377.

Spencer, M. B., & Markstrom-Adams, C. (1990). Identity processes among racial and ethnic minority children in America. *Child Development, 61,* 290-310.

Steinberg, L., Dornbusch, S. M., & Brown, B. B. (1992). Ethnic differences in adolescent achievement: An ecological perspective. *American Psychologist, 47,* 723-729.

Sue, S., & Kitano, H. H. L. (1973). Stereotypes as a measure of success. *Journal of Social Issues, 29,* 83-98.

Sue, S., & Morishima, J. (1982). *Mental health of Asian Americans.* San Francisco: Jossey-Bass.

Sue, S., & Okazaki, S. (1990). Asian-American educational achievements: A phenomenon in search of an explanation. *American Psychologist, 45,* 913-920.

Sue, S., & Sue, D. W. (1971). Chinese-American personality and mental health. *Amerasia Journal, 1,* 52-63.

Takaki, R. (1989). *Strangers from a different shore: A history of Asian Americans.* Boston: Little, Brown.

Ting-Toomey, S. (1981). Ethnic identity and close friendship in Chinese American college students. *International Journal of Intercultural Relations, 5*, 383-406.

Uba, L. (1994). *Asian Americans: Personality patterns, identity, and mental health.* New York: Guilford.

Wooden, W. S., Leon, J. J., & Toshima, M. T. (1988). Ethnic identity among sansei and yonsei church affiliated youth in Los Angeles and Honolulu. *Psychological Reports, 62*, 268-270.

Yeh, C. J., & Huang, K. (1996). The collectivistic nature of ethnic identity development among Asian-American college students. *Adolescence, 31*, 645-662.

8. Ecological Correlates of the Social and Emotional Adjustment of African American Adolescents

Ronald D. Taylor
Leanne Jacobson
Debra Roberts

In recent years, there has been an increase in attention paid to the development and functioning of African American adolescents and their families. Several special issues in the journal *Child Development*, the major outlet for child development research, have been devoted to minority children and families and matters concerning their functioning. An important feature of this work has been a broader focus on the contexts and conditions affecting the nature of family life in African American homes. Thus, for example, more research has examined the processes through which families' economic resources, family structure, and other related factors influence parents' and children's functioning. Also, work has begun to examine the manner in which important social ecological factors (neighborhood, school, peers) are associated with family functioning and adolescent adjustment.

In this chapter, we review research on the social and emotional development of African American adolescents. Our review is guided by Bronfenbrenner's (1979, 1986) ecological perspective. Thus, we consider how contexts in which adolescents interact influence their behavior. We consider how relationships and processes in the family influence adolescents' psychological adjustment and competence. Bronfenbrenner argued that it is also important to understand how contexts beyond the family may help shape adolescent functioning through their influence on the family. The contexts considered here include adolescents' peers, their schools, and

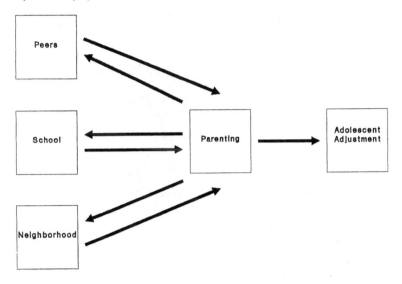

Figure 8.1. Conceptual Model of the Links Between Contextual Variables and Adolescent Adjustment

their neighborhoods or communities. We consider these contexts and their association with family functioning and, in turn, the relations of family processes with adolescent adjustment.

The conceptual model guiding the presentation is shown in Figure 8.1. The model suggests that the social contexts in which adolescents live have both direct and indirect effects on their behavior. Thus, for example, adolescents who associate with peers who value school achievement may be more likely to do well in school. A finding of this sort would be evidence of the direct effects of the peer context on adolescent behavior.

Evidence of the indirect effects of peer environmental variables on adolescent adjustment would be findings revealing, for instance, that to the extent that adolescents engage in problematic behavior with peers, their parents may become more firm in their discipline and vigilant in their supervision. Adolescents, in turn, may be less inclined to engage in problem behavior as their parents' behavior changes.

In line with the model, we first characterize the association with adolescent adjustment of key contexts in which adolescents interact, namely peers, schools, and neighborhoods. Second, we examine the evidence that the links of these contexts to adjustment exist because processes operating in these contexts affect the parenting experiences to which adolescents are exposed. Finally, we examine links between parenting practices and adolescent functioning. Before discussing the empirical evidence underlying the conceptual model, we review key demographic characteristics of African American adolescents and families.

DEMOGRAPHIC CHARACTERISTICS

African American children represent 11 million, or 13%, of the nation's children (Bennett, 1995). Of the nation's 11 million African American children, 31% are individuals between the ages of 12 and 17 years. It is estimated that by the year 2050, 20% of American children will be African American. Sixty-one percent of African American adolescents live in single-parent households. The majority of African American adolescents in single-parent households reside with the mother, with just 3% residing with their father. Twelve percent of African American children reside with their grandparents. Thirty-eight percent of the African American adolescents living with their grandparents also live with their mother present in the household.

In terms of their geographic distribution, the majority of African American families (56%) reside in central cities, and 35% live in suburban areas. Fifty-five percent of African American families live in the South, 17% live in the Northeast, 20% live in the Midwest, and 8% live in the West. Current population projections suggest that the majority of African Americans are likely to live in the South well into the next century (Bennett, 1995).

Median family income of African American families is $21,550; in comparison, the median income of European Americans is $39,310. The gap in family income has much to do with differences in the economic resources of single-parent families. The median income of African American married-couple families is $35,230; in comparison, the median income of households headed by mothers is $8,690. The rate of poverty for African American families is 46%, which is more than twice the rate of 17% for European American families.

Seventeen percent of African Americans have managerial or professional specialty jobs, and 43.5% have service occupations. The high school completion rate for African American youngsters is 73%. By age 25 years, 13% of African Americans have completed college with a bachelor's degree.

PEER, SCHOOL, AND NEIGHBORHOOD LINKS TO ADOLESCENT ADJUSTMENT

Peers

Peers are an important social context that may influence adolescents' attitudes and behaviors in important areas. Indeed, some have argued (Steinberg, Dornbusch, & Brown, 1992) that in the area of academic achievement and attitudes about school, peer influence may outweigh parental influence for African American youngsters. Unfortunately, research on peer relationships among minority youngsters is in short supply. Much of the available literature focuses on the role of peers in adolescents' problem behavior (Taylor, 1994). In recent research on peer relationships, the peer crowds existing in typical high schools have been identified and their influence on important behaviors assessed (Brown, 1990; Brown, Mounts, Lamborn, & Steinberg, 1993). However, the high schools examined in this research are not typical of those that African American adolescents attend. African American adolescents attend public schools in which they are the predominant ethnic group, although much of the research has been conducted in schools that are predominantly European American and ethnically mixed. Brown (1990) has shown that peer groups found in some high schools include "jocks," "brains," "loners," Asians, "rogues," "druggies," "populars," and "nerds." These groups appear similar to those that Ogbu (1985) suggested are present in urban, inner-city settings. Empirical research is needed on the composition of peer groups in African American schools.

For all adolescents, peer acceptance becomes increasingly more important. Brown et al. (1993) showed that adolescents' behavior and adjustment are associated with the kind of peers with whom they associate. For example, the more that adolescents associate with peers who have positive attributes (e.g., populars, brains) the better they perform in school. Conversely, affiliating with negative groups (e.g., druggies, outcasts) is not associated with academic achievement. Taylor (1994) found that African American adolescents' grades were positively associated with their report of having friends who valued education. Also, research (Brook, Gordon, Brook, & Brook, 1989) has shown that for African American youngsters, the more they have achievement-oriented friends the less likely it is that they will use drugs.

In ethnographic research with African American adolescents, several investigators (Anderson, 1991; Fordham & Ogbu, 1986) found similar peer influences. For instance, Fordham and Ogbu showed that African American adolescents, with peers who reject school achievement as an act of opposing mainstream culture, may openly avoid school achievement. In comparison, in school settings in which there is a peer culture supportive or accepting of school achievement, African American adolescents do well in school (Spencer & Dornbusch, 1990).

Anderson (1991) suggested that whether inner-city, African American female teenagers become pregnant depends partially on the nature of their peer relationships. Youngsters are less likely to become pregnant when their parents are able to monitor the teens' peers and steer them toward peers who support the families' values of the "work ethic, common decency, and moral and social responsibility." In comparison, pregnancy is more likely for those teens whose peers are accepting of their pregnancy and view pregnancy as an affirmation of the girl's passage into adulthood. Anderson's (1991) work focuses on the risk of pregnancy primarily for low-income, inner-city African American adolescents. He maintained that teen pregnancy is one of the outcomes of living in conditions in which economic resources are scarce and youngsters' options for upward mobility are limited. It seems reasonable to assume that a different set of forces would determine whether girls in other contexts become pregnant.

It is important to note that the work of Anderson (1991) and Fordham and Ogbu (1986) identified an important theme evident in the findings of a number of investigations. Thus, a factor placing African American adolescents at risk for problems in adjustment are feelings of alienation and isolation from the social and economic mainstream. The more that adolescents perceive that their resources are scarce and their options limited, the more likely they are to make risky decisions with long-term negative consequences. Taylor (1991) drew similar conclusions, suggesting that as adolescents perceive substantial barriers to their economic and social well-being, they may embrace a "subculture of disengagement from the wider society" (p. 140). Adolescents who are disengaged from the wider society are likely to be vulnerable to risks that range from the investment of insufficient time and motivation in school to involvement in dangerous and illegal activities.

Schools

School as a social context "brings economic, political, and social forces to bear on all phases of adolescent development" (Entwisle, 1990). Much of the research on schools with African American adolescents has focused on achievement problems. Research has shown that African American adolescents' grades and achievement test scores are lower than those of any other group (Reed, 1988). A variety of explanations has been offered for this problem, ranging from genetic (Jensen, 1969) to cultural explanations (Boykin, 1986; Shade, 1982). In this section, we focus mainly on the social ecology of schools.

Ethnic composition. Research on the effects of minority representation and desegregation in schools on African American adolescents' achievement is mixed. Findings (Entwisle, 1990) have revealed that in predominantly European American schools, African American youngsters in the North and those in predominantly European American schools under "desegregation plans with a metropolitan scope" had higher levels of achievement. In comparison, a number of researchers (Epps, 1981; Hawley, 1981; Stephan, 1978) have reported weak effects of desegregation on African American adolescents' achievement. For instance, Mayer (1991) found that a school's racial composition (integrated vs. racially isolated) had no effect on African American students' drop-out rate when the socioeconomic makeup of the schools was controlled. Mayer's findings suggest that, for African American youngsters, the economic mix of schools makes more of a difference on achievement than does the racial or ethnic composition.

Teacher behavior. Research on the impact of teachers' behavior on the achievement of African American adolescents has shown that although teachers perceive their behavior as similar with African American and European American students, observations reveal that European American youngsters receive more praise and have more meaningful interactions with teachers than do African American teenagers (Longshore & Prager, 1985). Irvine (1990), in a review of research on teacher expectations, showed that teachers tend to have more positive expectations of European American than of African American students. Teachers also tend to give African American students less attention, less encouragement, less praise, and more criticism. For example, Simpson and Erickson (1983) found that, more than any other group, African American boys were the recipients of teachers' criticism. Irvine's review also revealed that teachers' race is an important factor to consider, in that African American and European American teachers, when rating the same students, tend to have quite different perceptions. For example, although the majority of African American teachers rated African American students to be of "average or better ability," the majority of European American teachers rated the same children to be of "average or lesser ability" (Griffin & London, 1979).

Jussim, Eccles, and Madon (1996) showed that teacher expectation effects have a powerful influence on African American students' grades. Jussim et al. (1996) found that teachers' expectations regarding students' performance had an impact equal to "a 4-unit change in grade (e.g., going from C to B+)." These findings may have both positive and negative implications. On the positive side, if teachers have high expectation for their students these findings suggest that African American students are likely to respond with higher levels of performance. Indeed, Steele (1992) has described academic programs in which African American college students with a history of low academic performance successfully completed difficult courses. Among the factors likely to be responsible for the students' performance were high teacher expectations within a supportive environment. On the negative side, if teachers' expectations are low, African American students can be expected to respond in kind with changes in performance which validate teachers' perceptions. Importantly, findings of Jussim et al. (1996) also indicate that teacher expectancy effects may be even more powerful for low-income African American students.

School climate. In Coleman's (1961) pioneering work on the social ecology of high schools, he argued that schools may have the attributes of small societies in which there is social stratification along such factors as gender and grade. Also, he suggested that at some schools peers are influential enough to compete with parents and school staff for students' values. However, there has been little evidence found of a monolithic youth culture, at times espousing values in opposition to those of parents or other adults (Brown, 1990). Indeed, findings have revealed that, on important issues, adolescents are more likely to rely on their parents or their own judgment rather than on peers. Also, there is evidence of strong similarity between parents and adolescents on political, moral, and religious values (Brown, 1990). However, work focusing on African American youngsters suggests different conclusions. Research, although not addressing the matter of a monolithic youth culture, has implicated African American adolescents' peers as possessing values somewhat at odds with school achievement. Steinberg et al. (1992) obtained results revealing that African American adolescents were less likely than European American or Asian American teens to believe that academic failure had negative ramifications for their future. The belief that academic problems have negative implications for the future is a significant predictor of academic success and school engagement. Steinberg et al. (1992) also found that for African American youngsters, peers were more influential than parents in academic achievement. Ogbu (Fordham & Ogbu, 1986; Ogbu, 1990) reported that the peers of African American youngsters may criticize and sanction those who do well in school. School achievement is labeled "acting White," and peers may ridicule those who engage in behavior aimed at school engagement. Clearly, these findings are troubling and need confirmation in additional work, particularly work that examines the wide array of school contexts in which African American youngsters are students. It is important to know whether peers with values similar to those identified by Steinberg and Ogbu exist, for example, in urban public academic magnet schools that may have a substantial number of high-achieving African American youngsters, or in parochial schools that also may have a substantial African American population. It is important to understand under what circumstances schools may develop a social climate in which school achievement is devalued.

Neighborhoods

Research assessing the effects of neighborhood context on adolescent adjustment, although increasing, remains scarce. Much of the work focuses on the role of neighborhood characteristics in adolescent problem behavior. Crane (1991) showed that the drop-out rate for African American youngsters decreased as the proportion of individuals in the community holding professional or managerial positions increased. Also, teenage pregnancy decreased with an increase in the proportion of high-status workers. Brooks-Gunn, Duncan, Klebanov, and Sealand (1993) found that neighborhood poverty was positively correlated with teenage pregnancy. Also, African American girls living in low-status neighborhoods were less likely to use contraception in their first sexual experience than were girls living in high-status neighborhoods. In other research, Taylor (1996a) found that the more parents reported their neighborhood as physically deteriorated and run-down, the lower adolescents' self-esteem. Also, the less parents reported that their neighborhood had access to important resources (markets, banks, law enforcement, recreation), the higher adolescents' psychological distress.

Summary

There is a scarcity of empirical research on peer relationships among African American adolescents. The available research suggests that similar peer groups may exist in schools that are predominantly African American and in those that are mainly European American, and the effects of positive and negative peers appear to be similar across groups. Research on schools indicates that African American adolescents perform better in integrated than in racially isolated schools. However, the economic composition of the school may be more important than the racial mix for adolescents' school achievement. An important factor in African American youngsters' achievement is the expectations of their teachers. Adolescents' performance varies as a function of the positive or negative expectations of their teachers. Teacher expectancy effects are significantly stronger for African American than for European American adolescents. Research on neighborhood effects on adolescents' adjustment has shown that in dangerous, risky communities adolescents report greater psychological distress.

The question of whether African American adolescents' peers are the significant source or factor in negative behavior (low achievement, delinquency, teen pregnancy) suggested in an array of research needs further study. Also, the matter of whether peers may have a stronger influence than parents on the behavior of African American than of European American adolescents needs to be examined. An important and clearly controversial implication of this work is that across contexts (school, home), the adults in the lives of African American youngsters are unable to maintain social conditions conducive to their adjustment. However, conclusions of this sort are highly premature until the influence of potentially critical factors such as social class, community characteristics, or school attributes has been considered.

PEER, SCHOOL, AND NEIGHBORHOOD LINKS TO PARENTING

In the conceptual model guiding this work, social environmental contexts (peer, school, neighborhood) are linked to adolescent adjustment because they influence the nature of the parenting experiences to which adolescents are exposed. Specifically, our rationale is that the parents serve as the principal link between environmental settings and adolescent functioning. Thus, for example, if neighborhoods are unsafe, school experiences are problematic, or peers are a problem, parents are likely to intervene when possible, and their actions are likely to affect their children. Indeed, parents' parenting practices may determine how adolescents respond when confronted with problematic environments, negative peers, or poor-quality schools.

Peers

Work on the association between peer relationships and parenting has focused mainly on the manner in which parents' behavior influences adolescents' peer group affiliations. For example, Brown et al. (1993) showed that parents influence their adolescents' peer relationships by influencing the youngsters' behavior. By engaging in behaviors like monitoring adolescents' actions and emphasizing academic achievement, parents influenced youngsters' grades, self-reliance, and drug use. In turn, the behaviors adolescents displayed were linked to their peer-group affiliations. For example, adolescents whose parents were lower in monitoring their behavior were more likely to use drugs and, in turn, were more likely to associate with other adolescents who used drugs (i.e., druggies). These adolescents were also less likely to associate with peers who were known as brains or normals. These findings were apparent regardless of ethnicity. Other work also has revealed a link between parenting and peer-group affiliation (Durbin, Darling, Steinberg, & Brown 1993). Specifically, this work has shown that parental acceptance and firm control are associated with adolescents' affiliation with peers who have adult-oriented values (e.g., jocks, normals, populars, brains). In comparison, low acceptance and firm control were linked to affiliation with groups such as druggies or "partyers," whose behavior runs counter to adult values. Durbin et al. (1993) did not include African American adolescents in their analyses and thus it is not clear whether these findings would hold true for African American families. However, research (Taylor, Casten, & Flickinger, 1993; Taylor & Roberts, 1995) has shown that parental acceptance and firm control and supervision are dimensions of parenting that are associated with important outcomes for African American adolescents (self-reliance, avoidance of problem behavior). It seems reasonable to assume that African American adolescents who are more self-reliant and who avoid problem behavior would be less likely to associate with problematic peers. Research directly on the question of whether these areas of parenting are also associated with African American adolescents' peer-group relationships is needed.

As noted previously, most of the recent work has focused on the ways in which parents influence adolescents' peer-group choices. Less work has focused on the ways in which peer relationships may influence parents' behavior. For example, it is important to understand how parents react when, despite monitoring of their adolescent's behavior at a high level, the adolescent nevertheless associates with negative peers. Although direct research on this question is not available, recent relevant research has been conducted. In this work, Mason, Cauce, and Gonzales (in press) examined the impact of parental warmth and control when the quality of adolescents' peer relationships is considered. The basic question guiding this research is, Does the nature of parental influence vary as a function of the nature of adolescents' peer relationships? Findings from this research have revealed that among African American adolescents with "problematic peers," a close relationship with their mother buffered them from the harmful effects of problem peers. These adolescents exhibited lower rates of problem behavior than did youngsters without supportive mothers. Interestingly, findings also revealed curvilinear relations when the peer environment and parental control were examined as predictors of problem behavior. Specifically, when adolescents were part of a negative peer group, a curvilinear relation was found between mothers' control (firm and restrictive control) and adolescents' problem behavior. This finding indicated that either too much or too little control was associated with an increase in youngsters' problem behavior when adolescents associated with negative peers. In other words, finding the right mix of parental control, or what Mason et al. (in press) call "precision parenting," was important for mothers whose adolescents associated with negative peers. This work is important because it indicates ways in which the peer environment may influence the family environment.

Schools

Recent work has examined the links between adolescents' schooling and parents' parenting practices and primarily has assessed the ways in which parents' behavior influences adolescents' performance and engagement in school. Less work has focused on the manner in which adolescents' school experiences influence parents' behavior. Empirical research on the effects of schools on parents' behavior is particularly important for African American adolescents. Some authors (Ogbu, 1987) have suggested that because of negative personal experiences with schools in the past and suspicions regarding the treatment of minority children, parents' experiences with their children's schooling may have important effects on parents' behaviors and attitudes that, in turn, may affect their adolescents' performance. It is also important to know how adolescents' school performance influences parents' behavior and attitudes. For example, it is important to know whether and in what ways parents alter their parenting behavior when their adolescent fails in school. It also would be interesting to note whether parents' views of themselves as effective parents change when their adolescent experiences problems in school. Unfortunately, research of this kind is in short supply.

In a series of studies (Dornbusch, Ritter, Liedermann, Roberts, & Fraleigh, 1987; Lamborn, Mounts, Steinberg, & Dornbusch, 1991; Steinberg, Emlen, & Mounts, 1989), it has been shown that authoritative parenting—parenting that combines acceptance, firm control of behavior, and encouragement of maturity—is positively associated with adolescents' school achievement. For example, Dornbusch et al. (1987) found that the more adolescents reported their parents as accepting, democratic, and encouraging, the higher their grades. Steinberg et al. (1992) examined the processes linking authoritative parenting to adolescents' school performance. This work revealed that adolescents in authoritative homes tend to have positive attitudes about their skills and capacity for achievement, and, in turn, they are more likely to do better in school. Also, authoritative parents tend to be involved in their adolescents' schooling (attending school functions, helping with homework, etc.), and parental involvement, in turn, is positively associated with adolescents' grades. This research also has examined the question of the causal direction of the relationships and has shown that authoritative parenting leads to adolescents' school success. It is important to note, however, that it is still plausible that adolescents' school achievement and experiences lead to changes in parenting. There may, in fact, be a reciprocal relation between school achievement and authoritative parenting.

It is important to note that authoritative parenting is not a strong predictor of achievement among African American adolescents. Possible explanations for this lack of association are discussed in a later section. However, authoritative parenting is a predictor of adolescent adjustment in other important areas, such as problem behavior or self-reliance and autonomy for African American youngsters (Steinberg, Mounts, Lamborn, & Dornbusch, 1991; Taylor et al., 1993), areas that are related to adolescents' school achievement. These findings indicate, as Mason et al. (in press) argued, that when considering the impact of parenting on outcomes for African American adolescents, it is important to consider the influence of moderating factors that may enhance or impede parenting effects.

Other work examining the links between parenting and schooling have revealed a positive association between school achievement and engagement and parents' family management practices. Taylor

(1996b) found that the more parents worked to organize the home environment (maintaining routines, assigning chores, etc.) the better adolescents did in school. Also, the more parents were involved in adolescents' schooling (attending activities, helping with homework) the more engaged adolescents were in their schoolwork. *Engagement in school* was defined as attending school regularly, completing homework assignments, and concentrating in class on schoolwork.

It is important to note that these findings are correlational; it is possible that parents were more involved in adolescents' schooling because of their adolescents' strong engagement or high grades in school. Indeed, research indicates that some schools in their operating practices may compel parents to be involved in their children's schooling and may influence the nature of parents' child-rearing practices (Coleman & Hoffer, 1987).

Coleman and Hoffer (1987) suggested that the finding that students in parochial schools often outperform students in public or private schools has in part to do with the connection between schools and parents. Parents with adolescents in parochial schools may participate in functional communities in which parents share values represented in the school and support those values in their parenting behavior. Parents are further compelled to monitor their children's grades and behavior because the youngsters' attendance at the school is determined by the adequacy of their grades and their avoidance of problem behavior. These findings are merely suggestive of ways in which the nature of adolescents' school environment may influence parenting. More direct research on these issues is needed because parochial schools in inner cities include among the students they serve substantial numbers of African American students.

Along related lines, the School Development Program (Comer, 1980) is a system-level school improvement approach designed to enhance the school experiences of teachers, parents, and students in predominantly African American schools. One facet of the program is the involvement of parents in the planning of school operations at all levels, spanning from curriculum development to school governance. An important aim of the program is to create a school climate in which parents feel welcome at school and participate in its management. The program also has focused on the ways in which staff at school and parents at home can enhance the development of youngsters' social and cognitive skills. Research examining the program's impact has shown positive effects on standardized achievement test scores, suspensions, and self-esteem (Haynes, Comer, & Hamilton-Lee, 1988). Research is needed on the mechanisms through which increased involvement in children's schooling by parents is linked to children's school achievement and adjustment.

Neighborhoods

Despite calls for more research on the links between neighborhood-community context and family functioning (Dornbusch, Ritter, & Steinberg, 1991), relatively little progress has been made. Furstenberg (1993) found that African American families living in transitional neighborhoods—communities in which resources were declining and social ties among residents were tenuous—began to shift from "collective to individualistic strategies of family management." Parents who had once relied on formal (churches and schools) and informal (friends and neighborhood associates) sources of support in their child-rearing began to look outside the neighborhood for such resources. Parents who once were willing to delegate authority to other parents and willing to accept responsibility for others' children became less inclined to do so as the conditions of the neighborhood worsened. Some parents planned and worked toward moving their family to a better neighborhood. Parents also sought to develop social networks for their children outside the community.

Furstenberg (1993) also examined family management strategies of African American parents living in a low-income neighborhood with scarce social and financial resources. In this neighborhood, shared values and social trust were low. Families here perceived the environment to be unsafe and the risk of exploitation high. Parents looked almost exclusively outside the neighborhood to develop social networks for their children. Parents also restricted their children's contact with the neighborhood environment and used confinement as a method of enhancing their youngsters' safety.

Several authors (Baldwin, Baldwin, & Cole, 1990; Baumrind, 1991) suggested that African American parents may be typically more authoritarian in parenting than European American parents because African American parents are more likely to live in dangerous communities. Authoritarian parenting in the context of a risky neighborhood environment is thought to buffer adolescents from harm. Little research has addressed the questions of (a) whether perceptions of neighborhood risk lead parents to engage in more restrictive behavior, and (b) whether the effectiveness of restrictive parenting is enhanced in dangerous neighborhoods. On the question of whether neighborhood risks influence parents' behavior, Taylor (1996a) showed that the more that parents reported their neighborhood as isolated from important services (health, law enforcement, etc.), the less accepting and more restrictive adolescents reported their parents' behavior to be. Also, on the question of whether the effectiveness of restrictive parenting for African American families differs depending on the families' neighborhoods, Lamborn, Dornbusch, and Steinberg (1996) showed that authoritarian parenting is stronger when African American adolescents live in predominantly European American neighborhoods. Also, the positive effects of authoritarian parenting are found regardless of the kind of community in which African American families live.

Summary

Research on the links of peers to parenting has shown that to the extent that parents are supportive and monitor adolescents' behavior, adolescents are more well adjusted and, in turn, associate with more positive peers. Although more empirical work is needed, these findings appear to exist regardless of youngsters' ethnicity. Research on the effects of peers on parents' behavior is in short supply, but relevant work suggests that the effectiveness of parents' parenting practices depends on the nature of adolescents' peer affiliations. The research linking schooling and parenting has shown that African American adolescents perform at higher levels when their homes are well organized and their parents are involved in their schooling. Findings also have shown that youngsters' performance increases in schools that work to increase parents' participation in important facets of the school (curriculum, governance, etc.) and in which there are shared values and goals between school and home. Parents in questionable neighborhoods tend to limit their adolescents' contact within the community and look to resources and social networks outside the community for support in child-rearing. Parents also tend to be more restrictive and less emotionally supportive in dangerous neighborhoods.

The influence of adolescents' peer affiliation and school experiences on parental behavior needs further study. Little is known about how parents' behavior is influenced by the kind of peers with whom their adolescents associate and by their awareness of their adolescents' school performance and experiences.

LINKS BETWEEN PARENTING PRACTICES AND ADOLESCENT ADJUSTMENT

The final step in examining the conceptual model underlying our review is to assess the links between parenting and the family environment and adolescent adjustment. Ogbu (1985) argued that to understand parents' parenting style and child-rearing practices, it is necessary to understand the adaptive competencies characterizing the families' particular ecological niche. He contends that through their socialization practices, parents attempt to teach their children the skills and competencies "needed within their effective environment." The skills and attributes needed are those that promote the children's chances at attaining social and material success as they are defined in their social surroundings. The adaptive competencies and skills and the child-rearing techniques used to teach them are expected to be common among most persons in the population living in the particular environment. Different populations living in different settings will develop alternative adaptive competencies and differing child-rearing practices. Thus, according to Ogbu's thesis, poor African American families living in urban neighborhoods or communities are expected to develop parenting strategies for insuring their children's adaptive competence, as competence is defined in this ecological context. A defining characteristic of the ecology of poor African American families is the lack of social and material resources. In comparison, working- and middle-class African American parents, because they occupy an environment more plentiful in environmental, technological, and social resources, would be expected to develop child-rearing strategies that differ from those of the poor.

Empirical studies testing Ogbu's (1985) proposition are in short supply. Based on a review of the literature, Ogbu (1985) suggested that there is evidence that poor urban African American parents display parenting behaviors designed to enhance their children's functioning under conditions of scarce resources. For example, it is suggested that high levels of punitive and restrictive parenting are displayed by poor urban African American parents as a means of enhancing their children's adaptive competence in areas such as self-reliance and independence. The assumption is that self-reliance and independence are valued attributes in conditions of scarce resources in which youngsters may need to rely on their own skills to satisfy their needs. Ogbu (1985) also maintained that adaptive competencies, such as interpersonal skills aimed at manipulating persons and situations, are valued and taught early in life in the course of mother-infant interaction. Ogbu's thesis has received little attention empirically. His suggestion that inner-city African American parents are restrictive and harsh in parenting is similar to assertions made by others (Baldwin et al., 1990; Baumrind, 1972); however, it is based on somewhat different reasoning. It is important to note, as Bronfenbrenner (1985) suggested, that Ogbu's model—and indeed much of the existing research—addresses the parenting of poor urban African American parents, with little attention paid to families in other ecological contexts.

Much of the research on family relationships and adolescent adjustment has not directly examined the association between the ecological context of family life and the nature of parenting, as Ogbu has recommended. An increasing body of research has examined the association of parenting styles and practices with measures of adolescent development. Much of this work is based on Baumrind's (1971, 1973) research on typologies of parenting and their association with children's cognitive and social competence. Baumrind has shown that parenting styles can be characterized in three primary ways: authoritative, authoritarian, and permissive. *Authoritative* parents are those who set and enforce clear standards of conduct but also value and encourage adolescents' independence and autonomy. *Authoritarian* parents value and enforce obedience and respect for authority; independence, individuality, and verbal give and take are not encouraged. *Permissive* parents tend to make few demands and permit their children ample opportunity for self-regulation. Research has assessed the association of parenting styles with various indexes of adolescent adjustment (Dornbusch et al., 1987; Steinberg et al., 1991; Taylor et al., 1993) and has shown that authoritative parenting generally is positively associated with adjustment assessed by a variety of indicators. Interestingly,

Dornbusch et al. (1987) found little association between any of the parenting styles and the school achievement of African American youngsters.

An important question to address is why parenting variables assessed in Dornbusch et al. (1987) were associated with the school achievement of European American adolescents but not African American adolescents. There are several possible explanations for this finding. First, as discussed previously, it may be, as Steinberg et al. (1992) maintained, that the effects of peers on African American adolescents' school achievement are stronger than the effects of parents. Steinberg et al. (1992) showed that African American adolescents believe that low school achievement is less an obstacle to social mobility than do European American adolescents. The adolescents' views on the importance of schooling were significant predictors of their grades, whereas their parents' parenting style was not.

Second, it is possible that the measures of parenting style examined in the parenting style research do not adequately assess the parenting practices of African American parents. The styles of parenting identified and measured are based on investigations of middle-class European American parents. The question of whether the parenting styles assessed measure parenting practices typical of African American parents has not been addressed. Chao (1994) showed that parenting styles and their meaning vary as a function of the cultural background of the families assessed. Thus, for example, authoritarian parenting, when understood in the context of Asian cultural values and traditions, does not have the negative connotations apparent for middle-class European American parents. In work similar in nature to that of Chao (1994), Brody et al. (1994) identified the parenting goals and behavior used to achieve the goals of rural African American families. The researchers also used focus groups of individuals from the same rural communities to evaluate the accuracy of their measures in characterizing family processes. This work is important because it first identified the behaviors of African American parents used to enhance the competence of their children and then assessed the impact of the practices on adolescents' behavior. Findings revealed that variables identified as valid and important features of parenting, such as maternal involvement in schooling or family cohesiveness, were positively associated with adolescents' self-regulatory skills. Adolescents' self-regulation, in turn, was positively associated with their academic competence (Brody, Stoneman, & Flor, 1994; Brody, Stoneman, & Flor, in press).

In additional work relevant to the links of parenting style to African American adolescents' adjustment (Wilson, Cooke, & Arrington, in press), it has been argued that African American parents generally value and work to instill discipline and hard work in their children. Slaughter (1977) found that maternal warmth and affection and communication of their aims and support for children's schooling are positively associated with academic success. Wilson and Allen (1987) also showed a positive association between maternal and adolescent education. Finally, McLoyd, Jayaratne, Ceballo, and Borquez (1994) showed that mothers' harsh discipline is positively associated with adolescent depression and difficulty making decisions.

Other research on parenting practices has revealed patterns of behavior that are linked to adolescent adjustment. Taylor (1996b) found that families with more adequate management practices, families who were organized, and families in which parents were involved in their children's schooling had adolescents who did better in school, were self-reliant, and avoided delinquent and problem behavior. Organized families were those who had clear routines and regular and predictable schedules. Parental involvement in schooling ranged from awareness of and help with homework to attendance at extracurricular activities and involvement in school governance matters. Clark (1983), in an ethnographic investigation of factors separating families of high- from low-achieving African American adolescents, also obtained findings suggesting the importance of family organization and parental involvement.

A number of researchers have found that social support in African American families enhances family functioning (McAdoo, 1982; Taylor, 1996b; Taylor et al., 1993; Taylor & Roberts, 1995), and more adequate family processes are positively associated with adolescents' adjustment (Taylor, 1996b; Taylor et al., 1993; Taylor & Roberts, 1995). For example, McAdoo found that the extended families of a population of African American families were a source of emotional and instrumental support (e.g., counseling and information and child care), especially during periods of high stress.

Finally, additional parenting behaviors associated with adjustment concern parents' racial socialization. Bowman and Howard

(1985) showed that the more parents attempted to help their young-sters prepare for the experience of racial discrimination, the better the adolescents' academic performance. Peters (1985) also argued for the importance of parents' preparing their children to face racism by enhancing their racial self-perceptions and self-esteem. However, although racial socialization may have important implications for areas of youngsters' adjustment, Spencer (1985) showed that only approximately 15% of parents actually sought to prepare their children for the possible experience of discrimination.

Summary

Ogbu (1985) suggested that parents' parenting behavior across cultures is shaped by the ecology in which families live and is designed to promote children's competence within the particular ecological context in which the family resides. Thus, according to Ogbu (1985), the assessment of parenting behavior should include the assessment of valuable attributes in a given social context and how parents act to promote those behaviors. Little research has examined Ogbu's (1985) formulation. Recent research has examined the association of parenting styles with adolescent adjustment and has shown that authoritative parenting is associated with adjust-ment in many areas but not with the school achievement of African American adolescents. Research also has revealed the importance of identifying the parenting goals of African American parents and the association with adolescents' adjustment. Findings also have revealed that support, warmth, the communication of high expecta-tions, and a stable, structured home environment are associated with adolescents' psychosocial adjustment and school achievement.

The question of why measures of parenting are associated with the school achievement of European American but not African American adolescents needs further examination. This finding may be indicative of general conceptual and methodological problems in this area. It is not clear that the parenting practices assessed in this work are universal in their application to families regardless of fam-ily ethnicity. In this work, the evaluation of the validity of the mea-sures in assessing family processes in African American homes is needed. Also, the question of how African American families address the issue of racism and racial discrimination is an important question that has not received adequate attention in empirical research.

CONCLUSIONS AND
FUTURE DIRECTIONS

The increase in attention in recent years to the development and adjustment of minority children has served to highlight areas in the literature in which there is scarce information. There is a need for theoretical and empirical work addressing the broad range of environments in which African American adolescents are raised. Theoretical formulations concerning the adjustment of African American youngsters focus primarily on adolescents living in conditions of poverty and economic disadvantage (Ogbu, 1985). This focus is justifiable in light of the high rates of poverty among African American families and the need to develop social policy grounded in empirical data. However, little is known about the conditions of life for working- and middle-class African American families.

Also, greater attention needs to be devoted to the ways in which culture may shape and give meaning to behaviors examined. There is growing recognition, for example, that the meaning of some parenting behaviors varies across cultural groups (Chao, 1994; Mason et al., in press). Thus, parenting behaviors that may be associated with negative outcomes for European American adolescents may not have similar correlates for African American adolescents because the behaviors have different meanings in the social and cultural context of African American family life. It is important, as Ogbu (1985) has argued, to address the questions of what are the behaviors in their youngsters that parents value and believe are important, why do families value these particular behaviors, and how do parents seek to enhance and sustain the development of these behaviors in their adolescents. The work by Brody and associates (e.g., Brody et al., 1994; Brody et al., 1995) is an example of research responsive to Ogbu's recommendations.

In addition, more work is needed in the areas of how adolescents and parents perceive and manage their neighborhood or community environment. Research needs to address the question of what assets and liabilities parents and youngsters perceive in their neighborhood and how do families manage to negotiate the positive and negative aspects of their social environment.

More research also is needed on African American adolescents' peer relationships. We currently know little about the peer groups that exist in high schools in which African American adolescents are typically found. Research on peer relationships is especially needed given the possibility that peers may rival parents in their influence on adolescents' behavior in some important areas (Steinberg et al., 1992). More research also is needed on how parents influence adolescents' choice of peers.

Finally, in our conceptual model and the research reviewed here, adolescent behavior is examined as an outcome of the factors and processes involved in different contexts. An important next step, however, is to examine to a greater degree the ways in which adolescents' behavior and adjustment help shape the contexts in which they reside. For example, adolescents who engage in problem behavior are likely to restrict their peer relationships and thus change the nature of their peer environment. Changes in the nature of the adolescents' peer affiliations are likely to have ramifications in other contexts, including in their home and school. Similarly, when adolescents experience difficulties in school, their problems are likely to affect parents' behavior and parents' perceptions of themselves as parents and as effective agents promoting their child's well-being.

REFERENCES

Anderson, E. (1991). Neighborhood effects on teenage pregnancy. In C. Jencks & P. E. Peterson (Eds.), *The urban underclass* (pp. 375-398). Washington, DC: Brookings Institution.

Baldwin, A. L., Baldwin, C., & Cole, R. E. (1990). Stress resistant children. In J. Rolf, A. S. Masten, D. Cicchetti, K. Neuchterlein, & S. Weintraub (Eds.), *Risk and protective factors in the development of psychopathology* (pp. 257-280). Cambridge, UK: Cambridge University Press.

Baumrind, D. (1971). Current patterns of parental authority. *Developmental Psychology Monograph, 4,* 1-103.

Baumrind, D. (1973). The development of instrumental competence through socialization. In A. D. Pick (Ed.), *Minnesota symposium on child psychology* (Vol. 7, pp. 3-46). Minneapolis: University of Minnesota Press.

Baumrind, D. (1991). Parenting styles and adolescent adjustment. In J. Brooks-Gunn, R. Lerner, & A. C. Peterson (Eds.), *The encyclopedia on adolescence.* New York: Garland.

Bennett, C. E. (1995). *The Black population in the United States: March 1994 and 1993* (Current Population Reports Series P20-480). Washington, DC: Government Printing Office.

Bowman, P., & Howard, C. (1985). Race-related socialization, motivation, and academic achievement: A study of Black youth in three-generation families. *Journal of the American Academy of Child Psychiatry, 24,* 134-141.

Boykin, A. W. (1986). Reading achievement and social-cultural frame of reference of Afro-American children. *Journal of Negro Education, 53,* 464-473.

Brody, G. H., Stoneman, Z., & Flor, D. (1995). Linking family processes and academic competence among rural African-American youths. *Journal of Marriage and the Family, 57,* 567-579.

Brody, G. H., Stoneman, Z., & Flor, D. (in press). Parental religiosity, family processes, and youth competence in rural two-parent African-American families. *Developmental Psychology.*

Brody, G. H., Stoneman, Z., Flor, D., McCrary, C., Hastings, L., & Conyers, O. (1994). Financial resources, parents' psychological functioning, parent co-caregiving, and early adolescent competence in rural two-parent African-American families. *Child Development, 65,* 590-605.

Bronfenbrenner, U. (1979). *The ecology of human development: Experiments by nature and design.* Cambridge, MA: Harvard University Press.

Bronfenbrenner, U. (1986). Ecology of the family as a context for human development: Research perspectives. *Developmental Psychology, 22,* 723-742.

Brook, J. S., Gordon, A. S., Brook, A., & Brook, D. W. (1989). The consequences of marijuana use on intrapersonal and interpersonal functioning in Black and White adolescents. *Genetic, Social, and General Psychology Monographs, 115,* 351-369.

Brooks-Gunn, J., Duncan, G. J., Klebanov, P. K., & Sealand, N. (1993). Do neighborhoods influence child and adolescent development? *American Journal of Sociology, 99,* 353-395.

Brown, B. (1990). Peer groups and peer cultures. In S. S. Feldman & G. R. Elliot (Eds.), *At the threshold: The developing adolescent* (pp. 171-196). Cambridge, MA: Harvard University Press.

Brown, B. B., Mounts, N., Lamborn, S., & Steinberg, L. (1993). Parenting practices and peer group affiliation in adolescence. *Child Development, 64,* 467-482.

Chao, R. K. (1994). Beyond parent control and authoritarian parenting style: Understanding Chinese parenting through the cultural notion of training. *Child Development, 65,* 1111-1119.

Clark, R. (1983). *Family life and school achievement: Why poor Black children succeed or fail.* Chicago: University of Chicago Press.

Coleman, J. S. (1961). *The adolescent society.* New York: Free Press.

Coleman, J. S., & Hoffer, T. (1987). *Public and private high schools: The impact of communities.* New York: Basic Books.

Comer, J. P. (1980). *School power: Implications of a intervention project.* New York: Free Press.

232   ADOLESCENT DIVERSITY

Crane, J. (1991). The epidemic theory of ghettos and neighborhood effects on drop-
    ping out and teenage childbearing. *American Journal of Sociology, 96,* 1226-1259.
Dornbusch, S. M., Ritter, P. L., Leiderman, P. H., Roberts, D. F., & Fraleigh, M. J.
    (1987). The relation of parenting style to adolescent school performance. *Child
    Development, 58,* 1244-1257.
Dornbusch, S. M., Ritter, P. L., & Steinberg, L. (1991). Community influences on the
    relations of family status to adolescent school performance among African-
    Americans and non-Hispanic Whites. *American Journal of Education, 99,* 543-567.
Durbin, D. L., Darling, N., Steinberg, L., & Brown, B. (1993). Parenting style and peer
    group membership among European-American adolescents. *Journal of Research
    on Adolescence, 3,* 87-100.
Entwisle, D. R. (1990). Schools and the adolescent. In S. Feldman & G. Elliot (Eds.),
    At the threshold: The developing adolescent. Cambridge, MA: Harvard University
    Press.
Epps, E. (1981). Minority children: Desegregation, self-evaluation, and achievement
    orientation. In W. D. Hawley (Ed.), *Effective school desegregation: Equity, quality,
    and feasibility* (pp. 85-106). Beverly Hills, CA: Sage.
Fordham, S., & Ogbu, J. (1986). Black students' school success: Coping with the
    burden of "acting White." *Urban Review, 18,* 176-206.
Furstenberg, F. F. (1993). How families manage risk and opportunity in dangerous
    neighborhoods. In W. J. Wilson (Ed.), *Sociology and the public agenda* (pp. 46-52).
    Newbury Park, CA: Sage.
Griffin, A. R., & London, C. B. G. (1980). Students relations among inner city teachers:
    A comparative study by teacher race. *Education, 101,* 139-147.
Hawley, W. D. (Ed.). (1981). *Effective school desegregation: Equity, quality, and feasibil-
    ity.* Beverly Hills, CA: Sage.
Haynes, N., Comer, J. P., & Hamilton-Lee, M. (1988). The effects of parental involve-
    ment on student performance. *Educational and Psychological Research, 8,* 291-299.
Irvine, J. J. (1990). *Black students and school failure: Policies, practices, and prescriptions.*
    Westport, CT: Greenwood.
Jensen, A. R. (1969). How much can we boost IQ and scholastic achievement? *Har-
    vard Educational Review, 39,* 1-123.
Jones, E. E. (1986). Interpreting interpersonal behavior: The effects of expectancies.
    Science, 234, 41-46.
Jussim, L., Eccles, J., & Madon, S. (1996). Social perception, social stereotypes, and
    teacher expectations: Accuracy and the quest for the powerful self-fulfilling
    prophecy. In M. P. Zanna (Ed.), *Advances in experimental social psychology* (Vol. 29,
    pp. 281-387). San Diego, CA: Academic Press.
Lamborn, S. D., Dornbusch, S. M., & Steinberg, L. (1996). Ethnicity and community
    context as moderators of the relations between family decision making and ado-
    lescent adjustment. *Child Development, 67,* 283-301.
Lamborn, S., Mounts, N., Steinberg, L., & Dornbusch, S. (1991). Patterns of compe-
    tence and adjustment among adolescents from authoritative, authoritarian,
    indulgent, and neglectful families. *Child Development, 62,* 1049-1065.
Longshore, D., & Prager, J. (1985). The impact of school desegregation: A situational
    analysis. *Annual Review of Sociology, 11,* 75-91.
Mason, C. A., Cauce, A. M., & Gonzales, N. (in press). Parents and peers in the lives
    of African-American adolescents: An integrative approach to the study of prob-

lem behavior. In R. Taylor & M. Wang (Eds.), *Social and emotional adjustment and family relations among ethnic minority families.* Mahwah, NJ: Lawrence Erlbaum.

Mayer, S. E. (1991). How much does a high school's racial and socioeconomic mix affect graduation and teenage fertility rates? In C. Jencks & P. E. Peterson (Eds.), *The urban underclass:* Washington, DC: Brookings Institution.

McAdoo, H. P. (1982). Stress absorbing systems in Black families. *Family Relations, 31,* 479-488.

McLoyd, V. C., Jayaratne, T. E., Ceballo, R., & Borquez, J. (1994). Unemployment and work interruption among African-American single mothers: Effects on parenting and adolescent socioemotional functioning. *Child Development, 65,* 562-589.

Ogbu, J. U. (1985). A cultural ecology of competence among inner-city Blacks. In M. B. Spencer, G. K. Brookins, and W. R. Allen (Eds.), *Beginnings: The social and affective development of Black children* (pp. 45-66). Hillsdale, NJ: Lawrence Erlbaum.

Ogbu, J. (1986). The consequences of the American caste system. In U. Neisser (Ed.), *The school achievement of minority children: New perspectives:* Hillsdale, NJ: Lawrence Erlbaum.

Ogbu, J. (1987). Variability in minority school performance: A problem in search of an explanation. *Anthropology and Education Quarterly, 18,* 312-334.

Ogbu, J. (1990). Cultural model, identity, and literacy. In J. W. Stigler, R. A. Shweder, & G. Herdt (Eds.), *Cultural psychology: Essays on comparative human development* (pp. 520-541). Cambridge, UK: Cambridge University Press.

Peters, M. F. (1985). Racial socialization of young Black children. In H. McAdoo & J. McAdoo (Eds.), *Black children: Social, educational, and parental environments:* Beverly Hills, CA: Sage.

Shade, B. J. (1982). Afro-American cognitive style: A variable in school success. *Review of Educational Research, 52,* 219-244.

Simpson, A. W., & Erickson, M. T. (1983). Teachers' verbal and non-verbal communication patterns as a function of teacher race, student gender, and student race. *American Educational Research Journal, 20,* 183-198.

Slaughter, D. T. (1977). Relation of early parent-teacher socialization influences to achievement orientation and self-esteem in middle childhood among low income Black children. In J. Glidewell (Ed.), *The social context of learning and development* (pp. 101-131). New York: Gardner.

Spencer, M. B. (1985). Cultural cognition and social cognition as identity correlates of Black children's personal-social development. In M. B. Spencer, G. K. Brookins, & W. R. Allen (Eds.), *Beginnings: The social and affective development of Black children* (pp. 101-131). Hillsdale, NJ: Lawrence Erlbaum.

Spencer, M. B., & Dornbusch, S. M. (1990). Challenges in studying minority youth. In S. Feldman & G. Elliot (Eds.), *At the threshold: The developing adolescent* (pp. 123-146). Cambridge, MA: Harvard University Press.

Steele, C. M. (1992, April). Race and the schooling of Black Americans. *Atlantic Monthly,* 68-78.

Steinberg, L., Dornbusch, S. M., & Brown, B. B. (1992). Ethnic differences in adolescent achievement: An ecological perspective. *American Psychologist, 47,* 723-729.

Steinberg, L., Elmen, J. D., & Mounts, N. S. (1989). Authoritative parenting, psychosocial maturity, and academic success among adolescents. *Child Development, 60,* 1424-1436.

Steinberg, L., Mounts, N. S., Lamborn, S. D., & Dornbusch, S. M. (1991). Authoritative parenting and adolescent adjustment across varied ecological niches. *Journal
of Research on Adolescence, 1,* 19-36.

Stephan, W. G. (1978). School desegregation: An analysis of predictions made in
Brown vs. Board of Education. *Psychological Bulletin, 85,* 217-238.

Taylor, R. D. (1994, March). *Family-peer linkages: Social class and ethnic influences.*
Paper presented at the biennial meeting of the Society for Research on Adolescence, San Diego, CA.

Taylor, R. D. (1996a). *Association of African-American mothers' perceptions of their neighborhood with their parenting and adolescent adjustment.* Unpublished manuscript,
Temple University.

Taylor, R. D. (1996b). Kinship support, family management, and adolescent adjustment and competence in African-American families. *Developmental Psychology,
32,* 687-695.

Taylor, R. D., Casten, R., & Flickinger, S. (1993). The influence of kinship social
support on the parenting experiences and psychosocial adjustment of African-
American adolescents. *Developmental Psychology, 29,* 382-388.

Taylor, R. D., Casten, R., Flickinger, S., Roberts, D., & Fulmore, C. D. (1994).
Explaining the school performance of African-American adolescents. *Journal of
Research on Adolescence, 4,* 21-44.

Taylor, R. D., & Roberts, D. (1995). Kinship support and maternal and adolescent
well-being in economically disadvantaged African-American families. *Child
Development, 66,* 1585-1597.

Taylor, R. L. (1991). Poverty and adolescent Black males: The subculture of disengagement. In P. Edelman & J. Ladner (Eds.), *Adolescence and poverty: Challenge for
the 90's* (pp. 139-162). Washington, DC: Center of National Policy Press.

Wilson, K., & Allen, W. R. (1987). Explaining the educational attainment of young
Black adults: Critical familial and extrafamilial influences. *Journal of Negro Education, 56,* 64-74.

9. Conceptual and Methodological Issues in Studying Minority Adolescents

Michael Cunningham
Margaret Beale Spencer

There are currently more than 40 million teenagers in the United States alone, and this population is expected to increase by an additional 4 million by the 21st century (Greydanus, 1991). Each adolescent embarks on a unique life course pathway. However, often the particular developmental pathways challenge research efforts to describe adequately and understand fully the associated behaviors and psychological outcomes generally linked with the period. Research findings and theoretical perspectives presented in this chapter provide a particular synthesis for interpreting adolescent developmental pathways. In addition, in support of more informed programmatic research efforts, one goal of this chapter is to introduce alternative perspectives and practices for current and future adolescent programs of support.

Generally viewed as a critical point of transition, adolescence is greatly influenced by previous experiences. A youth's history in childhood with socializing others occurs in particularly structured ecological environments. Bronfenbrenner (1993) described the interaction between the person and two aspects of the environment. He surmised that individuals are influenced by the people present in the setting and "the physical and symbolic features of the setting

AUTHORS' NOTE: The research reported was supported by funds awarded to the second author from several sources: The Spencer, Ford, and W. T. Grant Foundations, the Commonwealth Fund, and the Social Science Research Council. In addition, supplemental funding was provided by the Annenberg Foundation.

that invite, permit, or inhibit engagement in sustained, progressively more complex interaction with and activity in the immediate environment" (p. 11). The interaction often engaged in by youth is influenced by adolescent attempts at exploration and discovery. Given youths' greater social mobility and psychologically unique developmental status, adolescents have more diverse experiences (and potentially more diverse outcomes) than do younger children. To illustrate, some youth demonstrate significant engagement to school, whereas others drop out. Some adolescents display stable and productive bonds with their parents, whereas others have challenging parent-child relationships. Attempts to interpret developmental pathways and outcomes of both resilient and vulnerable adolescents are aided by conceptual formulations that (a) acknowledge specific adolescent developmental concerns, (b) concede the interactive relations between culture and context, (c) consider the unique and cognition-dependent meaning-making processes of youth in general, and (d) incorporate and consider first a "normal" human developmental and context-sensitive perspective versus a set of pathology-assuming assumptions. This is particularly salient for research efforts that include diverse groups of adolescents (i.e., diversity that is associated with although not limited to gender, ethnicity, race, religion, color, national origin, body type, socioeconomic status [SES], and maturational rate).

There have been substantial research efforts that link adolescent characteristics and parental variables, although most research models represent nonminority experiences (e.g., Steinberg, 1987; Steinberg & Silverberg, 1987). When research studies do address minority experiences, parental characteristics are often limited to marital status, or research studies simply substitute traditional social address variables (e.g., race and gender) without specifically demonstrating and justifying their inclusion. Studies that specifically address minority adolescent and parent interactions are needed because, from recent studies, it is unclear whether parental psychological variables are most important (e.g., parental life satisfaction and depression) or are critical as a function of their impact on the quality of the home environment (e.g., availability of weapons, parental arguments, sibling fighting; see Spencer, Swanson, & Glymph, 1996). Furthermore, much of the research and representative studies inclusive of minority youth include conceptualizations and assumptions about normal developmental processes and pathways that are based on nonminority youth and their families.

Few programmatic research efforts provide foundational theoretical work and empirical examination of cultural patterns and contextual influences that are linked to one of the most critical themes of adolescence: identity formation. Research as foundational as identity processes during adolescence becomes more sparse when research efforts are focused on minority adolescents. Where such work exists, it rarely states the implications of parallel processes (e.g., undergirding perceptual and cognitive processes) for mental health in diverse ethnic and racial minority groups.

Another foundational theme of special importance among adolescents generally and minority adolescents specifically is the maturation process. Maturational processes generally are not addressed as a physical development factor of unique importance during adolescence. Identity themes are more often noted than physical development factors; unfortunately, the majority of available research seldom links these variables, although there are recent exceptions (see Spencer, Dupree, Swanson, & Cunningham, in press). Many researchers have illustrated that the process of maturation is universal and occurs with minor variations across racial and cultural groups. However, they acknowledge that individuals are subject to wide ethnic variations in behavioral manifestations of the process, their symbolic meanings, and their societal responses (Phinney & Rotheram, 1987; Spencer & Dornbusch, 1990; Spencer & Markstrom-Adams, 1990).

The existing theoretical and empirical literature is flooded with notions of pathology for urban minority youth and families (Cunningham, 1993). Despite this picture of pathology, many youth and families are quite successful in spite of the extreme coping efforts often required for life in high-risk environments (Spencer, Cole, Dupree, Glymph, & Pierre, 1993; Spencer, Dobbs, & Swanson, 1988). Furthermore, and at least as important, much diversity exists within groups (Coates, 1990; Spencer, 1986). The question that persists is what types of experiences are influential to all groups versus those types of experiences that are group-specific? There is a critical need for an improved understanding of conceptual and methodological issues when examining adolescent processes. An appreciation of developmentally appropriate adolescent responses for both ethnic and racial minority and nonminority adolescents and attendant parental experiences and practices is needed. Consequences of persistent scholarly neglect include the misuse and underuse of human and economic resources given that current prevention and intervention strategies remain inconclusive at best.

In this chapter, we integrate a phenomenological perspective (Spencer, 1985, 1995) with traditional ecological systems theory (Bronfenbrenner, 1979, 1983; Lewin, 1935, 1946). The combination affords a more dynamic theoretical framework and provides a heuristic device for understanding the complexity of adolescent behavioral patterns. This variation implies an appreciation of process within the person and context interaction and allows for the individual's perception and experience of gender role and racial stereotypes and biases to be considered in the research across five components. In addition, the framework sustains use of an exploratory structure for clarifying conceptual and methodological concerns—particularly those of special salience during the adolescent period. Accordingly, the Phenomenological Variant of Ecological Systems Theory (PVEST) (Spencer, 1995; Spencer & Dupree, 1996; Spencer, Dupree, & Hartman, 1997) proposes that human development processes, especially for diverse youth, are unavoidably associated with particular risk characteristics; involve the engagement of specific stresses; require the deployment of responsive coping methods; and, over time, become linked with specific identity processes that ultimately predict uniquely patterned outcomes, either productive or unproductive (Spencer, 1995, 1999). In Spencer's model, *risk factors* include one's appraisal of stereotypic and biased reactions to one's race, SES, gender, physical status, and neighborhood dangers. The risk factors are mediated by *stress engagement* experiences, that is, one's perceptions, experiences, and buffers of stress, which in turn affect the *coping methods* of youth (e.g., maladaptive and adaptive). From the coping methods, one's *identity* or *persona* emerges and contributes to life choices and behaviors that lead to sets of patterned *life outcomes*. The model illustrated in Figure 9.1 provides a phenomenological framework for assessing healthy psychological functioning that facilitates an understanding of pathways and possible mechanisms involved both in problem and productive outcomes. The themes noted in Figure 9.1 (i.e., risk, stress engaged, coping, identity processes, and disparate outcomes) aid in explaining the several mediating processes that link context and developmental pathways both for resilient youth and more vulnerable youngsters. Spencer's

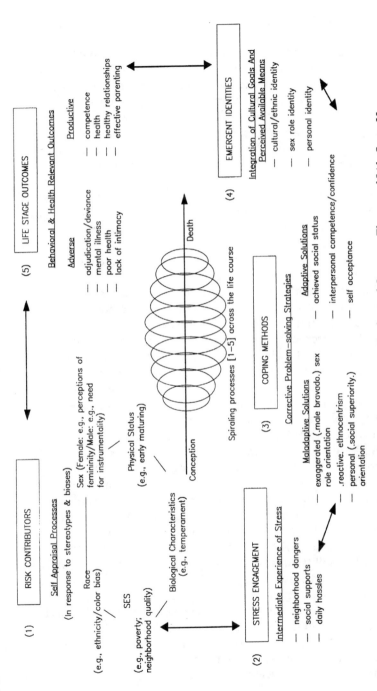

Figure 9.1. A [Revised] Phenomenological Approach to an Ecological Systems Theory of Life Span Human Development

SOURCE: Adapted from Spencer, 1995.

model demonstrates the idea that the meaning-making experiences of youth of color (particularly those easily identified by color and gender) are key to understanding the relative and interactive impact of high-risk environments. As suggested by the spiral depicted at the core of Figure 9.1, the dynamic set of themes represents a compelling set of relations that occur (i.e., as spiraling sets of development-specific thematic relations) across the life span. The particular type of risk factor, specific stress engaged, coping methods used, identity response, and outcome produced will appear different as a function of the particular period of interest. For example, the methods of coping available to a 2-year-old will be different from those generally employed by an adolescent. Similarly, middle-aged adults do not lack significant risk conditions and attendant stresses, although the mechanisms used to cope with them and associated identifications will vary.

Consistent with our overall theme of addressing adolescent specific-influences, the PVEST framework provides an Identity-Focused Cultural Ecological (ICE) perspective that (a) enhances our analyses concerning the ways in which both vulnerable and resilient families interpret their experiences, (b) provides an alternative lens that illustrates how such families (responsively) attend to their families' needs, and (c) conceptualizes those interpretations first from a framework of normal developmental processes that are linked to specific cultural-ecological conditions rather than an exclusive and narrow consideration only of constructs of pathology.

When attempting to interpret adolescent outcomes, the PVEST perspective allows researchers to address developmentally appropriate themes that are consistent with the adolescent period generally. For example, possible mediators include, but are not limited to, neighborhood characteristics, parent-adolescent relationships and parenting styles, school climate, youths' own attitudes and beliefs about opportunity, maturational processes, and level of psychological vulnerability to mental health and competence outcomes. The particular mediators of importance will vary as a function of the particular developmental point in the life span of concern.

This chapter provides a theoretical synthesis, a PVEST, as a template for critiquing and discussing conceptual and methodological concerns. We offer a general background for perspectives involving adolescents, their parents, and the context in which they develop. In addition, we demonstrate the efficacy of PVEST by discussing findings from programmatic research efforts that were influenced by the framework. We provide two types of illustrations. First, the PVEST framework is used to discuss methodological issues and measurement concerns for minority populations. Second, the framework is employed to interpret research findings for African American youth that provide a more developmentally appropriate and sensitive perspective and acknowledge the diverse ways of considering context.

BACKGROUND

Resiliency and vulnerability often occur in the same environment. The "bidirectional" set of outcomes (resiliency for some and vulnerability for others), in fact, often is observed in the same family and neighborhood contexts. Attempts to understand these concerns must consider both the developmental issues as well as the contexts in which development occurs and behaviors are expressed. Our discussion is embedded in themes that consider basic developmental process for the interaction between adolescents and parents and the environments in which youth develop.

Adolescence

As a point of transition, adolescence is greatly influenced by what comes before, including the unique psychohistorical period. Adolescence also undergirds the expected quality of the adult outcomes that follow. The transition from adolescence to adulthood occurs in particular contexts. When the effects of race and ethnicity are factored in, significant symbolic and structural variations become evident in both the quality of problems encountered and objective outcomes experienced across settings (e.g., school and peer group). For African American and other minority adolescents, the patterned nature evident for some (e.g., teen pregnancy, youth incarceration, male aggression, school failure) influences the types of research questions frequently pursued because the assumption is that the patterned outcomes for some represent the potential and only expectation for the entire group. Also affected are the specific scientific constructs included, the research cited, the interpretations of empirical data made, and the policies initiated from research findings.

The issue of ethnic and racial influences on identity, competence, and mental health concerns during adolescence is understudied and frequently misunderstood. Relative to the social sciences, DeVos and Romanucci-Ross (1982, p. vii) noted that many methods of classification in societies have been stressed. From kinship systems of simple preliterate, preindustrial societies to the stratified economic classes of complex industrial societies, each class-based category has enjoyed significant attention. On the other hand, ethnic divisions generally have remained unnoticed, thereby reinforcing the assumption that societies are unitary and possess homeostatic cultural traditions that represent the norm. However, as indicated for American ethnic-minority adolescents (particularly those from disfavored ethnic-racial groups, such as African Americans, Chicanos, and Native Americans), all show significant and patterned outcomes. These outcomes are often different from those of nonminority or Anglo-American youth although not unlike the outcomes described by Ogbu (1985) for parallel disfavored groups in other countries (notably, these outcomes are significantly influenced by a group's visibility due to skin color). Such patterned adolescent outcomes are important in that they shape, undergird, and texture the most protracted period of the life course: adulthood (Lerner, Villarruel, & Castellino, 1999). Although stressing the importance of phenotypical visibility, Spencer (1985) suggested that the structure of opportunity and the degree of discrimination, prejudice, and identity difficulties encountered by a minority group also serve a deterministic function. From a PVEST perspective, the issues raised by Spencer affect the context because the stress engaged increases, level of coping required changes, and responsive methods of reacting can be conceptualized as stable identity processes that have implications for the quality of outcomes experienced.

The resurgent and continued interest by researchers in the period of adolescence is not surprising. What is unexpected is the limitation of the research questions generated, particularly when examining minority youth, unless the research is concerned with deviance, identity confusion, assimilation efforts, school failure, or early sexual activity and parenthood (Cunningham, 1993). This limitation has led to implicit linkages between minority status and pathology and to assumptions that cultural difference implies cultural deviance. An alternative view that should be pursued as an aspect of context might well be that society responds to cultural differences with abhorrent expectations, stereotypes, and conditions of chronic risk that require reactive and persistent coping efforts if one is to survive both physically and psychologically. The family and the role of parenting as an important cultural context could bear more proactive and thoughtful scrutiny.

Parenting

Raising an adolescent can be stressful under the best conditions. Multiple factors need to be considered simultaneously to understand the complex and dynamic interactions between parents and adolescents. With a few exceptions (see Spencer, Dupree, Swanson, & Cunningham, 1996; Spencer, Swanson, et al., 1996), empirical research that stresses the interactive nature of parent-adolescent links is virtually nonexistent—particularly for minority youth. Advanced levels of cognitive abilities accompanying adolescent pubertal changes influence choices that may not be agreed on by adolescents and their parents. Interactions between parents and adolescents often can be misinterpreted or misunderstood (Smetana & Asquith, 1995). Adolescent perceptions of parental-based hassles may not be problematic but instead may be an indication of parental monitoring (see Spencer, Dupree, et al., 1996). Furthermore, in general, parents' experiences in the workplace may affect the quality of life at home (Brookins 1985, 1988).

Research has tended to look narrowly at the relation between environmental conditions or demographic characteristics and developmental outcomes (e.g., the relation between single-parent homes and school failure) or at the relations between individual characteristics and outcomes (e.g., race or gender and violence). This narrow or unidimensional approach tells us nothing about the processes that make the difference between school success and school failure for a child from a single-parent home; it does not address the etiology of "peaceful" versus aggressive outcomes for an African American boy growing up in a violent community setting versus his male sibling who copes more aggressively, although the two were reared in and shared the same biological child-rearing context. Both resiliency and vulnerability can be evidenced in the same family setting.

Family and Neighborhood Contexts

The idea that development does not occur in a vacuum but rather in a context of environmental influence is gaining increased attention (see Bronfenbrenner, 1979; Hambrick-Dixon, 1990; Markstrom-Adams & Spencer, 1994; Spencer, 1985, 1995; Spencer & Markstrom-Adams, 1990; Washington & LaPointe, 1989). Exposure to physical environmental stressors poses risks for all humans. However, of particular concern is that lower-income African Americans, whose options are restricted by conditions associated with SES and race, are more likely to be exposed disproportionately to environmental stressors, with few opportunities to escape (Bullard & Wright, 1987).

As suggested by Jacob (1990), it appears that the gap between minority-status Americans and nonminority-status citizens extends well beyond a simple plotting of poverty and unemployment rates and also should include the significant effects of specific environmental constraints. From infant mortality rates that are at Third World levels in some resource-poor neighborhoods, to high levels of crime due in part to the lack of police visibility, to problems with housing where residents experience overcrowding and segregation, too frequently African Americans' development and life-course opportunities are hampered by the physical environment (see Jacob, 1990). Hambrick-Dixon (1990) speculated that the prevalence of environmental stressors in the communities of Black America serves as a harsh reminder that racial inequity still thrives.

Although representing different disciplines, numerous economists, sociologists, city designers, and planners have documented the positive and negative attributes of different patterns of neighborhood spacing. However, rarely have the consequences of these varying community designs and general environmental confounds been examined in terms of their impact on behavioral development and psychological growth (Wohlwill, 1985). More importantly, few studies have examined the differential direct effects of neighborhood as a function of the youngster's own stage of development. Adolescents engage the environment and transition through diverse settings much more directly, frequently, and independently than do infants, toddlers, or middle-childhood youngsters. The effects on the latter are mediated more often by parental variables. Spencer's (1985) work on the impact of economic conditions on cognitive processes explored the interactive effects between affect, maturation-linked cognitive processes, and context characteristics. Analyzed together, the findings suggest explanations for pathways that lead to vulnerable mental health outcomes versus demonstrated resiliency. Relatedly, Heckler's (1985) observations suggested that attention span, memory, language, and cognition, along with physiological functions, can be compromised for individuals confronted with spacing problems and environmental stressors. Evidence suggests that both neighborhood spacing schemes and the overall physical environment affect developmental processes.

RESEARCH BASED ON PVEST

The PVEST framework is supported by culturally sensitive perspectives and programmatic research efforts. Spencer (1986) and Spencer et al. (1988) examined the effects of poverty and youth victimization as life stressors. Spencer (1985) and Spencer, Cunningham, and Swanson (1995) explored normal identity processes under high race-stigmatizing conditions. Spencer et al. (1995) and Cunningham (1993, 1994) included peer group experiences as significant variables that influence adolescent development. Connell, Spencer, and Aber (1994) and Spencer, McDermott, Burton, and Kochman (1997) examined neighborhood and parenting effects on adolescent development. Spencer and Markstrom-Adams (1990) and Spencer and Dornbusch (1990) explored the relation between minority status and identity. Chestang (1972) depicted the consequences of development in a "hostile environment" and its potential contribution to vulnerability. Spencer's perspective and conceptual synthesis represent an identity-focused and cultural-ecological developmental framework (i.e., ICE), left generally unexplored in contemporary theorizing about African Americans and other people of color.

Measurement and Methodological Concerns

Spencer's PVEST framework has been influenced by a long and consistent mental health-related research history of examining resilient outcomes among African American children and families. Alternative theorizing such as the PVEST framework (Spencer, 1995) introduces a focus (i.e., ICE) that invites new constructs. Cunningham and Spencer (1997) demonstrated the theoretical and practical uses of an ICE perspective. In developing the Black Male Experience Measure, the effort provides a social and developmentally relevant context-sensitive construct. As depicted in Figure 9.1, the constructs consistent with the themes of the measure afford an examination of phenomenological processes and suggest that youth's social stresses, identity, and adaptations are associated with Black male youths' unique cultural-ecological niche.

The PVEST framework has been used to address methodological issues. One example of the framework's efficacy is noted in an analysis of the validity of the Child Behavior Checklist (CBCL) and Youth Self-Report (YSR) with African American adolescents (Weiss, Spencer, Schaefer, & McDermott, 1997). The measurement of child and adolescent behavior has relied frequently on the CBCL (Achenbach, 1991a; Achenbach & Edelbrock, 1983) and its associated rating scale, the YSR (Achenbach, 1991b; Achenbach & Edelbrock, 1987). In reported research with children and adolescents during the period 1990 to 1994, hundreds of investigators used the CBCL, and more than 75 administered the YSR (Achenbach, 1999). The authors (Weiss et al., 1997) used common factor analysis with orthogonal and oblique rotation of first-order dimensions to identify method effects and not trait effects. Higher-order analysis failed to discover significant trait dimensions. Canonical correlation confirmed that little of the variation in one instrument was common to the other, and the broad-band internalizing and externalizing dimensions in each scale showed substantial overlap. The results were replicated with data from the same measures administered again a year later to those students and parents who continued to participate in the study. Challenging popular usage, Weiss et al. (1997) concluded that the frequently used measures are unable to assess and interpret low levels of clinical and subclinical behavior in African American populations. Although the measures are widely used, the CBCL and YSR's usefulness may be limited to clinical conditions and environments. In attempting to assess behavioral and emotional problems of minority adolescents, researchers must be cognizant of the interaction of an individual in an ecological context (Allen & Majidi-Ahi, 1998). Because behaviors are embedded in multiple environments (Bronfenbrenner, 1993), and because adolescent cognitive and behavioral outcomes are bidirectional and reciprocal (Bell & Harper, 1977), researchers using measurement tools like the CBCL and YSR have to consider adolescent behaviors in regard to an ecological niche. Using the PVEST perspective, attention is given to interactive person-context *processes* involved in developing the internalizing and externalizing dimensions discussed by Achenbach and his colleagues.

In Spencer et al. (1993), researchers examined self-efficacy among urban African American early adolescents growing up in low-resource families and often in violence-plagued settings. To examine child-perceived context, the authors developed measurement scales from items selected from instruments that focused on the child's perceptions of family, school, and neighborhood (e.g., "Are you afraid of the people in your neighborhood?"). A principal components analysis of 60 items revealed five context factors: (a) violent context (Cronbach's $\alpha = .69$), (b) family conflict ($\alpha = .70$), (c) weapons (in) context ($\alpha = .68$), (d) afraid ($\alpha = .65$), and (e) turf wars ($\alpha = .61$). Summary scores for each of the five factors were calculated by summing z scores of the raw scores of the items that loaded on the factors. Higher scores indicated higher levels of perceived violence, family conflict, weapons, and fear of turf wars. The authors used a phenomenological perspective to examine how adolescents "make meaning" of their environment. Furthermore, the authors focused specifically on the development of competence and resilience. Their analyses offered an example of specific components of the much broader theoretical framework that integrates a phenomenological perspective with ecological systems theory (Spencer, 1995).

Other work by Glymph (1994) has been influenced by the PVEST perspective. He conducted a study with the purpose of developing an instrument that measured children's perceptions of violence and aggression in their neighborhoods. The resulting scales facilitate the measurement of opinions and the development of a composite of neighborhood experiences. Also, Glymph's study investigated whether there were gender differences in students' perceptions of environmental violence. He noted that boys more often reported perceptions of violence in their neighborhoods. For each of the six factors that demonstrated gender differences, boys had higher scores. The results suggest, as do the national data on crime, that boys are disproportionately experiencing violence. Overall, it seems male students reported living in a more violent context when describing their neighborhoods. Moreover, these results justify PVEST conceptualization that influenced Glymph's Student Perceived Neighborhood subscales.

The study's results and national crime data indicate that adolescent boys are experiencing violence at higher rates than are girls. Glymph's (1994) results support Spencer's (1995) discussion of the PVEST framework. Also noted is that it appears critical to understand the methods boys use to cope with experiences of violence. For example, Glymph's results note a significant correlation of the crime data with a Spiritual Support scale. The scores for boys suggest that they are coping with their lives in a violent context through the use of some form of spirituality (e.g., prayer, use of a deity as a source of guidance when experiencing difficult situations). This finding appears counterintuitive because African American adolescent boys (along with their male elders) tend to excuse themselves from organized religious services. However, the results suggest that African American adolescent boys are influenced by spirituality but may well be obtaining their spiritual sustenance from sources outside of an organized church unit, which traditionally has served that institutional purpose, particularly in many Black communities.

Overall, the findings from Glymph's (1994) study suggest useful information for educators and researchers concerned about youth violence. Yet more research is needed to understand the short- versus the long-term perceptions of violence in one's neighborhood. As suggested by Glymph, adolescents demonstrate coping skills in high-risk environments. His study indicates that the issue of students' perceptions of violence are related to specific objective conditions in their environments. However, concretized understanding supporting the effects of perceptions of violence is needed.

Psychosocial Outcomes

The PVEST framework and previously noted examples are important and provide alternative ways of exploring resilient outcomes; the approach is different from traditional studies that have ignored a research focus that explored underlying processes for the prediction of resiliency, which remains the predominant outcome for minority youth (i.e., as opposed to a narrow and exclusive focus on vulnerability and pathology). An early exception are research findings by Spencer et al. (1988), which indicated that own-group cultural identity processes (i.e., Black youths' Afrocentric belief systems) during middle childhood and very early adolescence support greater resiliency during periods of unusual stress. Both academic and mental health outcomes were more positive for middle-childhood and early adolescent youth who valued their own ethnic heritage as opposed to identification with the dominant group. The findings and interpretation are consistent with theorizing by Anthony (1987), who views such identificatory processes as responsive coping methods.

Several other projects have demonstrated the methodological and conceptual usefulness of the PVEST framework. Cunningham (1994) examined contextual experiences that influence educational outcomes and mental health functioning for African American adolescent boys. He used the PVEST framework to analyze findings from his study. The results suggested that for adolescent African American boys, low emotional support needs, feelings of alienation, and high contextual hassles (i.e., peer/gang/turf hassles) were associated with bravado attitudes. Specifically, the sense of personal or social alienation was associated with callous sex attitudes toward women. Also, a low match between self and context was a significant predictor of beliefs associated with the attitude that violence is manly. Thus, as adolescent boys perceive negative experiences in the context of their peers (i.e., stress engagement), they cope by expressing exaggerated masculine traits.

Furthermore, as adolescent boys experience puberty, they struggle with notions concerning appropriate adult male role behavior (i.e, societal expectations for boys). During the pubertal developmental period (i.e., when the majority of boys are approximately age 13), many youth appear to use more reactive coping styles. Using PVEST's components to examine how risk contributors influence adolescent stress engagement and coping methods, Cunningham (1994) noted that boys who expressed fewer bravado attitudes take more responsibility for their academic successes and failures. Specifically, boys who had low levels of callous attitudes toward women took more responsibility for their academic success. Furthermore, positive environmental experiences influenced more positive educational achievement-oriented attitudes. For example, taking responsibility for academic failure was associated with less negative environmental experience and more positive environmental incidents. Also, taking responsibility for academic success was associated with less negative self-perceptions and less alienation.

Furthermore, academic success is associated with emotional support from friends, family members, and other significant others in the adolescent's context. The results suggested that taking responsibility for academic failure influences emotional support needs. Moreover, this finding implies that adolescents are more cognizant of psychosocial emotional needs as they learn to take more responsibility for their academic failures.

As in Cunningham's (1994) analysis, Dupree (1994) used the PVEST framework to demonstrate how contextual experiences influence cognitive functioning in African American adolescent boys and girls. Dupree's analyses were concerned with the effects of experience with violence on affective and cognitive functioning. He defined experiences with violence as being a victim of a violent act, having a family member who was the victim of a violent act, or knowing others who were shot, cut, or killed. It was hypothesized that such experiences would lead to fear related to the school context as well as cognitive distraction: Both have implications for academic outcomes. The assumption was that both the fear and the cognitive distraction would be a result of inordinately high levels of attention being placed on the source of one's fear or anxiety. Implications of the results are quite evident for mental health preventive and intervention opportunities. The PVEST framework facilitates understanding different coping strategies that either would exacerbate or diminish the affective and cognitive responses associated with violent encounters. A major finding was that for both boys and girls, school-related fear was associated with reactive aggressive coping. School-related fear was determined by students' responses to the items "I am afraid of going to school." and "I cut classes or skip school." Reactive aggressive coping was measured by responses to the items "How often do you get into fights?" "Do you carry a weapon?" and "I feel like injuring somebody."

Dupree's (1994) results link problem outcomes to contextual experiences. He noted that the association between school-related fear and reactive aggressive coping suggests that aggressive behavior and attitudes may be, in many instances, a response to fear. Aggressive attitudes and behaviors actually may represent coping strategies. In addition to reactive aggressive coping, there were active cognitive-behavioral coping and avoidant cognitive coping. Analyses conducted with these variables suggested an interesting gender difference. For boys, the greater the use of active cognitive-behavioral coping, the more avoidant the cognitive coping. Boys coped with problems by attempting to avoid thinking about them. Although a similar relation was not found for girls, analyses did indicate that girls in the study were more likely to engage in active cognitive-behavioral coping in response to experience with violence. These results implied that the same activity may have different outcomes for boys and girls. Although active cognitive-behavioral coping may lead to avoidant cognitive coping for boys, the findings and other research suggest that the same strategy may lead to further rumination for girls (e.g., Nolen-Hoeksema, 1987).

Gender Influences

A seminal aspect of the PVEST framework considers the importance of examining results by gender. Dupree's (1994) results support this notion. For both boys and girls, high self-esteem was associated with lower levels of school-related fear and distraction. In other research, self-esteem has been found to be negatively associated with self-focused attention and distractibility (Klein, 1992), that is, high distractibility and high self-focused attention are related to low self-esteem. These findings offer insight into the cognitive mechanisms involved when self-esteem serves as a buffer to negative experiences.

Benefits accrued from use of the alternative theorizing by Spencer (1995) are consistent with results from a study conducted by Swanson (1994). She used multiple regression analyses in her application of the PVEST framework for her study of African American adolescents. She included mental health measures of self-esteem and racial identity along with SES variables to predict language, math, and overall academic performance on the Iowa Test of Basic Skills. Swanson's results noted that self-esteem, racial identity, and SES were predictive of language performance for boys and girls on the standardized exam. Within this model, Parental Status (a SES subscale reflecting parental education and occupation) was a strong contributor to both. Pre-encounter racial identity (i.e., Eurocentric or dominant group preferential beliefs) showed a negative relation with language performance for girls.

Furthermore, Swanson's (1994) application of PVEST components of coping methods and emergent identities' influence on academic outcomes is noted. She demonstrated that self-esteem, racial identity, and SES were predictive of mathematics for boys and girls. The significant contributing variables in this model for boys were Parental [SES] Status and Encounter Racial Identity (i.e., transitional [neither White nor Black bias] period racial identity). For girls, the contributing variables included Parental Status and Pre-encounter (i.e., Eurocentric cultural values). In addition, math performance was negatively predicted by girl's grade level in school (i.e., poorer performance associated with later grade level).

In addition to the Parental Status findings, Swanson's (1994) research indicated the importance of discussing gender influences. Her general findings for overall academic performance for boys and girls indicate that pre-encounter and immersion (i.e., reactive [or stereotypic behaviors] Afrocentrism) variables were negatively associated with performance for boys. SES and encounter identity scores, however, are positive contributors. The most salient contributors to girls' overall performance were Parental Status and Pre-encounter racial identity.

When using the self-esteem, racial identity, and overall academic performance variables to predict behavioral outcomes statistically, Swanson (1994) obtained significant results. Among boys, this model suggested that grade in school was the strongest contributing variable. For girls, the model was not statistically significant, but overall academic performance was a significant variable in the model.

As in Swanson's (1994) study, Pierre (1994) conducted a project that explored the effects of variables such as family structure, poverty level, and school efficacy processes on adolescent school performance and examined how the Home/Parental Support of School Performance Scale (H/PS) adds to the value of an ecological cultural model for predicting academic achievement. Pierre's findings indicate that parents' high academic expectations for their children play an important role in students' performance on standardized tests regardless of gender, poverty level, family structure, and content assessed. This would suggest that the home provides another vital source of motivation available to the school system as a source of encouragement for maximizing adolescents' effective school functioning.

Consistent with the PVEST framework, Pierre's (1994) study supports alternative methods of addressing the needs of families of color. Pierre noted that actual parent involvement in schools is not the only aid for success. High expectations for success are important. A belief that children have unlimited and often underused potential could well become a self-fulfilling prophecy to spur achievement. Furthermore, perceptions of parental communication were predictive of scores on standardized tests. The questions that loaded on this factor asked about time and conversation demanded by parents. The responses indicated that when the participants thought that there was a higher demand from parents on their time and conversation, their scores on the test were lower.

As suggested by Spencer's (1995) theorizing, the meaning individuals give to experiences is linked to self-appraisal processes, such as race, gender, and SES. Pierre's (1994) analysis further supports the PVEST framework. She noted that acceptance of responsibility for achievement positively affected test scores of boys rather than girls. This could all be a part of a beneficial "Catch-22" situation for boys. Those who performed well felt good about their performance and were spurred on to maintain achievement. The relation between acceptance and achievement was not apparent for girls.

CONCLUSION

Conceptual and methodological issues concerning cultural and economic diversity in adolescent development were presented. We noted that interest in developmental outcomes for adolescents and families of color is not new. However, integration of person characteristics with environmental and contextual concerns remains, unfortunately, quite rare. Use of a phenomenological perspective facilitates understanding of adolescent developmental concerns and identity formation. Conceptualizations such as the PVEST perspective afford alternative ways of thinking about and depicting adolescent experiences. Our synthesis of theoretical ideas and empirical demonstrations supports the notion that development is dynamic, interactive, and bidirectional. While attempting to understand adolescent outcomes, one cannot ignore basic development concerns. Furthermore, the "meaning-making" process for an adolescent is linked directly to contextual experiences. However, more important is Spencer's (1995) advancement of ecological issues raised by Bronfenbrenner's (1979) and Lewin's (1935) work. The PVEST framework is an acknowledgment of the phenomenological aspect that affords more crystallized understanding of behaviors and attitudes in specific contexts.

The implications of research that uses the PVEST framework will support notions that negative attitudes are learned and are associated with negative contextual experiences. As adolescents experiment with potential adult roles, support systems are needed to help interpret adolescent experiences and to aid the youth's productive application. The support systems need to be found in schools, neighborhoods, homes, and so forth. An enhanced understanding of the developmental processes that lead to negative outcomes affords opportunities to know when, how, and with whom to implement intervention and prevention programs.

REFERENCES

Achenbach, T. M. (1991a). *Manual for the Child Behavior Checklist/4-18 and 1991 Profile.* Burlington, VT: University of Vermont Department of Psychiatry.
Achenbach, T. M. (1991b). *Manual for the Youth Self-Report and 1991 Profile.* Burlington, VT: University of Vermont Department of Psychiatry.
Achenbach, T. M. (1999). The Child Behavior Checklist and related instruments. In M. E. Maruish (Ed.), *The use of psychological testing for treatment planning and outcomes assessment* (2nd ed., pp. 429-466). Mahwah, NJ: Lawrence Erlbaum.
Achenbach, T. M., & Edelbrock, C. (1983). *Manual for the Child Behavior Checklist and Revised Behavior Profile.* Burlington, VT: University Associates in Psychiatry.
Achenbach, T. M., & Edelbrock, C. (1987). *Manual for the Youth Self-Report and Profile.* Burlington, VT: University of Vermont Department of Psychiatry.
Allen, L., & Majidi-Ahi, S. (1998). African American children. In J. T. Gibbs & L. N. Haung (Eds.), *Children of color: Psychological interventions with culturally diverse youth* (pp. 143-170). San Francisco: Jossey-Bass.
Anthony, E. J. (1987). Risk, vulnerability, and resilience: An overview. In E. J. Anthony & B. J. Cohler (Eds.), *The invulnerable child* (pp. 3-48). New York: Guilford.
Bell, R. Q., & Harper, L. U. (1977). *Child effects on adults.* Hillsdale, NJ: Lawrence Erlbaum.
Bronfenbrenner, U. (1979). *The ecology of human development: Experiments by nature and design.* Cambridge, MA: Harvard University Press.
Bronfenbrenner, U. (1993). The ecology of cognitive development: Research models and fugitive findings. In R. H. Wozniak & K. W. Fischer (Eds.), *Development in context: Acting and thinking in specific environments* (pp. 3-44). Hillsdale, NJ: Lawrence Erlbaum.
Brookins, G. K. (1985). Black children's sex-role ideologies and occupational choices in families of employed mothers. In M. B. Spencer, G. K. Brookins, & W. R. Allen

(Eds.), *Beginnings: The social and affective development of Black children* (pp. 257-272). Hillsdale, NJ: Lawrence Erlbaum.

Brookins, G. K. (1988). Making the honor roll: A Black parent's perspective on private education. In D. T. Slaughter & D. J. Johnson (Eds.), *Visible now* (pp. 12-20). Westport, CT: Greenwood.

Bullard, R. D., & Wright, B. H. (1987). Blacks and the environment. *Journal of Social Relations, 14,* 165-184.

Chestang, L. W. (1972). *Character development in a hostile environment* (Occasional Paper No. 3, p. 1-12). Chicago: University of Chicago Press.

Coates, D. L. (1990). Gender differences in the structure and support characteristics of Black adolescents' social networks. *Sex Roles, 17,* 667-687.

Connell, J. P., Spencer, M. B., & Aber, J. L. (1994). Education risk and resilience in African-American youth: Context, self, action and outcomes in school. *Child Development, 65,* 493-506.

Cunningham, M. (1993). African American adolescent males' sex role development: A literature review. *Journal of African American Male Studies, 1,* 30-37.

Cunningham, M. (1994). Expressions of manhood: Predictors of educational achievement African American adolescent males. *Dissertation Abstracts International, 34*(5-A), (University Microfilms No. 1223).

Cunningham, M., & Spencer, M. B. (1997). The Black Male Experiences measure. In R. L. Jones (Ed.), *Handbook of tests and measurements for Black populations* (pp. 301-310). Hampton, VA: Cobb & Henry.

DeVos, G., & Romanucci-Ross, L. (1982). *Ethnic identity: Cultural continuity and change.* Chicago: University of Chicago Press.

Dupree, D. M. (1994). The effects of experience with violence on the affective and cognitive functioning of African-American adolescents. *Dissertation Abstracts International, 34*(4-B), (University Microfilms No. 1686).

Glymph, A. (1994). *Assessing youths' perception of their neighborhood: Development of the student perception of neighborhood.* Unpublished master's thesis, Emory University, Atlanta, GA.

Greydanus, D. E. (Ed.). (1991). *Caring for your adolescent.* New York: Bantam.

Hambrick-Dixon, P. J. (1990). The effect of the physical environment on the development of Black children. *Journal of Environmental Psychology, 8,* 299-314.

Heckler, M. (1985). *Report of the secretary's task force on Black and minority health.* Washington, DC: Government Printing Office.

Jacob, J. E. (1990). *The state of Black America 1990.* New York: Urban League.

Klein, H. A. (1992). Temperament and self-esteem in late adolescence. *Adolescence, 27,* 689-694.

Lerner, R. M., Villarruel, F. A., & Castellino, D. R. (1999). Adolescence. In W. K. Silverman & T. H. Ollendick (Eds.), *Developmental issues in the clinical treatment of children* (pp. 125-136). Boston: Allyn & Bacon.

Lewin, K. (1935). *A dynamic theory of personality.* New York: McGraw-Hill.

Lewin, K. (1946). Action research and minority problems. *Journal of Social Issues, 2,* 34-46.

Markstrom-Adams, C., and Spencer, M. B. (1994). A model for identity intervention with minority adolescents. In S. Archer (Ed.), *Interventions for adolescent identity development* (84-102). Thousand Oaks, CA: Sage.

Nolen-Hoeksema, S. (1987). Sex differences in unipolar depression: Evidence and theory. *Psychological Bulletin, 101,* 259-282.

Ogbu, J. U. (1985). A cultural ecology of competence among inner-city Blacks. In M. B. Spencer, G. K. Brookins, & W. R. Allen (Eds.), *Beginnings: The social and affective development of Black children* (pp. 45-66). Hillsdale, NJ: Lawrence Erlbaum.

Phinney, J. S., & Rotheram, M. J. (1987). *Children's ethnic socialization: Pluralism and development.* Newbury Park, CA: Sage.

Pierre, P. (1994). *Exploration of how home and parental characteristics support achievement and effective school functioning of adolescents.* Unpublished doctoral dissertation, Emory University, Atlanta, GA.

Smetana, J., & Asquith, P. (1995). Adolescents' and parents' conceptions of parenting authority and personal autonomy. *Child Development, 65,* 1147-1162.

Spencer, M. B. (1985). Cultural cognition and social cognition as identity factors in Black children's personal-social growth. In M. B. Spencer, G. K. Brookins, and W. R. Allen (Eds.), *Beginnings: The social and affective development of Black children* (pp. 215-230). Hillsdale, NJ: Lawrence Erlbaum.

Spencer, M. B. (1986). Risk and resilience: How Black children cope with stress. *Journal of Social Sciences, 7,* 22-26.

Spencer, M. B. (1995). Old issues and new theorizing about African-American youth: A phenomenological variant of the ecological systems theory. In R. L. Taylor (Ed.), *Black youth: Perspectives on their status in the United States* (pp. 37-70). New York: Praeger.

Spencer, M. B. (1999). Social and cultural influences on school adjustment: The application of an identity-focused cultural ecological perspective. *Educational Psychologist, 34,* 43-57.

Spencer, M. B., Cole, S. P., Dupree, D., Glymph, A., & Pierre, P. (1993). Self-efficacy among urban African American early adolescents: Exploring issues of risk, vulnerability, and resilience. *Development and Psychopathology, 5,* 719-739.

Spencer, M. B., Cunningham, M., & Swanson, D. P. (1995). Identity as coping: Adolescent African-American males' adaptive responses to high-risk environment. In H. W. Harris, H. C. Blue, and E. H. Griffith (Eds.), *Racial and ethnic identity: Psychological development and creative expression* (pp. 31-52). Boston: Routledge & Kegan Paul.

Spencer, M. B., Dobbs, B., & Swanson, D. P. (1988). Afro-American adolescents: Adaptational processes and socioeconomic diversity in behavioral outcomes. *Journal of Adolescence, 11,* 117-137.

Spencer, M. B., & Dornbusch, S. (1990). American minority adolescents. In S. Feldman & G. Elliot (Eds.), *At the threshold: The developing adolescent* (pp. 123-146). Cambridge, MA: Harvard University Press.

Spencer, M. B., & Dupree, D. (1996). African American youths' eco-cultural challenges and psychosocial opportunities: An alternative analysis of problem behavior outcomes. In D. Cicchetti & S. Toth (Eds.), *Rochester Symposium on Developmental Psychopathology: Vol. 7. Adolescence: Opportunities and challenges* (pp. 259-282). Rochester, NY: University of Rochester Press.

Spencer, M. B., Dupree, D., & Hartman, T. (1997). A phenomenological variant of ecological systems theory (PVEST): A self-organization perspective in context. *Development and Psychopathology, 9,* 817-834.

Spencer, M. B., Dupree, D., Swanson, D. P., & Cunningham, M. (1996). Parental monitoring and adolescents' sense of responsibility for their own learning: An examination of sex differences. *Journal of Negro Education, 65,* 30-43.

Spencer, M. B., Dupree, D., Swanson, D. P., & Cunningham, M. (in press). The influence of physical maturation with family hassles in African American adolescent males. *Journal of Comparative Family Studies, 29.*

Spencer, M. B., & Markstrom-Adams, C. (1990). Identity processes among racial and ethnic minority children in America. *Child Development, 61,* 290-310.

Spencer, M. B., McDermott, P. A., Burton, L., & Kochman, T. (1997). An alternative approach to assessing neighborhood effects on early adolescent achievement and problem behavior. In J. Brooks-Gunn, G. Duncan, & J. L. Aber (Eds.), *Neighborhood, poverty: Context and consequences for children* (pp. 145-163). New York: Russell Sage Foundation.

Spencer, M. B., Swanson, D. P., & Glymph, A. (1996). The prediction of parental psychological functioning: Influences of African American adolescent perceptions and experiences in context. In C. D. Ryff & M. M. Seltzer (Eds.), *The parental experience in midlife* (pp. 337-380). Chicago: University of Chicago Press.

Steinberg, L. (1987). Impact of puberty on family relations: Effects of pubertal status and pubertal timing. *Developmental Psychology, 23,* 451-460.

Steinberg, L., & Silverberg, S. B. (1987). Influences of marital satisfaction during the middle stages of the family life cycle. *Journal of Marriage and the Family, 49,* 751-760.

Swanson, D. P. (1994). Self-efficacy and racial identity: Effects of psychosocial processes on academic and behavioral problems. *Dissertation Abstracts International, 34*(4-A), (University Microfilms No. 915).

Washington, V., & LaPointe, V. (1989). *Black children and American institutions: An ecological review and resource guide.* New York: Garland.

Weiss, R. V., Spencer, M. B., Schaefer, B. A., & McDermott, P. A. (1997). *Construct validity of the Child Behavior Checklist and Youth Self-Report with urban African-American adolescents.* Manuscript submitted for publication.

Wohlwill, J. F. (1985). The confluence of environmental and developmental psychology: Signpost to an ecology of development? *Human Development, 23,* 354-358.

10. The Variety of Adolescent Experiences

Raymond Montemayor

The authors of the chapters in this volume summarize and integrate theory and research on adolescents from a diversity of ethnic, economic, and geographic contexts. Adolescents who are African American, Mexican American, Asian American, Native American, rural, and poor have been underrepresented in research on normal adolescent behavior and overrepresented in studies of problem behavior (Graham, 1992). In the popular media, negative stereotypes abound about Black teenagers who are drug addicts, Hispanic gang members, Asian math whizzes, Indian alcoholics, the desperate and alienated poor, and rural hicks. Lacking in these descriptions of dysfunction has been a fuller description of the typical adolescent experiences of these racial, cultural, and economic minority adolescents, experiences that often include resilience and success. One goal of this volume is to present a more balanced picture of these understudied and misunderstood adolescents. To this end, authors were asked to focus on positive, healthy development, because much previous work has examined, and continues to focus on, problem behavior.

Several themes emerge from the chapters in this volume. In this final chapter, I discuss some of the issues that cut across discussions about particular groups of adolescents.

LIVING IN TWO WORLDS

Several authors discuss the idea that adolescents from ethnic minorities are "caught between two worlds," the traditional culture of their parents and family and the modern culture of White middle-class America. Adolescents cope with this division in several ways: through biculturalism, which is an attempt to maintain ties to both the majority and their own minority culture; by assimilation and adopting the majority culture's norms and standards; through separation, or associating only with members of one's own culture and rejecting the majority culture; or by becoming marginal, living within the majority culture but feeling estranged from it (Phinney, 1990). Castro, Boyer, and Balcazar (Chapter 6, this volume) discuss two typical pathways among Mexican American adolescents—*assimilation* and *biculturation*. According to these authors, assimilation involves the replacement of Spanish-language and Mexican traditions and behavior with spoken English and Euro-American behaviors. In contrast, biculturation involves successfully integrating components of Mexican culture with those of the European American culture. As an example of biculturation, many Mexican American adolescents speak Spanish at home and in their neighborhood and English at school.

The difficulty of maintaining some connection with one's ethnic heritage in a modern urban society such as the United States is a theme that runs through descriptions of ethnic minorities in this book and in public discourse. What is new about this idea is that several authors in this volume show that this theme is present in rural and Appalachian youth as well as in ethnic-minority adolescents.

Adolescence is a time when young people make important decisions about their educational and occupational futures and about their family goals. According to Crockett, Shanahan, and Jackson-Newsom (Chapter 3, this volume), rural adolescents also think about these issues but are faced with the additional problem that some answers to these questions require the adolescent to leave behind—at least temporarily and perhaps permanently—family, friends, and community. Some rural adolescents abandon their past and assimilate into big-city modern America. Others attempt to integrate traditional values with modernity, and still others make choices that keep them close to home and heritage.

Wilson and Peterson (Chapter 4, this volume) discuss the problem Appalachian youth have of trying to integrate their past with their future. They point out that traditional folk culture emphasizes family closeness, kinship, obligation to kin, localism, and fundamentalist religion, whereas the values of urban-contemporary culture are achievement, competition, geographic mobility, individualism, and secularism. For Appalachian youth, these different worlds result in different types of identities, which Wilson and Peterson call "Appalachian-identified," "biculturally identified," and "urban-identified."

Searching for a way to resolve the tension between one's background and modern life is a problem not only for ethnic minority adolescents but also for adolescents from traditional cultures, many of whom leave their heritage and their physical roots when they go to college. The achievement of material success in contemporary America requires some acceptance of modern, secular, consumer values. The task facing many adolescents is how to resolve this disjunction between their personal past and the future.

ETHNIC IDENTITY

Discussion about the difficulty some adolescents have of living in two worlds blends into a discussion about ethnic identity. Several authors make the point that positive mental health among ethnic-minority adolescents includes all the components of health found in middle-class White adolescents but, in addition, requires the development of a positive ethnic identity. The process of establishing a positive ethnic identity is exacerbated by the fact that many minority adolescents have a negative view of the history and customs of their own ethnic community, based on popular images and negative stereotypes.

The issue of coming to grips with one's ethnicity is at the heart of discussions about the development of non-White adolescents. A process similar to the development of an ethnic identity is a central concern for adolescents who are Caucasian but who did not grow up in a secular urban environment. One task for many rural and Appalachian adolescents is forming an identity that includes one's cultural heritage and is rooted in a particular geographic place but also reflects the modern world.

In contrast to discussions about identity development among mainstream adolescents that emphasize issues of commitment to occupation and relationship, ethnic identity focuses deeply on the commitment of adolescents to their heritage. The authors in this volume suggest that adolescents essentially have three choices in regard to their ethnicity: to deny or minimize its importance, to view it negatively, or to accept their past with pride and to find some way to integrate their cultural heritage with their current circumstances.

No single model of ethnic identity formation is widely accepted. There are several that offer different perspectives on this issue and bring to the foreground important components of this multi-dimensional concept. Jean Phinney's (1989) formulation is based on Erik Erikson's (1968) theory of identity development and focuses on issues of intrapersonal conflict and exploration, leading to commitments to personal and social goals. Atkinson, Morten, and Sue (1983) proposed a framework of ethnic identity development based on intrapersonal and interpersonal conflict. Although the theory emerged from clinical work with Asian American adolescents, its essential structure—conformity, conflict, questioning, and achievement—seems applicable to identity development among adolescents whose culture and traditions are not supported by the majority culture.

Surprisingly, research on the process of ethnic identity formation and on the impact of ethnic identity on adolescent health and competence is either lacking or equivocal. Several authors report positive correlations between ethnic identity and self-esteem, although reviews of this literature show inconsistency in these findings (Phinney, 1990). It appears that some non-White adolescents experience a deep need to examine their ethnic heritage and to incorporate that examination into their self-concepts, but it is unclear what advantages accrue as a result of this examination.

COMPETENCE

Several authors examine the meaning of competence for non-White, poor, and rural adolescents. Yoshikawa and Seidman (Chapter 2, this volume) make the important point that *competence* generally is defined as cognitive competence and is measured by school performance. Examination of minority adolescents who are poor and live in cities shows that this definition is too narrow and does not capture the multiple dimensions of competence that are demonstrated by non-White and non-middle-class adolescents. For example, many adolescents, especially daughters, from poor and minority families are expected to take part in the routine care of younger siblings, and young men often are expected to help supplement family income through part-time work or through "off the books" jobs. The general point raised by this discussion is that competence is embedded in context and needs to be examined in terms of the behaviors necessary to succeed in one's immediate environment, which for adolescents who are poor, minority, or rural often includes competencies that are family- and neighborhood-based rather than school-based.

THE FAMILY

Until recently, much of the discussion about non-White and non-middle-class families was based on a "cultural deficit model," which was an attempt to trace the academic and social problems of minority and poor youth to maladaptive parenting styles (Parke & Buriel, 1998). These parenting styles were viewed as deeply embedded in the customs and traditions of non-middle-class culture and highly resistant to modification. More recent approaches, as reflected by the discussions in this volume, focus on the family-in-context and examine the impact of the often harsh environment of non-middle-class families on parenting. From this perspective, parenting styles are viewed as adaptational responses of parents to their environments and attempts by parents to teach their children how to survive in those environments.

Every author in this volume emphasizes the importance of the family as an influence on adolescent development, whatever the ethnicity, economic background, or geographic residence of the adolescent. But the authors go beyond merely showing that the family is a powerful force in the lives of adolescents and argue that many minority and rural parents and adolescents hold a set of values about family life termed *familism*, which involves strong family identification, obligations, and loyalty.

Familism takes different forms in different groups. Leong, Chao, and Hardin (Chapter 7, this volume) show that the academic success of Asian American students is not due only to the emphasis parents place on teaching industry, discipline, and order but also to a strongly held Asian cultural ideology in which adolescent behavior is viewed by others and by the adolescent as reflecting on the family. Asian American adolescents understand that they are working not only for their own success but also for the good name of their family.

Another version of the ideology of family is illustrated in the lives of some African American adolescents, especially girls. According to Taylor, Jacobson, and Roberts (Chapter 8, this volume), in many African American families, female children take on the responsibilities of child care for younger siblings at an early age. In many White middle-class families, taking care of a younger sibling is often the responsibility of a baby-sitter, or an older sibling is paid for the care of the younger sibling. The important point here is that this difference in sibling care is not the result of the fact that middle-class families have money to pay for child care; it is due to a different emphasis on individuality and family responsibility. In White families, adolescents are allowed and even expected to develop apart from the family. In non-White families, children are considered part of a family, which means that family members do things for each other without pay.

Although families are central to the development of adolescents, whatever their ethnicity, economic status, or geographic location, families are embedded in communities of related and unrelated adults who also play an important role in the lives of adolescents. The deterioration of urban neighborhoods due to drug addiction, crime, and unemployment has led to the loss of connection among neighbors and the isolation of families from each other (Wilson, 1987). As a result, the socialization of adolescents involves the community less and the isolated, overburdened family more.

Among American Indian families, community involvement in the lives of adolescents is so great as to constitute a kind of surrogate parenting. According to Beauvais (Chapter 5, this volume), in many American Indian families parents do not exert strong control over their adolescents. Instead, it is the community in the form of relatives and unrelated adults who give advice to adolescents and reprimand them when they do wrong. A tradition of the involvement of relatives and neighbors in the upbringing of adolescents works when relatives live close by and neighborhood communities are cohesive. When these circumstances are not present—and they are not in most modern Indian tribal societies—adolescents do not develop the internal controls over their own behavior that they need.

PEERS

In addition to parents, and sometimes even more than parents, peers exert a powerful influence on adolescents. Some even have argued, although not in this volume, that peers matter more than parents (Harris, 1998). The high correlations between the behavior of adolescents and their friends should be viewed cautiously, however. As several authors in this volume point out, the association between peer standards and adolescent behavior is reciprocal—adolescents choose peers who are like themselves, and peers, both directly and indirectly, shape adolescent behavior.

Much of the research on peer influence on poor and minority adolescents examines the impact of peers on unhealthy and antisocial behavior. A recurring theme in this literature is that many minority and poor adolescents come to feel alienated from socially accepted goals and develop a sense of hopelessness about success in school and the workplace. Although these feelings are based on a realistic appraisal of life in contemporary America, feelings of hopelessness are also the result of the development of an ideology of mistrust and victimhood learned from parents and peers. Several authors in this volume examine the other side of this equation and show that peers can be forces for positive development. Having friends who value academic achievement, who do not abuse alcohol or drugs, and who do not commit crimes is highly related to success in school and later life.

SCHOOL

Many adolescents perform poorly in school. Most explanations for low grades focus on low motivation and a lack of self-discipline. According to the authors in this volume, the school problems of adolescents who are poor, minority, or rural arise from two additional sources: an impoverished background and school systems that are generally inadequately equipped to deal with adolescents who are not from conventional middle-class backgrounds.

Several authors discuss the impact of peers on the academic achievement of minority, poor, or rural adolescents. The conclusion that can be drawn from these discussions is that although parents matter, peers may matter more, especially when students attend schools with a peer culture that de-emphasizes academic success. For many middle-class White adolescents, peers and parents hold similar high standards for achievement. In contrast, for some poor, minority, and rural students, achievement in school is seen as selling out. Such a norm puts students in the position of having to choose between parents and peers, between academic success and academic indifference or rejection.

Risking rejection from peers because one is interested in school and in doing well academically is a peril for many academically talented adolescents whatever their racial and economic background. Research suggests that some peers do not support academic achievement, and some part of the adolescent culture does not value an emphasis on schoolwork (Brown, 1990). What is different for a minority student is that the pressure to minimize schoolwork takes the insidious form of a rejection of one's ethnic background.

Taylor et al. point out that the more adolescents feel alienated, isolated, and cut off from mainstream culture, the more they feel that barriers exist to their economic and social well-being. When adolescents believe that paths to achievement are blocked because of their race or culture or background, they are more likely to do poorly in school.

THE PERIOD OF ADOLESCENCE

Traditional notions of adolescent development may not capture the experience of many minority, poor, and rural adolescents. For example, the emphasis on the achievement of autonomy and separation from family (Erikson, 1968) is foreign to some Hispanic and Asian cultures, which emphasize familism, the placement of needs of the family before needs of individuals.

In addition, several authors make the point that the period of childhood is truncated among some minority, poor, and rural children. Adolescence may be reached earlier in these groups than among European middle-class children. Many minority children take on adult roles at an earlier age than do middle-class White children, whose educational trajectories take them to college and beyond, forestalling entry into adulthood. In African American and Hispanic cultures, older children are expected to take care of younger siblings, and young Native American boys take on adult responsibilities of care for family livestock but are treated as children by teachers. In general, youth who live on farms take on adult roles and responsibilities at an earlier age than do metropolitan youth. Adolescence as a distinct period of the life cycle between childhood and adulthood may be more characteristic of White middle-class Western Europeans than of other ethnic and cultural groups.

DIVERSITY WITHIN GROUPS

Every author in this volume makes the point that there is much diversity within ethnic and economic groups in the behavior of adolescents. "American Indian" encompasses a range of tribes with different customs and peoples. "Rural" is an overly inclusive term that describes a variety of types of youth. Rural includes not only areas based on agriculture but also those based on mining and retirement. Rural varies also by population size, employment opportunities, poverty rates, and ethnic composition. Regional differences are important also, and life in rural Appalachia is quite different from farm life in Nebraska. Such differences influence community settings and provide different backgrounds for the unfolding of adolescent development.

Differences also were noted between rural adolescents and urban adolescents, but differences were more profound when farm families were compared to nonfarm families in rural settings. The context of shared farm responsibilities makes farm life a unique setting for coming into adulthood, different from growing up in a small town.

Several authors point out that within-group differences for an ethnic or economic group are great. For example, although differences exist between Black and White adolescents, equally great differences also exist between Black adolescents from middle-class professional families and Black adolescents living in impoverished inner-city neighborhoods. Leong et al. show that, contrary to the stereotype that Asian Americans are a "model minority," some Asian American adolescents do not do well in school, suffer mental illnesses, and have behavioral problems.

Concern about the negative effects of poverty on urban adolescents in America is warranted, given increases over the past decade in the severity of poverty-related risks in cities. Although these trends present ample cause for concern and intervention, the majority of urban poor children do not become delinquents, school drop-outs, or teenage mothers. Adolescents living in urban poverty show a range of competent outcomes that belie common assumptions about their low abilities and achievements, as Yoshikawa and Seidman show. Assumptions about the poor underlie the tendency to focus on negative outcomes among poor children and adolescents. Emphasis on between-group differences masks the range of individual differences among adolescents, particularly the range of competent outcomes that many achieve.

HISTORICAL AND GENERATIONAL
CHANGE WITHIN GROUPS

The culture of any group is not static but is itself changing in response to economic and social change. Little attention is paid in the research to the history of cultural groups or about how the meaning of one's ethnicity or background has changed over time. Writers sometimes are guilty of describing a tradition that once was central to a group or a region, with the assumption that the tradition holds true today with the same meaning and intensity that it once had. Ethnic groups are an "amalgam," to use the word of Beauvais, of traditional and contemporary, and minority and majority, culture.

Traditional ways of doing things are changing in many groups. Adolescents have contact with a wide range of other adolescents in school and through television, experiences that alter them and their relations with the past. For example, although many Indian tribes retain their traditional rites of passage, there is a sense of ambivalence and ambiguity about these ceremonies, as they have become increasingly divorced from the lives of modern Indian youth.

ETHNICITY AND
SOCIOECONOMIC STATUS

Discussions about ethnicity often do not distinguish between ethnicity and socioeconomic status. Many observers attribute behaviors, especially those that are maladaptive, to cultural traditions and customs, when these behaviors may be the result of economic and social conditions. To what extent are the behaviors of poor, rural, and non-White adolescents the result of their ethnicity versus their socioeconomic status? Surprisingly little research has attempted to tease apart these two great forces.

Several authors in this volume discuss this issue in regard to high school achievement. Crockett et al. show that differential high school dropout rates between urban and rural adolescents are mainly accounted for by economic differences and not social-psychological factors. Taylor et al. also show that, for African American adolescents, high school dropout rates decline as do teenage pregnancy rates as the proportion of adults who hold professional or managerial positions increases in the neighborhoods in which the adolescents live. More research is needed on the main and inter-active effects of ethnicity and socioeconomic status.

AN ECOLOGICAL PERSPECTIVE

In general, research on ethnic, economic, and geographic diversity among adolescents has been guided by Bronfenbrenner's (1979, 1989) ecological perspective. Family, peer, school, neighborhood, town, economic, social, and historical contexts are all shown to in-fluence adolescent behavior. Interestingly, some authors, such as Taylor et al., also point out that adolescent behavior affects these contexts. For example, street crime leads to the physical deteriora-tion of a neighborhood, alters the behavior of residents, and changes perceptions of the neighborhood and of neighbors. These research-ers have an interesting discussion about how Black families react to the decline of their neighborhood, moving from the use of informal social supports of other neighbors to the formal government sup-ports outside their neighborhood.

Cunningham and Spencer (Chapter 9, this volume) make the additional point that it is not the environment per se that has the significant influence on adolescent behavior but the "symbolic fea-tures of the setting" that affect behavior. They examine this idea in relation to Black adolescents, but perceptions of the environment may influence the behavior of all adolescents.

One of the least-studied aspects of cultural and economic diver-sity is the influence of the size of one's reference group on adolescent development. Growing up in a community with many others like oneself may be quite different from growing up in a community where one's status is unusual and different. Being a Mexican American adolescent in San Antonio, Texas, where I grew up, and being a Mexican American adolescent in Columbus, Ohio, where I now live, is the difference between being one of 437,016 out of 786,000—about one out of two—versus being one of 6,215 out of 565,000—about one out of 100. In San Antonio, connection with the Mexican culture is a natural daily event. In some neighborhoods, the Mexican American population approaches 100%, Spanish is spoken more than English, and Mexican culture is the backdrop of daily life. In Columbus, that culture is largely invisible and confined to a yearly festival and few Mexican restaurants (mostly bad). One wonders whether the individual development of minority adolescents is affected by the size of the minority population. For example, is the need to develop an ethnic identity lessened in a community where a minority is the majority?

From an ecological perspective, Taylor et al. discuss Ogbu's (1985) point that people develop the skills they need to survive in their environments; they develop adaptive competencies for their particular life setting. According to Ogbu, for many African American adolescents those skills include self-reliance and the ability to manipulate other people. These abilities are valued and taught as an adaptational response to conditions of scarce resources. Performing this kind of functional analysis for the variety of contexts in which adolescents live might help shed light on why adolescents in different contexts behave as they do.

RELIGION

An unexpected theme that appeared in several of the chapters in this volume was the importance of religion to adolescents who are poor, non-White, or rural. Little attention is paid to religion in the lives of adolescents in America, although religion is fundamentally important to large numbers of adolescents, especially nonmajority youth (Benson, Donahue, & Erickson, 1989). Wilson and Peterson specifically mention the centrality of religious beliefs in the lives of Appalachian youth and families. Some research has shown that religion is a protective factor that can decrease the risk that adolescents will become involved in unhealthy and illegal behaviors, although it is unclear how this process operates (Benson et al., 1989). Religion also affects adolescents indirectly through parenting style. Wilson and Peterson show that Appalachian styles of parenting emphasize nurturance combined with rigid control, including physical punishment. They argue that the use of corporal punishment is rooted in fundamental religious beliefs that legitimize child-rearing approaches that reflect the biblical injunction to "spare the rod and spoil the child."

CONCLUSION

Much progress has been made in the last few years to broaden and deepen our understanding of the diversity of adolescent development. Unfortunately, most of the research on adolescents who are non-White, poor, or rural has focused on problem behavior. We know much about the unhealthy and illegal behavior of adolescents in these groups and less about competence and resiliency. My hope is that this book will be part of a new look at adolescents who are poor, rural, or non-White, a look that will encompass the fullness of their experiences, good and bad, and that will lead to a more complete understanding of the variety of adolescent experiences.

REFERENCES

Atkinson, D. R., Morten, G., & Sue, D. (1983). *Counseling American minorities.* Dubuque, IA: William C. Brown.

Benson, P., Donahue, M., & Erickson, J. (1989). Adolescence and religion: Review of the literature from 1970-1986. *Research in the Social Scientific Study of Religion, 1,* 153-181.

Bronfenbrenner, U. (1979). *The ecology of human development: Experiments by nature and design.* Cambridge, MA: Harvard University Press.

Bronfenbrenner, U. (1989). Ecological systems theory. *Annals of Child Development, 6,* 187-251.

Brown, B. B. (1990). Peer groups and peer cultures. In S. S. Feldman & G. R. Elliot (Eds.), *At the threshold: The developing adolescent* (pp. 171-196). Cambridge, MA: Harvard University Press.

Erikson, E. H. (1968). *Identity: Youth and crisis.* New York: Norton.

Graham, S. (1992). "Most of the subjects were White and middle class": Trends in published research on African Americans in selected APA journals, 1970-1989. *American Psychologist, 47,* 629-639.

Harris, J. R. (1998). *The nurture assumption.* New York: Free Press.

Ogbu, J. U. (1985). A cultural ecology of competence among inner-city blacks. In M. B. Spencer, G. K. Brookins, & W. R. Allen (Eds.), *Beginnings: The social and effective development of black children* (pp. 45-66). Hillsdale, NJ: Lawrence Erlbaum.

Parke, R. D., & Buriel, R. (1998). Socialization in the family: Ethnic and ecological perspectives. In W. Damon (Editor-in Chief) & N. Eisenberg (Vol. Ed.), *Handbook of child psychology: Vol. 3. Social, emotional, and personality development* (5th ed., pp. 463-552). New York: John Wiley.

Phinney, J. (1989). Stages of ethnic identity development in minority group adolescents. *Journal of Early Adolescence, 9,* 34-49.

Phinney, J. (1990). Ethnic identity in adolescents and adults: A review of research. *Psychological Bulletin, 108,* 499-514.

Wilson, W. J. (1987). *The truly disadvantaged: The inner city, the underclass, and public policy.* Chicago: University of Chicago Press.

Name Index

276

ADOLESCENT DIVERSITY

Haignere, C., 22
Haller, E. J., 59, 60
Hambrick-Dixon, P. J., 244
Hamilton-Lee, M., 222
Hammond, W. R., 148
Hansen, T. D., 59
Hardesty, C., 64
Harper, A. C., 148
Harper, L. U., 247
Harrington, M., 83
Harris, J. R., 264
Hartman, T., 238
Harwood, A., 148
Hastings, L., 226, 229
Hauser, R. M., 98
Hawkins, J. D., 24, 27, 155, 165
Hawley, W. D., 213
Haynes, N., 24, 222
Heckler, M., 245
Hektner, J. M., 60, 65, 66
Helge, D., 45, 61
Henderson, R., 10
Hennon, C. B., 90
Henry, C. S., 85, 90, 92, 98, 99, 100
Herdman, R., 115, 129
Hicks, G. L., 84, 85, 88, 89, 91
Hiraga, Y., 22
Hirschfelder, A., 120, 122, 123
Hobbs, D., 44, 45, 47, 52, 53, 64, 67
Hoffer, T., 221
Hogan, J., 164
Hogan, R., 164
Hollenbeck, A., 128, 129
Howard, C., 227
Hoyt, D. R., 49, 50
Hser, Y., 142
Hsia, J., 183
Huang, K., 190
Huang, S. L., 183, 185
Hubbard, L., 17
Huberman, A. M., 172
Hummon, D. M., 47, 50
Humphrey, R. A., 87
Huston, A. C., 14

Ianni, F. A., 43, 59
Indian Health Service, 115, 116, 129
Institute of Medicine, 32
Irvine, J. J., 214

Jacob, J. E., 244
Jacob, S., 47
James, F., 12, 15
Janovitz, M., 50
Jargowsky, P. A., 9
Jarrett, R. L., 10, 14, 25
Jayaratne, T. E., 13, 227
Jemmott, J. B., 10
Jemmott, L. S., 10
Jencks, C., 12, 24
Jensen, A. R., 213
Jensen, L., 44
Jessor, R., 14, 143, 155, 165
Jessor, S., 155, 165
Joe, J., 121, 124
Johansen, H. E., 45
John, R., 118, 148
Johnson, D. J., 14
Johnson, K. M., 53
Johnson, L., 89
Johnson, T. G., 98, 99
Johnston, G. M., 51
Johnston, L. D., 61, 62
Jumper-Thurman, P., 130, 133
Jussim, L., 214

Kagitcibasi, C., 85
Kao, G., 181, 182, 184, 185, 186
Kaplan, E., 61
Karoly, L. A., 11
Kasarda, J. D., 50
Kasser, T., 21
Kazdin, A. E., 143, 144
Keane, E., 129
Keefe, S. E., 80, 84, 85, 87, 88, 156, 157
Kelleher, K. J., 63
Kenkel, W. F., 79, 98, 99, 100
Kenny, D. A., 28

Trickett, P. K., 16
Trimble, J., 123, 128, 129, 130
Trimble, J. E., 111, 171
Trowbridge, N., 61
Truesdell, L. E., 46
Tyler, F. B., 14, 18
Tyler, L. E., 60
Tyler, S. L., 14, 18

U.S. Census Bureau, 1, 2, 9, 15, 43, 141, 142, 146, 147, 210
U.S. Department of Agriculture, 53
U.S. Department of Commerce, 147
Uba, L., 196
University of Minnesota Health Center, 135, 136

Vasquez, R., 152, 153, 171
Vaughan, R. D., 22
Vega, W. A., 148, 150, 151, 155, 158
Ventura, A. M., 18
Vicary, J. R., 59, 61, 65
Villanueva, I., 17
Villarruel, F. A., 242
Virkler, S. J., 59, 60

Walter, H. J., 22
Ward, J. V., 18
Warheit, G. J., 148, 155
Washington, V., 244
Waters, M. C., 18
Watt, N. F., 27
Waxman, H. C., 183, 185
Weinberg, D. H., 11
Weiss, R. V., 246
Weller, J., 85, 87, 88, 89, 90, 94
Wenk, D., 64
Werner, E. E., 27
West, S. G., 27
Weston, R., 149
Whisnant, P. E., 81
Whitbeck, L. B., 61
White, L. K., 52

Whitmore, J. K., 18, 20
Wiehe, V. R., 94, 95
Williams, T. M., 11, 18
Williamson, L., 190, 192
William T. Grant Foundation, 45
Willits, F. K., 47, 51
Wilson, G. T., 144
Wilson, J. L., 59, 61, 65
Wilson, K., 227
Wilson, P., 79, 88, 90, 97, 98, 99, 100
Wilson, S. M., 50, 78, 79, 80, 85, 86, 88, 89, 90, 92, 94, 95, 96, 97, 98, 99, 100, 101
Wilson, W. J., 11, 12, 263
Wirth, L., 46
Wohlwill, J. F., 244
Wolf, W., 133
Wooden, W. S., 192
Woodhead, H., 117, 123
Wozniak, P. H., 52
Wright, B. H., 10, 244
Wright, D., 181, 184, 185
Wu, C., 61
Wyatt, G. E., 148

Yee, B. W. K., 148
Yeh, C. J., 190
Yokley, R. T., 51
Yoon, G., 85
Yoshikawa, H., 10, 26, 27, 30, 33, 35
Youniss, J., 95
Yung, B. R., 148

Zamsky, E. S., 21
Zax, M., 21
Zdep, S. M., 61
Zelizer, V. A. R., 56
Zhang, Y., 14, 18
Zhou, M., 15, 25, 26
Zigler, E., 16, 17
Zimmerman, C. C., 46
Zimmerman, M. A., 21
Zimmerman, R. S., 148, 155

Subject Index

Academic achievement, 23
  authoritative parenting and, 21
  church involvement and, 26
  family context research and, 20-21
  parental emotional support and, 21
  See also specific ethnic/racial/geographic groups; Academic competence; Model minority myth
Academic competence, 16, 26, 30
  peers and, 22
Acculturation, 150, 155
  ethnic identity and, 191
Acculturation theory, 188, 190-193
  Asian American, 191-192
Adaptability-flexibility capacity, 145
Adaptive adjustment, 144
Addiction careers, 142
Adolescence:
  definition, 14
  emergence of, 113-114
  identity formation, 237
  influence of previous experience on, 235, 241-243
  maturation process, 237
  See also Adolescents, studying minority

Adolescent competence categories:
  bravado group, 30
  competent groups, 30
  ethnically disidentified group, 30
  intrapsychically vulnerable group, 30
  unhappy underemployed group, 30
Adolescent Pathways Project, 19, 23, 26, 30
Adolescents, minority:
  competence issues, 261-262
  ethnic identity issues, 260-261
  ethnicity/socioeconomic status issues, 267-268
  experience of adolescence among, 265-266
  family issues, 262-263
  peer issues, 264
  religion as issue, 269-270
  school issues, 264-265
  traditional versus modern culture issues, 258-260
  within-group diversity issues, 266-267
  within-group historical/generational change issues, 267

About the Editors

Raymond Montemayor is Associate Professor of Psychology at Ohio State University. His research interests include parent-adolescent relations, especially the study of conflict and stress between parents and adolescents. In addition, he is interested in emotional development during adolescence and gender issues. He is a Fellow of the American Psychological Association. He is on the Editorial Boards of the *Journal of Adolescent Research* and the *Journal of Early Adolescence*. He teaches undergraduate and graduate courses in adolescence at Ohio State University.

Gerald R. Adams is Professor of Family Relations and Human Development at the University of Guelph in Guelph, Ontario. His research interests focus on personality and social development in adolescence and primary prevention. He is coauthor of *The Adolescent Experience* (4th ed.). He has been recognized for his accomplishments through Fellow distinctions with the American Psychological Association and the American Psychological Society. He is the Editor of the *Journal of Adolescent Research*.

Thomas P. Gullotta, MA, MSW, is CEO of Child and Family Agency of Southeastern Connecticut. He is the Editor of the *Journal of Primary Prevention*. He is a senior book series editor for *Issues in Children's and Families' Lives.* He is a series editor for *Prevention in Practice.* He holds editorial appointments on the *Journal of Early Adolescence* and the *Journal of Educational and Psychological Consultation.* He serves on the board of the National Mental Health Association and is an adjunct faculty member in the Psychology Department of Eastern Connecticut State University.

About the Contributors

Hector G. Balcazar, PhD, is Associate Professor in the Department of Family Resources and Human Development at Arizona State University. His research interests include Latino health issues, acculturation and health, maternal and child health, and chronic disease and prevention program development for Latinos.

Fred Beauvais is a senior research scientist with the Tri-Ethnic Center for Prevention Research at Colorado State University. He has worked for more than 20 years with numerous Indian communities collecting data for basic research that also enables them to design interventions for social problems more effectively. His primary work has been in the area of substance abuse, but he also has conducted studies on school dropouts, violence and victimization, and the training of mental health professionals. The development of procedures for conducting culturally sensitive research has been a parallel interest.

Gina R. Boyer is a graduate student in the clinical program of the Department of Psychology at Arizona State University. Her research interests include parenting, African American families, and cross-cultural issues in assessment and testing.

Felipe Gonzales Castro, MSW, PhD, is Professor of Psychology in the clinical psychology program of the Department of Psychology at Arizona State University. He served as Director of the Hispanic Research Center at Arizona State University from 1991 to 1997. He has conducted various research projects in the area of Hispanic/Latino health. His research areas include drug abuse and addiction, prevention and treatment, and health promotion in minority populations.

Ruth K. Chao, PhD, is Assistant Professor in the developmental program of the Department of Psychology at the University of California, Riverside. She received her PhD in educational psychology from the University of California, Los Angeles (UCLA), in 1992 and held a postdoctoral position for 2 years in the Department of Psychology at UCLA. Her research interests have primarily involved studies of East Asian immigrant families, focusing on the role of parenting in children's school achievement. Part of her research on parenting has included an alternative parenting style—training—to describe immigrant Chinese parents.

Lisa J. Crockett is Associate Professor of Psychology at the University of Nebraska–Lincoln. Her research interests include adolescent problem behavior, the development of behavioral trajectories, gender issues, and the transition to adulthood. She is coeditor, with Ann C. Crouter, of *Pathways Through Adolescence: Individual Development in Relation to Social Contexts* (1995) and coeditor, with Rainer K. Silbereisen, of *Negotiating Adolescence in Times of Social Change* (2000).

Michael Cunningham, a developmental psychologist, is Assistant Professor of Psychology and African & African Diaspora Studies at Tulane University. His primary research interests include examining adolescent development in diverse contexts. Specifically, he examines how self-perceptions influence how African American adolescent males develop proactive and reactive coping styles. Currently, he is examining the influence of context-specific perceptions on academic achievement orientation in African American youth.

Erin E. Hardin is a graduate student in the counseling psychology program at Ohio State University. She received her BA in psychology from Grinnell College in 1994. Her master's thesis examined the role of cultural factors in the measurement of career maturity among Asian American college students. Her other research interests include the acculturation and adjustment of Asian Americans, culturally appropriate counseling interventions, and cross-cultural psychology.

Julia Jackson-Newsom is a project coordinator for Tanglewood Research, Inc., in Clemmons, NC. Her research interests include adolescent problem behavior, sibling differences in sychosocial outcomes, and substance use prevention. Her master's thesis is titled *Predictors of Substance Use Trajectories in Adolescence.*

Leanne Jacobson is a graduate student in the developmental division of the Department of Psychology at Temple University. Her research interests include adolescent social and emotional adjustment and the etiology of juvenile delinquency.

Frederick T. L. Leong is Associate Professor of Psychology at Ohio State University (OSU). He obtained his PhD from the University of Maryland with a double specialty in Counseling and Industrial/Organizational Psychology. Currently, he serves as a faculty member in both the Counseling and Industrial/Organizational Psychology programs at OSU. He has more than 70 publications in various counseling and psychology journals and 30 book chapters. He is the editor of *Career Development and Vocational Behavior of Racial and Ethnic Minorities* (1995). His most recent book (coedited with James Austin) is *Psychology Research Handbook: A Guide for Graduate Students and Research Assistants* (1996, Sage). His major research interests are in vocational psychology, Asian American psychology, cross-cultural psychology (particularly culture and mental health), and personality and adjustment.

Gary W. Peterson, PhD, is Professor in and Chair of the Department of Sociology at Arizona State University. His areas of expertise include adolescent development within families and parent-child relationships. Specific topics have included parental contributors to adolescent social competence, autonomy, conformity to parents, and status attainment among samples of middle- and low-income urban and rural youth. Currently, he is examining these and ethnic and cultural issues in samples of adolescents from the People's Republic of China, Russia, and the United States. Samples from the United States include Mexican American youth and low-income rural youth from Appalachia. A related theme in his work has been the application of family and sociological theories to the study of adolescent development. Currently, he is a coeditor of the *Handbook of Marriage and the Family* (2nd ed.).

Debra Roberts is a Postdoctoral Research Fellow in the Department of Family Studies, University of Maryland, College Park. She received her PhD in Developmental Psychology from Temple University and her MS in Community Psychology from Florida A&M University. Her research interests include ethnic/cultural identity and the normative development of children of African descent.

Edward Seidman is Professor of Psychology at New York University. Previously, he was Vice President and Dean of Research, Development, and Policy at Bank Street College of Education, and Professor of Psychology at the University of Illinois at Urbana-Champaign and the University of Manitoba. He is the recipient of a Senior Fulbright Hays Research Scholar Award, and the award for Distinguished Contributions to Theory and Research in Community Psychology. He is editor of the *Handbook of Social Intervention* (1983), and coeditor of *Redefining Social Problems* (1986) and the *Handbook of Community Psychology* (2000). His earlier intervention research on the diversion of adolescents in legal jeopardy from the juvenile justice system received several national awards. His current research and scholarship focus on the social development of urban adolescents, primary prevention, and social policy.

Michael J. Shanahan is Assistant Professor of Human Development and Family Studies at Pennsylvania State University. His research interests include children in poverty, the ecology of adolescent work, and historical patterns in adult educational and occupational attainment. He is coeditor (with J. Tudge & J. Valsiner) of *Comparisons in Human Development: Understanding Time and Context* (1996).

Margaret Beale Spencer, a developmental psychologist, is the Board of Overseers Professor of Education in the Graduate School of Education at the University of Pennsylvania. She is also the director of the Interdisciplinary Studies in Human Development program (ISHD), the Center for Health, Achievement, Neighborhood, Growth, and Ethnic Studies (CHANGES), and the W. E. B. Du Bois Collective Research Institute. Her adolescent-focused research addresses resiliency, identity, and competence-formation processes, particularly among youth of color. Her current research is on the maturing cognitive capacities and socioemotional development of low-income African American adolescents and an examination of factors that differentially predict resilient and unproductive outcomes.

Ronald D. Taylor is Associate Professor in the Department of Psychology and Assistant Director of the Center for Research in Human Development and Education at Temple University. He received his PhD from the University of Michigan in Developmental Psychology. His research interests include the social and emotional development and family relations of ethnic-minority adolescents. His most current research focuses on the impact of neighborhood conditions on family processes and adolescent psychological well-being among poor, urban, African American and European American families.

Stephan M. Wilson, PhD, is Director of the Research Center for Families and Children, Professor of Family Studies, and an Appalachian Center Associate at the University of Kentucky. His areas of expertise include adolescent development within family and community contexts, parent-child interactions, rural and Appalachian adolescents and families, and work-family issues. He has investigated these and related topics in such journals as *Adolescence, Journal of Adolescent Research, Journal of Adolescence, Journal of Marriage and the Family, Family Relations, Family Science Review, Journal of the American Academy of Nurse Practitioners, Journal of Family Issues, Journal of Marriage and Family Therapy, Sociological Inquiry, Journal of Counseling and Development, Lifestyles, Family Life Educator,* and *American Journal of Health Promotion,* as well as in book chapters on family-of-origin influences on late-adolescent lifestyle decisions and on educational and occupational attainment and life satisfaction, rural and Appalachian youth, school-family relations, and family wellness.

Hirokazu Yoshikawa is Assistant Professor of Psychology at New York University, specializing in community psychology. His research areas include the effects of welfare policies on children and families, the experiences of working families in poverty, competence among children and adolescents in poverty, long-term effects of early childhood intervention programs, and community-level HIV prevention among Asian/Pacific Islander communities. He served recently on the Department of Health and Human Services Advisory Committee on Head Start Research and Evaluation. He is a coeditor of *A Quarter Century of Community Psychology* (in press) and *Design Issues in Prevention and Intervention Research* (in press). He received his PhD in clinical psychology from New York University.